The Encyclopedia of Regional Dolls of the World

The Encyclopedia of Regional Dolls of the World

Marjory Fainges

ROBERT HALE • LONDON

Acknowledgments

I wish to thank all those who have made this book possible, especially Dorothy and Jane Coleman, who encouraged me to get this book under way. Thanks also to all those who allowed me to photograph their interesting dolls at various doll shows. An especially hearty thanks goes to Jenny Miller; Shirleyanne McKay; Barbara Cooper and Audrey McMahon of the NSW Doll Collectors Club; Jean Krukelis and Vera Woodhead of the Brisbane Doll Society; and Sherry Morgan of Florida, USA, who so generously helped with photographs or allowed me to photograph their collections to fill in the gaps of the countries that I did not have in my own collection. Special thanks also go to various ethnic groups who went out of their way to help identify some of the dolls I had photographed, and to the girls at Rabbit Photos, Stafford City, who at times had to repeat the processing to get the finish I wanted. Special thanks to my husband for the meals he cooked and the phone calls he answered while I was preparing this book. I sincerely hope that, in reading this book, you will learn a little more about the dolls in your collections and the countries they represent.

Bibliography

Bachmann, Manfred and Hansmann, Claud, *Dolls the Wide World Over*, Harrap, 1971

Baten, Lea, *The Image and the Motif—Japanese Dolls*, Shufunotomo Co. Ltd, 1986

Eaton, Faith, *Dolls in Colour*, Blandford Press, 1975

Fainges, Marjory, *Australian Dollmakers—a History*, Kangaroo Press, 1986

Fainges, Marjory, *Encyclopedia of Australian Dolls*, Kangaroo Press, 1993

Frame, Linda Jean, *Folk and Foreign Costume Dolls*, Collector Books, 1980

Gordon, Lesley, *A Pageant of Dolls*, Edmund Ward

Holz, Loretta, *The How-to Book of International Dolls*, Crown Publishers Inc., 1980

Smith, Patricia R., *Oriental Dolls in Colour*, Collector Books, 1979

Turner Wilcox, R., *Folk and Festival Costume of the World*, Charles Scribner's Sons, 1985

White, Gwen, *Dolls of the World*, Mills & Boon, 1962

First published in Great Britain 1995

ISBN 0 7090 5612 5

Robert Hale Limited
Clerkenwell House
Clerkenwell Green
London EC1R 0HT

Printed in China through Global-Com Pte Ltd

Contents

Introduction 7
Origins 7
Starting a Collection 8

Afghanistan 11
Albania 11
Algeria 12
Andorra 12
Argentina 12
Armenia 13
Australia 13
Austria 15
Azerbaijan 16
Bahrain 16
Bangladesh 17
Barbados 18
Belarus 18
Belgium 19
Bolivia 21
Bosnia-Hercegovina 21
Brazil 22
BRIDES 22
Bulgaria 25
Burma 26
Cambodia 27
Cameroon 28
Canada 28
Canary Is. 30
Celebes 30
Channel Is. 30
Chile 31
China 31
Colombia 35
Cook Is. 36
Cornwall 36
Côte d'Ivoire 36
Crete 37
Croatia 37
Cuba 38
Cyprus 39
Czech Republic 40
DANCE 41
Denmark 43
Djibouti 44
Dominica 44
Ecuador 45
Egypt 46
England 47
Estonia 48
Ethiopia 48
Fiji 49
Finland 50
France 51
French Polynesia 55
Georgia 55
Germany 55
Ghana 58
Greece 59
Greenland 61
Grenada 62
Guatemala 62
Haiti 63
Honduras 64
Hong Kong 64
Hungary 65
Iceland 66
India 67
Indonesia 69
Iran 70
Iraq 71
Ireland 72
Israel 73
Italy 75
Jamaica 78
Japan 78
Java 82
Jordan 83
Kalimantan 84
Kashmir 84
Kazakhstan 85
Kenya 85
Korea (South) 87
Laos 88
Lapland 88
Latvia 89
Lebanon 90
Lesotho 91
Liberia 91
Liechtenstein 92
Lithuania 92
Luxembourg 92
Macedonia 93
Malaysia 94
Malta 94
Martinique 95
Mexico 95
Moldova 97
Monaco 97
Mongolia 98
Montenegro 98
Moravia 99
Morocco 100
MUSICIANS 101
Namibia 102
Nepal 103
Netherlands 103
New Caledonia 105
New Zealand 106
Nigeria 107
Northern Ireland 108
Norway 108
Pakistan 109
Palestine 111
Panama 111
Papua New Guinea 112
Peru 113
Philippines 114
Pitcairn Is. 116
Poland 116
Portugal 118

Puerto Rico 120
RELIGION 120
Romania 122
Romany 124
Russia 125
St Lucia 127
St Vincent 128
Samoa 128
San Marino 129
Saudi Arabia 129
Scotland 130
Senegal 131
Serbia 132
Sikkim 133
Singapore 133
Slovakia 134
Spain 135
South Africa 136
Sri Lanka 138
Swaziland 139
Sweden 140
Switzerland 141
Syria 142
Taiwan 143
Tajikistan 144
Thailand 144
Tibet 146
Tonga 146
Trinidad 147
Tunisia 147
Turkey 148
Turkmenistan 149
Uganda 150
Ukraine 150
USA 151
Uruguay 154
Uzbekistan 155
Vanuatu 155
Vatican 156
Venezuela 156
Vietnam 157
Virgin Is. 157
Wales 158
Zimbabwe 159
Index 160

Introduction

The custom of bringing or sending back home a souvenir, such as a doll dressed in costume, from one's travels is as old as travel itself. This book deals with just such dolls. Due to time and circumstance costumes worn by many nations and regions within these nations have changed considerably, and in some areas have been discarded altogether and can now only be seen on rare special occasions or in museums.

A collection of full-size national costumes of the world would take up an enormous amount of space, but a collection of costumed dolls, while still very colourful, needs a comparatively small area for display, and at a glance an onlooker can take in the great diversity of colours, materials and styles used in costumes worn around the world, both now and in the past. People have been, and still are, fascinated by other countries' costumes, especially if they differ from what they are accustomed to.

What many collectors and non-collectors alike do not realise is that a collection of dolls dressed in folk, ethnic or regional costumes is a microcosm of the world's cultures, occupations, history and religions.

Origins

For the origin of these small dolls we must go back approximately two hundred years to when dolls first began to be commercially produced in Europe and Asia. Dolls produced then were usually dressed in the local costume, either simply or ornately, and in historic or ethnic style, depending on the country concerned.

In those days one valley often had little to do with the next, and the everyday and festival costumes worn by the people (and represented in the dolls' clothing) differed considerably from one area to another. These old dolls still in their costume have significant historical value.

With the industrial revolution people began to travel further from home due to better shipping facilities and the reach of the railways, and many travellers wanted to take home souvenirs or relics of their travels to show the loved ones at home the types of costume worn in the places they had visited. So the words souvenir dolls or relics began to be used in conjunction with these little ambassadors of another country.

Such dolls were usually made in the materials commonly used in the manufacture of dolls during the nineteenth century. This is the reason why you find the white unglazed china or the old glazed china-headed dolls so often dressed in the different regional costumes of Germany. Traders in other countries, not wanting to miss out on a possible bonanza with sales of such dolls, often ordered dolls or doll parts and either had them dressed in Germany or in small workshops in the country where they were sold. This situation is the same today, with the modern manufacturers of dolls in Korea, Hong Kong and Taiwan supplying dolls throughout the world for the same purpose.

1840s wax doll made to represent what Europeans thought was worn in the Middle East and Asia Minor.

With England, Germany, France, Spain and Portugal spreading their empires into the far-flung corners of the world, many of these outposts wanted to send small mementoes home to explain the costume of those around them. This is one of the reasons why you sometimes find old wax dolls dressed in eastern attire, or beautiful French and German bisque-china-headed dolls in mulatto or dark brown tonings dressed in eastern or African style costumes.

Japan was rather an exception as for many years the Japanese made dolls associated with their historical customs, and it wasn't until Japan opened itself up to trade with the world that others became aware of this part of their culture.

The terms used to describe these small dolls dressed in various types of local costume have changed considerably over the years. They include souvenir, national, international, folk, ethnic and regional. All are correct within reason, but due to the rapidly changing politics of our modern world, and the ever-increasing use of mass-produced dolls, the words 'regional dolls' would seem to be the most appropriate at the time of writing.

This is the reason I have chosen to title this book *Encyclopedia of Regional Dolls of the World*, as many of the terms that have been used may cover a specific type of doll only, and I wish this book to encompass all types of doll: old, new, ethnic, folk, souvenir, national and International. The word regional covers all and is the most comprehensive.

Regional dolls

A doll dressed in regional costume depicts clothing worn by people belonging to an area rather than a particular country. A classic example is Lapland. It is not a separate country, but encompasses the northern sections of three countries, Finland, Sweden and Norway. The Lapps have lived in these areas for many years and, although paying allegiance to a country, they still have their own customs and way of life. Another such region is the Tyrol, a mountainous region that takes in part of Italy, Switzerland and Austria.

The Orient and Middle East are much vaguer regions, but many of the earlier dolls of France and Germany were dressed in Oriental and Eastern style, although not necessarily depicting a particular country or costume. Similarly, Africa, the West Indies, and even some of the islands of the Pacific, because of their vast regions and the sparse facts that emerged about them before the Second World War and the rise of mass media, caused many manufacturers to dress dolls vaguely under a general classification, making it hard to definitely identify any actual area that these dolls are supposed to represent.

Another reason I prefer to refer to these dolls as regional is that since the beginning of this decade so much has happened in the political sense, with the break-up of the once-vast Soviet Union, the reunification of divided Germany, the split of Czechoslovakia into two countries and the sad plight of Yugoslavia.

In this book most countries are described as a whole, with the various dolls shown wearing regional costume so that collectors and students alike can learn more of past costumes, through dress, in this fast-changing world.

Ethnic dolls

This term covers dolls actually made and dressed in the region portrayed by the doll and its clothes.

Folk dolls

Often a very crude rendition of what the western world looks upon as a doll, these are nevertheless ethnic dolls. They are usually hand made from materials on hand, and are to be found in Africa and some of the other undeveloped regions of the world.

National dolls

These dolls are dressed in a particular country to portray the accepted local national or regional costumes, using dolls manufactured elsewhere. Over the years many countries have used dolls manufactured in Germany, France, the United Kingdom, the USA, Japan, Hong Kong and Taiwan for dressing souvenir dolls in their national costume.

International dolls

These dolls are manufactured and dressed by a firm to portray a foreign country's costume. Such firms include Pedigree (England), Madame Alexander, Carlson and even Mattel of the USA, Eros and Lenci of Italy, Peticollin of France and the many old and well-known manufacturers of both France and Germany who dressed their beautiful bisque-china-headed dolls, often made and painted to suit the region concerned.

Souvenir dolls

Souvenirs they definitely were. With the colonisation of countries by France, Germany, Spain, Portugal and Britain, and the consequent travel to these areas, the need to send or give gifts to those at home, particularly to children in the form of a doll dressed in the costume of the area visited, became the nucleus of what today is a thriving industry throughout the world catering to the mass tourist market.

Historical dolls

Many countries produce dolls depicting famous historical personages or typical important eras of their history, and feature these among their souvenir dolls.

Religious dolls

This is another important aspect of regional dolls, as many dolls over the years have been dressed in the various costumes of the religions and beliefs found in particular regions. Examples are the straw dolls of Indonesia, and dolls depicting the devil dancers of Sri Lanka, the gurus of India, the various orders of the Catholic and other Christian churches, as well as those representing some Jewish customs.

Benefit dolls

Other dolls were dressed in costume to raise funds, and prime examples are the lovely Door of Hope dolls made and dressed in China, dolls made in the orphanages of Korea to raise funds, the dolls made by refugees in Jordan, and the WPA dolls produced in the USA to raise funds during World War II.

Collecting regional dolls is an exciting facet of antique, old and modern doll collecting that is all too often overlooked by doll collectors. The emerging interest in collecting and keeping old dolls in their original costume or dress is now causing many doll collectors to have a second look at this once disdained section of a marvellous hobby.

Starting a Collection

Many doll collectors are introduced to this fascinating hobby when a family member or friend brings back a small souvenir from overseas — a doll. This doll often stands on its own in the corner of a cabinet to be joined later, and again later, by other such dolls, and without actually realising it the doll owner has become a collector.

Other dolls, after years of seclusion in the back of a cupboard, may find themselves on a church, charity or school white elephant stall or at a flea market, to be eagerly picked up by a very happy collector of these small dolls that are only now attaining their rightful position in the ever-increasing world-wide activity of doll collecting.

These small dolls (only occasionally of a larger size) have been the silent ambassadors of many countries for well over a hundred years, especially since the beginning of the industrial revolution and the subsequent mass production of dolls.

Many dolls were dressed with their clothing depicting in detail the costume of the regions they represent, whereas others gave and still give only a suggestive outline of a general area. In the last 20 years Taiwan firms have produced many small ranges of what they have termed national dolls, but unfortunately many of these dolls leave a lot to be desired as to the correctness of the regional costume they are said to represent.

The aim of this book

With the migration of many millions from what was referred to as the 'old' world due to the consequences of war, famines and religious persecution over the centuries, the displacement of people after World War II and the political refugees of this century, the traditional make-up of the population of many countries is changing.

The aim of this book is to help not only the collectors of these dolls to understand a little more about the dolls they collect, but more importantly children and even adults to learn more about the costumes and customs of other lands, and maybe make this world of ours a better place to live in.

The costumes found on the small dolls portrayed in this book are many and various and are an insight into many aspects of life in other countries. Some dolls depict fascinating dance costumes, while still others show regional musical instruments. On looking through this book you can not only learn about the various costumes of other places, but gain insights into the everyday life of both today and the past, through the medium of dolls.

To assist in finding the various countries whose dolls have been included in this book, the countries (and regions) have been listed in alphabetical order.

With each listing the relevant continent is indicated. The capital city of the country is also given and where possible the current population and a little history. Where the name of a country has changed over the last sixty years, former names are also included and cross indexed. In some cases regions, cantons, and so on are listed so that you can see where the different regional costumes are worn. Countries such as Switzerland with its 32 cantons, Italy, Germany, India and France have many different regional dolls, so only a representative selection is shown.

Unfortunately, in some cases only one costumed doll was available for me to photograph as a representation of a particular country. For other countries, such as Japan and Scotland, many more dolls dressed in regional costume were available. Dolls depicting the traditional dress of Scotland are widespread because Scots have migrated to many parts of the world over the years, and their love of tradition and their colourful costume has kept it in use for dressing dolls for generations.

Should there be a reason for a doll's particular costume, such as the much maligned and often misrepresented doll depicting the Australian 'Swaggie', an itinerant worker looking for work rather than a hobo, this will be noted with the doll.

The interest worldwide in these very diversified costumed dolls is evident in that there are a number of museums in the world devoted purely to this type of doll, with well-known ones in England, Germany and India. Shankars Doll Museum of New Delhi, India, produce beautifully made and detailed dolls in their own workshops which they still exchange with other museums worldwide. Many of the Indian dolls portrayed in this book are from an exchange made with Shankars by our old museum — Panaroo's Playthings, Brisbane. My husband and I exchanged forty dolls made by us and dressed to depict the costume worn during the first two centuries of white settlement in Australia. Other museums have sections in which a small display of such dolls is a feature.

Abyssinia See Ethiopia

Afghanistan (Democratic Republic of) Asia

Surrounded by Iran, Pakistan and parts of what were the Soviet Union, Afghanistan covers an area of 652 225 square kilometres (251 759 square miles) with nearly 75 per cent of its area mountainous terrain.

Once part of the mighty Persian Empire, until the overthrow of this empire by Alexander the Great, the first national Afghan/Pashtan emerged in 1747. After several attempts by Britain to take partial control, on 13 April 1919 Afghanistan became independent. Continual fighting during the 1980s between the rebel Muslim parties and a Soviet-backed government, continued after the withdrawal of Soviet troops in 1989, eventually degenerating into factional fighting between rival Muslim groups.

Capital Kabul.
Population Approximately 16 million.
Language Pashto and Duri (Persian).
Religion Muslim (mainly Sunni, some Shi'ite), some Hindus, Sikhs and a small Jewish minority.

The doll on the left is showing the fine pleating and head embroidery on the back of her chadar. The doll on the right is another Afghan doll showing her painted features and the way she is dressed under the chadar. The long sheer red headscarf can also be used to veil her face. The doll wears a long black tunic, decorated waistcoat, gold waistband and medallions, red tombons and black shoes.

Afghan couple. The woman is dressed in the all-enveloping chadar, finely pleated at the back and embroidered in the facial area, with eyelets to see through. Under the chadar the doll wears a headscarf, a long maroon tunic with a fancy waistcoat, gold waistband and silver medallions. White tombons (pants) and black shoes finish the outfit. The elderly male doll wears a white turban with a red crown. The turban is a straight piece of cloth 5–8 metres (6–9 yards) in length and so wound that, as a Muslim, when he prays to Allah his bare forehead can touch the ground. He wears a long navy tunic with the traditional red waistcoat, navy tombons and black shoes. Around the waist is a length of rope; he carries a bag or white cotton sack on his back and holds a staff in the left hand.

Dressed in pantaloons or 'tombons', a loose tunic of white cotton and a waistcoat of red gold-embroidered felt, this doll represents an Afghan horseman sitting astride his horse with a spear in the right hand.

Albania (Republic of) Europe

Located in the Balkans, Albania is bordered by the Adriatic Sea and adjoins Greece and Macedonia (formerly part of Yugoslavia). The coastal area, which is only about 30 per cent of the total area of 28 748 square kilometres (11 097 square miles, is fertile and used for agriculture, whereas the other 70 per cent is mainly mountainous and not well populated.

Between the ninth and fifteenth centuries foreign powers (Bysantium, Bulgaria, Serbia and Italy) fought for control of Albania's strategic coastline. The Ottoman conquest (1385–1417) began a Turkish occupation that lasted until 1912. Albania became independent during the Balkan Wars (1912–13), but due to its occupation by various armies during and after World War I no government was established until 1921. Albania was formally proclaimed a republic in 1946.

Capital Tirana.
Population Approximately 3.5 million.
Language Albanian.
Religion Muslim, Greek Orthodox, Roman Catholic and atheism.

Composition heads and hands. The man wears a black hat, white full-sleeved tunic over white shirt, black bolero, embroidered trim and multicoloured sash around his waist. The skirt is fully pleated. The long white trousers have bands and tassels at the knees. The woman wears a white headscarf and a flower at the front of her hair. A blouse of fine fabric is partly covered by a short black, gold-embroidered bolero/vest. The long jacket has black sleeves embroidered in red, and red fronts with red embroidery and black turned-up-toe slippers complete the outfit. (Courtesy Jenny Miller, Glenbrook, New South Wales)

Algeria (The Democratic and Popular Republic of) Africa

Covering an area of 2 381 740 square kilometres (919 352 square miles), Algeria is situated on the northern coast of Africa, with coastline to the Mediterranean Sea. To the east it has borders with Tunisia and Libya, to the south with Niger, Mali and Mauretania, and to the west with Western Sahara and Morocco.

Home of the nomadic Berber peoples, Algeria became a Roman province in 106 BC. The Vandals put an end to the rules of Rome in 429 AD, but the region came under Byzantine control early in the sixth century, and under the influence of Arabs, who brought Islam with them, in the seventh century. Apart from the capture of some coastal cities by Spain in the Middle Ages, Algeria remained under Arab rule until the middle of the sixteenth century when it became part of the Ottoman Empire.

Notoriously a stronghold of piracy and slave trading, Algeria seemed troublesome to other traders around the Mediterranean. After an insult suffered by the French consul in 1827, the French first blockaded Algiers, and then invaded it in 1830. Resistance from the Berbers was ferocious and it took until 1848 for the French to subdue the country; from then it became a colony with three departments.

By 1880 Europeans in Algiers had appropriated most of the fertile farmland. Many were French ex-soldiers, and others were from Italy, Spain and Malta.

In 1900 Algeria became locally autonomous under a governor-general. Two political movements developed among the Muslims after World War I: one called for full assimilation with France (the Muslims to be given French citizenship and equal rights with French settlers), while the other was nationalist and wanted independence.

Algeria became the Allied Armies' African base in World War II. France finally granted Algeria a national assembly in September 1947, but unfortunately only a few Muslims could qualify, thus keeping control firmly in European hands. Fighting broke out, and by 1956 the National Liberation Front controlled much of the country, despite considerable French resistance.

In September 1959 France was finally forced to concede to Algerians the determination of their own future. More resistance ensued, this time from those wishing to remain French.

After the Algerian people voted almost unanimously for independence, France recognised the new state on 3 July 1962. Constitutions have been made, suspended and new ones adopted over the last thirty years.

Capital Algiers.
Population 25.6 million, with 96 per cent of the population living in the north. 83 per cent are Arab, 17 per cent Berber, with a few French.
Religion Sunni Muslim 98 per cent with 60 000 Roman Catholics.
Language 75 per cent of the population speak Arabic, the official language, and 25 per cent speak Berber.

This French celluloid doll is dressed in a long sheer veil held to her dark pink bodice with gold-embroidered motifs. Across her face she has a short veil decorated at the hem. Her hip-length pink bodice has a yellow hem trim and is tied around the waist with a cream sash. She wears a long cream skirt and red shoes.

American Samoa See Samoa.

Andorra (Principality of) Europe

A small neutral co-principality since 1278, Andorra is situated in the Pyrenees mountains, roughly midway between Barcelona (Spain) and Toulouse (France). A small country, it covers only 453 square kilometres (175 square miles), is 30 kilometres (19 miles) long and 20 kilometres (12 miles) wide, and consists mainly of mountains, valleys and gorges. One of its main exports is hydroelectricity provided by the River Valira which flows south into Spain.

Tradition has it that Andorra was first granted self-government by Charlemagne for helping the King of the Franks in his war against the Saracens.

Capital Andorra la Velle.
Population Approximately 51 500.
Language Catalan, but some French and Castillian Spanish are more widely spoken.
Religion Roman Catholic, with a minority of Jewish, Jehovah's Witnesses and Protestants.

This little 17.75-cm (7-inch) vinyl doll is dressed in a black lace head-dress which extends past the shoulder. Her dress has a black bodice decorated with yellow braid. Her skirt is yellow cotton print, and she wears a black apron edged with lace and gold braid. The name Andorra and the coat of arms of Andorra are printed on the apron. The doll wears white undies and black shoes.

Argentina (Argentine Republic) South America

Occupying almost the whole of the southern part of South America, Argentina is bordered on the west by its slender neighbour Chile, on the east by the Atlantic Ocean and to the south are Cape Horn and the Antarctic Ocean. In

The 23-cm (9-inch) doll on the left represents an Argentine *gaucho* (cowboy). The doll wears a black felt hat turned up at the front and tied under the chin, and a blue headband and kerchief. Over a white shirt he wears a black jacket edged with gold braid. From the black leather belt hang the bolas, which when expertly thrown can bring down cattle. He carries a quirt (short whip) in the right hand and a serape (blanket) over the shoulder. The middle doll (plastic 24 cm, 9.5 inches) has black plaits with a white hair ribbon. Her red and white spotted everyday dress is completed with a frill at the hem, and a white neckerchief and apron. The third doll (plastic 23 cm, 9 inches) depicts a man from La Pampe. The doll has short black hair and wears an orange helmet-like cap with purple and yellow trim. Over the white shirt he wears a wide woven jacket with yellow trim. The doll has black trousers and black shoes and a drum slung over his shoulders (early 1970s). The female doll wears a white felt hat over a white headscarf, white blouse, yellow waistcoat decorated with braid in brown shades. Her orange skirt is also decorated with braid. She carries a small baby with an orange cap on her back. (Courtesy Audrey McMahon, New South Wales. Photograph: Shirleyanne McKay)

the north, Argentina has common borders with Bolivia, Paraguay, Brazil and Uruguay. The area of 2 766 889 square kilometres (1 068 000 square miles) encompasses 22 provinces and includes the fertile Pampas plains, as well as the Cordilleras range, with its highest point Mt Aconcagua (6960 m (22 834 ft). Extensive archaeological research has discovered that hunter-gatherers and fishermen were present in the area almost 12 000 years ago. The Spanish arrived in the first half of the sixteenth century, founding Buenos Aires in 1536. Today's Argentina was part of the Spanish vice-royalty of Peru until 1776 when Charles III of Spain established the vice-royalty of Rio de la Plata (which also included the present-day countries of Paraguay, Uruguay and Bolivia). Argentina was declared independent in 1816. Various rebellions and boycotts over an often unfair electoral system prevented stabilisation of the administration and electoral system until 1912.

Capital Buenos Aires.
Population Approximately 32.3 million, of which 85 per cent live in urban areas.
Language Spanish 95 per cent, 3 per cent Italian, 1 per cent Guaran (an Indian language), 1 per cent other languages.
Religion Christianity, 91 per cent Roman Catholics.

Armenia Asia Minor

Bordered by Georgia to the north, Azerbaijan to the east, Iran to the south and Turkey to the west, Armenia covers a total area of 30 000 square kilometres (11 580 square miles).

Part of the Turkish (Ottoman) and Russian Empires before World War I, Armenia became independent in 1918, only to be occupied by Russia and grouped with Azerbaijan and Georgia to form the Transcaucasian Federated Soviet Republic in 1921. The group was dissolved in December 1936 and Armenia became the Armenian Soviet Socialist Republic. The country regained independence after the dissolution of the Soviet Union in 1991.

Capital Yerevan.
Population 3.4 million of which 89.7 per cent are Armenian, 5.3 per cent Azerbaijani, 2.3 per cent Russian and 1.7 per cent Kurd.

This 28-cm (11-inch) plastic doll made in the USSR wears a grey turban and sash and a multi-striped jacket worn over breeches tucked into knee-length boots.

Wax-like plastic doll made in the USSR wears a mustard pillbox hat with gold decoration around the front and bead ornamentation at the sides. The hat is black over her sheer white gold-edged veil and two plaits hang down her back. Over her cream blouse she wears a purple dress with deep neckline decorated with gold. Gold is also used down the front and at the cuffs and hem. A mustard apron is decorated with gold and brown and the doll wears a mustard belt.

Australia (Commonwealth of)

The sixth largest continent, and also the only one-country continent, Australia is bordered on all sides by oceans or seas. These include the Pacific, Indian and Antarctic Oceans and the Tasman Sea.

The mainland is divided into six separately governed states and two territories: Western Australia, the Northern Territory, South Australia, Queensland, New South Wales, the Australian Capital Territory and Victoria, and together with the island state of Tasmania these make up the Commonwealth of Australia. Australia also administers the external territories of the Australian Antarctic Territory, the Cocos (Keeling) Islands, Christmas Island, Norfolk Island, Heard and McDonald Islands, the Territory of Ashmore and Cartier Island, and the Territory of Coral Sea Islands.

The land area of 7 682 300 square kilometres (2 965 368 square miles) includes tropical rainforest and desert regions, plateaus and basins of the Great Dividing

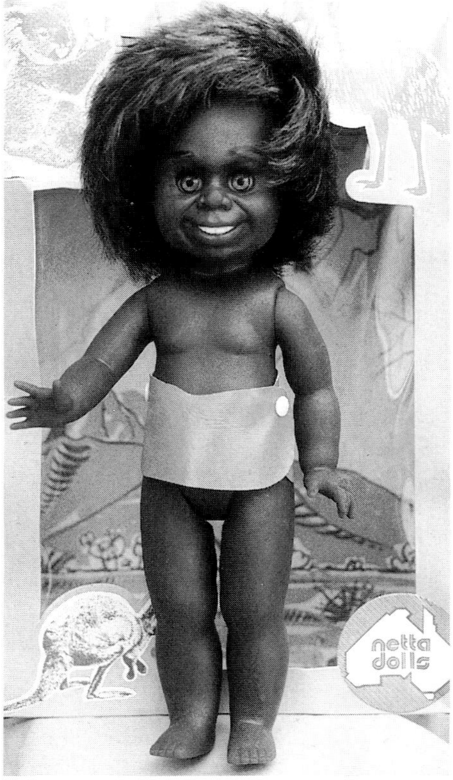

A truly Australian doll—'Bindi'. This 35.5-cm (14-inch) vinyl doll was designed in the 1960s to represent an Australian Aboriginal child, and was first manufactured by Metti of Adelaide, South Australia. The doll was continued by another Adelaide company, Netta, who bought Metti in 1976. This is a Netta doll and wears a vinyl wrap-around skirt; earlier dolls wore cloth wrap skirts. 'Bindi' was remodelled and copyrighted in 1992, and the new version is similar but with a closed mouth. The pre-1993 boxes were decorated with Aboriginal motifs and Australian fauna.

Three renditions of the popular Australian character doll the 'Swaggie' or swagman. Rather than a hobo or layabout as some people think, the doll represents an honest itinerant worker who in the late 1880s and again during the 1930s depression often had to walk vast distances to get work. The swagman was made famous by the Australian national song 'Waltzing Matilda' by Banjo Paterson. The doll on the left is the normal 17-cm (6.75-inch) plastic doll found in many souvenir shops. The middle doll is a very well made felt doll, and the doll on the right is an unusual version popular in some areas about 20 years ago. This doll has a cloth body and a well-painted mango-seed head with the pith acting as whiskers. All dolls have a felt hat, two with corks dangling from the brim. The swaying motion of the corks helped deter the bush flies found in vast numbers in inland Australia. A check, white or patterned shirt is worn, often with sleeves rolled up, and a vest over. The cord tied round the trouser leg (known as bowyangs) was to stop unwanted insects running up a leg, while the flapping lower leg deflected biting snakes. Over the shoulder the dolls carry a swag (hence the name swaggie) or bluey or 'Matilda': all three names were used for what is actually a blanket and bedding roll with clean clothes in the folds. Around the neck they wear their tea, flour and sometimes sugar bags. With these they could make tea, and bush bread called damper. The 'billy' is a fire-blackened tin for boiling water.

Wooden character dolls depicting early colonial costumes. These turned wooden dolls (9–14 cm, 3.5–5.5 inches) were made in the 1980s by Sugar Creek Toymakers of Bungwahl, New South Wales. (Courtesy Shirleyanne McKay, New South Wales)

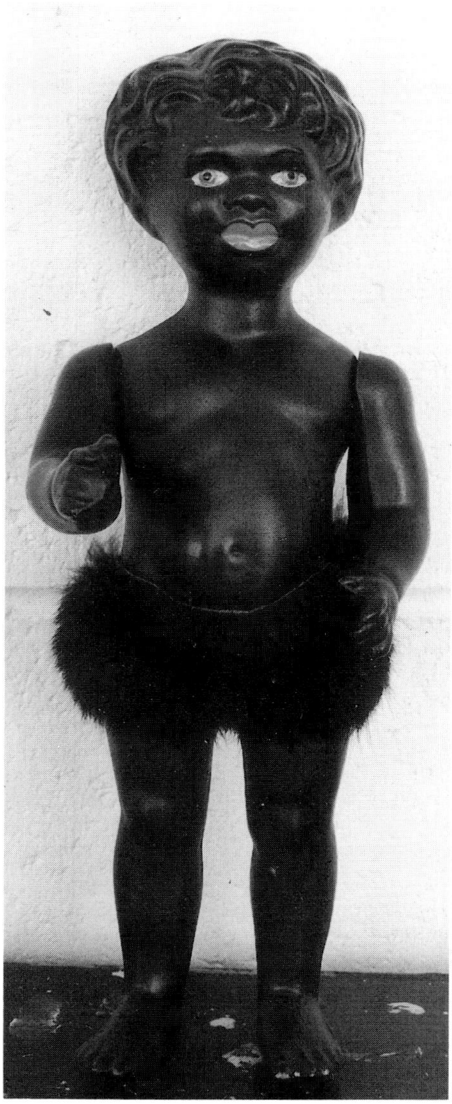

A clay/latex doll of the late 1940s and early 1950s with moulded hair and wearing a fur-like skirt. On the back of the doll is a map of Australia with state borders outlined. (Private collection, Sunshine Coast, Queensland)

Range, and in winter quite large snow-fields between New South Wales and Victoria. The highest mountain is Mt Kosciusko (2228 m, 7310 ft).

Archaeological research indicates that the Aborigines (the indigenous people) have lived in Australia for at least 60 000 years.

The first European settlement was the British penal colony established at Port Jackson (now Sydney, New South Wales) in 1788. Transportation of convicts from Britain ended in New South Wales in 1840, in Tasmania in 1853, and in Western Australia in 1867.

Free settlers migrated to Australia from the 1790s and representative government was granted in 1850. Depite the differing ideas of the then independent states, particularly with regard to railway gauges, postal systems and defence, the colonies of New South Wales, Victoria, Queensland and South Australia, Western Australia and Tasmania joined together in a Federation of States on 1 January 1901 and became the Commonwealth of Australia. The Northern Territory was divided from South Australia to become a separate member of the Commonwealth in 1911.

Capital Canberra (in the Australian Capital Territory).

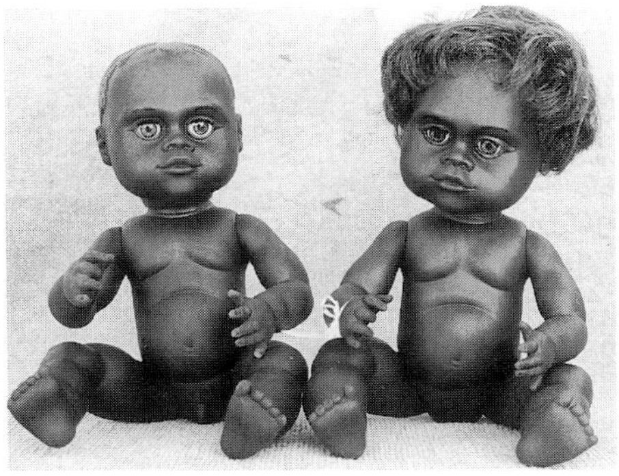

The Aboriginal baby dolls (vinyl 35.5 cm, 14 inches) made by Netta of South Australia and first released in early 1993. They depict Australia's indigenous people, whose children were often called piccaninnies.

Three foreign versions of the Australian Aborigine often sold in souvenir shops. On the left is a young girl made of stockinette. The 16.5-cm (6.5-inch) plastic doll in the middle has a headband and painted totem marks on the body and bark shield. The right-hand doll, of stockinette, is a hunter, also with headband and bark shield. These dolls are not good representations of the Australian Aborigine.

Population 17 million of which 86 per cent live in urban areas, mainly on the coastal fringe, due to the poor quality of land and lack of water inland. Approximately 94.4 per cent of the population is of European extraction, 2.1 per cent Asian and only 1.1 per cent the indigenous Aborigines. In 1987 3.49 million Australians had been born overseas: 1.2 million in the United Kingdom and Ireland, 1.5 million in Europe (Italy, Greece, the former Yugoslavia, Germany, The Netherlands, Poland, Malta, Lebanon), 606 000 in Asia and over 230 000 in New Zealand. In 1986 there were under 230 000 Aboriginal Australians and Torrest Strait Islanders.

Language English (official), but some native languages are spoken by the Aborigines living in their tribal areas.

Religion (optional census question) 73 per cent Christian, 0.5 per cent Muslim, 0.4 per cent Jewish, 0.2 per cent Buddhist.

Austria (Republic of) Europe

A land-locked country in central Europe, Austria borders on eight other countries: Germany, the Czech Republic, Slovakia, Hungary, Slovenia (once part of Yugoslavia), Italy, Switzerland and Liechtenstein. It is divided into nine federal states or lander with an overall area of 83 855 square kilometres (32 368 square miles) of which 64 per cent comprises the Austrian Alps, part of the large alpine system (commonly called the Tyrol) that connects Germany, Liechtenstein, Switzerland and Italy. The country's highest peak is the Grossglockner (3797 m, 12 457 ft). The very fertile Vienna Basin supports virtually all of Austria's arable land.

Hard-plastic dolls (14 cm, 5.5 inches). *Left* This female doll wears a tall black hat with upturned sides and braid band, a brown dress with scooped neckline with mauve drape insert, a braid waistband, green check apron, white stockings and black shoes. *Middle* The male doll wears a black truncated cone hat trimmed with flowers and feathers. He has a white shirt, red vest trimmed in gold/green, and a red jacket trimmed in gold/green with green cuffs. A white cord is draped around his shoulders, and he has a grey waistband, black breeches, white stockings and black shoes. *Right* This female doll wears an open-weave gold brocade cap tied into a top knot. She wears a maroon brocade dress with yellow brocade shawl held at the front with a gold button, light grey brocade apron, white stockings and black shoes.

These two 22-cm (8.75-inch) dolls by the Austrian firm Baitz have wire armature bodies covered with felt, and cellulon heads with painted features. The male doll has a black, slightly conical felt hat with gold cord bands, worn over short brown hair. Under his brown felt jacket with red lapels is a red waistcoat trimmed in green with silver buttons, over a white shirt. Black trousers with silver buttons at the waist, white stockings and black shoes complete the outfit. 'Leni' is the name printed on the female doll's tag. She wears a black flat-crowned hat with gold trim on the brim. Her blonde hair, braided and brought forward over the ears, is tied with black ribbon on top of the head. The black neckband is trimmed with gold, and a white blouse, gathered at neck and cuffs and trimmed with lace, is worn under a pink dirndl top trimmed with a gold insert and straps. Over the pink skirt is an embroidered apron trimmed with light taupe braid and a large black velvet bow at the waist. The doll wears white stockings and black shoes.

The present area of Austria was conquered by the Romans at the end of first century BC and was overrun by Germanic and Asiatic tribes in the fourth and fifth centuries AD. It became the eastern province (Ostmark) of the Frankish Empire in 790, and part of the Holy Roman Empire in 800. After many bloody years, Rudolf declared the Austrian ducal title hereditary in 1282.

During the next three centuries, combinations of war, diplomacy and judicious marriages expanded the Hapsburg domains, with the main setback

Both these small 16.5-cm (6.5 inch) plastic dolls have a tag with the *edelweiss* (Austria's national flower) on it. The male doll has 'Wachau' on the back of his tag. He has short brown hair under a black hat with slightly turned-up brim, trimmed at the back with feathers. He wears a long-sleeved white shirt and red tie under a black embroidered waistcoat trimmed with braid, black knee breeches, white stockings and black shoes. 'Wilten' is on the female doll's tag and the doll wears a tall stiffened black truncated-cone hat trimmed with cord, flowers and feathers. Over her white cotton blouse with lace ruffles at the elbows and ruffled lace collar with a black bow, she wears a red bodice with green trim and lacing. She has a black skirt and a blue figured apron. The undies are white knee-length panties, and she has white stockings and black shoes.

Two 22-cm (8.75-inch) dolls manufactured by Baitz, Austria, depict the *Alt-Wien* (old Vienna) costume. The female doll wears a pink poke bonnet, plain on the inside and check material on the outside, over blonde hair with ear puffs. The blue and white patterned dress has a bottom ruffle and is trimmed with lace. The doll wears white undies. The male doll sports a grey top hat with black band, and a white shirt with a mauve bow tie over which is worn a decorative waistcoat and a blue felt coat with black lapels. Blue check trousers, white socks and black shoes complete the outfit. The dolls have well moulded, painted cloth faces and bodies of felt over wire armatures.

Austria 'Bregenz' is marked on the back of the wrist tag. The doll wears a hat with an upstanding black lace brim over blonde plaits. The black velvet jacket is trimmed with narrow gold braid and worn over a red dirndl top. The black skirt is trimmed at the hem with red embroidered braid. The long white apron is trimmed with fine gold braid and lace. The doll has painted shoes and socks.

being the declaration of independence by Switzerland in 1453.

In 1804 Emperor Franz I renounced the title of Holy Roman Emperor. Then the defeat of Napoleon found Austria on the winning side, not only a principal territorial beneficiary of victory but also acknowledged as leader of a new German confederation.

The revolutionary upsurge in Europe led to Austria being compromised, until later it succumbed to Bismarck's version of a smaller Germany, finally being forced in 1866 to relinquish the German stage to Prussia. The 1914–1918 conflict led to the first Austrian Republic being proclaimed in 1919. The unopposed entry of German forces in March 1938 *(Anschluss)* meant that Austria was fully incorporated into Hitler's Reich.

After World War II Austria was occupied by the Soviet Union, United States, France and Britain, and a Second Republic was declared in December 1945. All occupation forces were withdrawn in 1955.

Capital Vienna.

Population Over 7.6 million, of which 55 per cent live in urban areas; 96 per cent Austrian, 1.7 per cent Yugoslav, 0.8 per cent Turkish, 0.5 per cent German.

Language German-speaking 97 per cent; others: Turks 60 000, Slovenes and Croats 32 000, Slovaks 23 000, Hungarians 19 000 and Czechs 10 000.

Religion Christianity, majority of which are Roman Catholic; 5.6 per cent Protestant and about 7000 Jews.

Azerbaijan (Republic of)

Covering a total area of 87 000 square kilometres (33 582 square miles), Azerbaijan has a coastline to the Caspian sea, and abuts the countries of Iran, Armenia and Georgia.

Part of the Turkish (Ottoman) and Russian empires before World War I, Azerbaijan became independent in May 1918. It was later occupied by Russian Communists and forged into the Trans-caucasion Soviet Socialist Republic (an amalgamation of Armenia, Azerbaijan and Georgia) which then became part of the USSR in 1922.

On 5 December 1936 the Trans-caucasian SSR was dissolved and the country became the Azerbaijan SSR.

In 1991 the country became independent.

Capital Baku.

Population 6.8 million, consisting of 78.1 per cent Azerbaijani, 7.9 per cent Armenian, 7.9 per cent Russian and 3.4 per cent Daghestani.

Bahrain (State of) Asia

The Independent State of Bahrain consists of a group of 35 low-lying islands situated in the Arabian or Persian Gulf, just 24 kilometres (15 miles) from the eastern

Azerbaijan (above and below) The male doll sits beside his red hookah. He wears a bright red turban, white shirt and long pink jacket hidden by his flowing white beard, white trousers and red shoes. (Courtesy Vera Woodhead, Queensland)

coast of Saudi Arabia and 28 kilometres (17 miles) from the western coast of the Qatar Peninsula. The total state area is 687 square kilometres (265.5 square miles). The central plateau on the island of Bahrain has a maximum elevation of 135 metres (443 ft). The islands are mainly barren due to poor soils, high salinity and semi-aridity; the 3 per cent of arable land is mostly located near springs and freshwater aquifers in the north of the island of Bahrain.

What is now Bahrain was the centre of the ancient civilisation of Dilmun between 2000 and 400 BC. In 1782 several families and tribes moved from Qatar to the nearby Bahraini islands, forming a ruling merchant class over the indigenous people, many of them of Persian descent. Bahrain finally came under British influence in 1820.

A treaty between Britain and the states on the southern side of the Persian Gulf was signed in 1835 prohibiting local fighting during the fishing and pearling season. When Britain withdrew in 1971 Bahrain became independent and its first parliamentary elections were held in December 1973.

Capital Manama.

Population 500 000 of which 78 per cent live in urban areas, 67 per cent are Bahrain Arab; 24 per cent Persian, Indian or Pakistani; 4.1 per cent other Arab and 2.5 per cent European.

Language Arabic (South Central Semitic) is the official language, although English is widely recognised as the commercial language. Farsi (Persian) and Urdu are also spoken.

Religion Islam. Of the 85 per cent Muslim, 60 per cent are Shi'ite, and 40 per cent Sunni; leaving 7.3 per cent Christian (24 600) and small minorities of Jewish, Baha'i, Hindu and Parsee.

This plastic and cloth doll (25 cm, 9.75 inches) wears a black pillbox hat with gold ornamentation around the brim, bead earrings, bead necklace, yellow blouse and a golden yellow jacket with gold ornamentation around the neck and down the front, and lemon lower sleeves. She wears a yellow belt with red buckle, yellow skirt with two-piece top flounce and black shoes.

This plastic doll (18.5 cm, 7.25 inches) from Bahrain wears a silver lace-fringed shawl over black plaits. She has heavy ornamentation at the forehead, and two large red flowers at ear level to which the thin face veil appears to be attached. A long silver brocade jacket open from just below the waist reveals a long brocade drape or apron concealing long blue trousers gathered at the ankles.

Bangladesh (People's Republic of) Asia

Situated between the foothills of the Himalaya and the Indian Ocean and bordered mainly by India and Myanmar (Burma), Bangladesh (formerly East Pakistan and previously part of Bengal and Assam) is approximately 144 036 square kilometres (55 598 square miles) in area and is dominated by three navigable rivers, the Ganges, Brahmaputra and Meghna. Their delta is the largest in the world and the country is predominantly low-lying fertile alluvial plain except for the highland regions in the north and northeast. Over two-thirds is arable and one sixth forested.

Bangladesh as a nation is compara-

An array of cloth dolls featuring the various costumes worn in Bangladesh including a doll with a cooking pot (second right back) and the doll on the right with a basket at her back carried by a rope on her head. The mother at the front is preparing food. (Courtesy Bangladesh Embassy, Canberra)

See also Brides.

A cloth doll from Bangladesh with painted features, black hair, a caste mark in the middle of her forehead and a fancy nose pin in the side of her nose. The sari is white with red trim. (Courtesy Bangladesh Embassy, Canberra)

tively new, although its history, due to its Indian origin, goes back thousands of years. Until 1947 Bangladesh was part of the British-ruled Indian provinces of Bengal and Assam. With independence granted to India and the creation of states along religious lines, Bengal was partitioned and the eastern part of the state, predominantly Muslim, combined with part of Assam to become the province of East Pakistan. Separated by 28 160 kilometres (11 000 miles) of Indian territory from its sister state West Pakistan, East Pakistan had more than half the country's total population. Bangladesh emerged as a separate state in 1971 after a civil war between West and East Pakistan. After years of military rule, presidential rule and martial law, Bangladesh returned to a Westminster-style parliamentary system of government in August 1991.

Three simple dolls from Bangladesh. The card reads CORR — THE JUTE WORKS, HANDMADE IN BANGLADESH, 100% JUTE FIBRE. Dressed in simple garments made from jute (hessian), the dolls depict a man (14 cm, 5.5 inches), wife (14 cm, 5.5 inches) and child (7 cm, 2.75 inches).

Capital Dhaka (Dacca).
Population Nearly 115 million of which only 13 per cent live in urban areas. 97.7 per cent are Bengali, 1.3 per cent Bihari and 1 per cent tribal, mostly in the Chittagong hills area.
Language Bangla/Bengali is the official language with English retained for legal and commercial use. There are also nearly 100 tribal dialects.
Religion Islam was declared the state religion in June 1988. About 86 per cent are Muslim (largely Sunni), 12.1 per cent Hindu, 0.6 per cent Buddhist and 0.3 per cent Christian (approximately 180 000 Roman Catholic and 26 500 Baptist).

Barbados (West Indies) North America

The Caribbean island of Barbados is situated approximately 435 kilometres (270 miles) northwest of Venezuela, and is 320 kilometres (199 miles) northeast of Trinidad. The island covers a total area of 430 square kilometres (165 square miles) and is divided into 11 districts. Predominantly low lying, with Mt Hillaby (340 m, 1115 ft) its highest point, the total land area is arable with sugar cane plantations covering 85 per cent of the cultivated terrain.

The earliest inhabitants of the Barbados were Arawak Indians, but the island was uninhabited immediately before the first European settlement in the 1620s. Although the first visitors were Portuguese, the first settlers were British and the island remained a British possession, becoming part of the Federation of the West Indies in 1958. It

A 23-cm (9-inch) cloth doll with embroidered features wearing a yellow turban with basket attached, red bead earrings, a blue blouse and white shawl caught at the front. The pleated skirt is two tone, yellow on top, dark check below, caught and gathered up at the centre front to show the white frilled slip (underskirt) trimmed in red. White panties.

was granted full internal self-government in 1961 and independence from Britain in November 1966.
Capital Bridgetown.
Population 300 000 of which 42.3 per cent live in urban areas. 91.9 per cent black, 3.3 per cent white, 2.6 per cent mulatto, 0.5 per cent East Indian.
Language English is the official language, although most speak an English-Creole dialect.
Religion Christianity. 39 per cent Anglican, 25.6 per cent other Protestant, approximately 24 000 Roman Catholic, with small communities of Hindus, Muslims and Jews.

Basutoland — see Lesotho.

Belarus (Byelarus, Byelorussia, White Russia) Europe

Belarus is a land-locked country covering an area of 208 000 square kilometres (80 288 square miles) with borders to the Russian Federation, Ukraine, Poland, Lithuania and Latvia.

Part of the Russian Empire until 1918, Byelorussia was formed out of the Tzarist provinces of Minsk, Mohilev, Viebsk and

A 28-cm (11-inch) plastic doll with a white headband with red decoration, white blouse with red decoration on the sleeves, neckband and down the front, red sleeveless jacket edged in red, blue plaid skirt, white apron with red bands and red/blue decoration, painted white stockings and black shoes.

This 28-cm (11-inch) plastic doll wears a long white shirt with simulated embroidery on the collar, front, sleeve cuffs and hem, and a yellow cord at the waist which should be tied at the left hand side. He has brown breeches and black boots.

Two small plastic dolls bought in Belgium in the 1970s depict the most common dolls found in this country. The Lacemaker doll sits on a wooden chair and is dressed in a hat with white pleated lace brim. A plum-coloured velvet dress has lace panels down the front, lace cuffs and apron, and a wide lace border with gold braid trim at the hem. Wooden sabots are worn on the feet. On the doll's lap is a check cushion from which hangs a piece of lace. On top of the lace are three turned wooden lace-making bobbins. The Orange-Seller doll wears a high white-plumed head-dress coming from a white tubular hat, with white side ribbons and gold 'V' trim; a white lace collar and white bow with a bell; beige top and trousers trimmed with black, yellow and red down the sleeves and sides of the trousers. The belt, also striped, has bells hanging from it. A red Belgian heraldic lion ornaments the front of the right leg, a black one the left leg. The doll wears sabots with yellow pompons, and has an orange in the right hand and a basket or oranges.

parts of Gomel and Grodno, becoming a constituent republic of the USSR along with the Ukraine and Russia. These were the basic Slavic republics when the USSR was officially created on 30 December 1922.

Because Byelorussia (sometimes referred to in the past as White Russia or Free Russia) was a land of open plains, it always had nebulous borders which shifted periodically with Russia, Poland and Lithuania. Besides the USSR, Byelorussia and Ukraine were the only Soviet Republics that were members of the United Nations during the years 1945–1991.

Known as Byelorussia from 1922–91, the country has chosen the name Belarus since the dissolution of the USSR in 1991 into separate republics and the Russian Federation.

Capital Minsk.

Population 10.1 million. Byelorussian 79.4 per cent, Russian 11.9 per cent, Polish 4.2 per cent, Ukrainian 2.4 per cent, Jewish 1.4 per cent.

Belgium (Kingdom of) Europe

Bordered by The Netherlands, Germany, Luxembourg, France and the North Sea (English Channel), Belgium is divided into nine provinces covering an area of 30 525 square kilometres (11 783 square miles) and including the forested Ardennes region (Mt Botrayes—694 m, 3277 ft) and a fertile and intensely cultivated central region. Fifty-two per cent of the total area is meadow, pasture or cultivated land (including the reclaimed polders on the North Sea coast), with 20 per cent forested.

Taking its name from a fierce Celtic tribe, the Belgae, conquered by Julius Caesar in 51 BC, Belgium was conquered by Germanic tribes, Christianised by the seventh century and absorbed into the Frankish Empire in the eighth century. By 1100 it was divided into four main domains, who regularly fought each other. With the end of the male Burgundian line in 1477, all the Low Countries passed by marriage to the House of Hapsburg, later becoming a province of Spain. After over 100 years, and some of the cruelest wars in history, the seven northern provinces of the Low Countries declared their independence from Spain, as The Netherlands, in 1581, while the 10 southern provinces (Belgium) remained under Spanish rule, later to pass to the Austrian Hapsburgs.

The armies of Napoleon Bonaparte finally ended Austrian rule in the Low Countries, and with the eventual defeat of France, the United Kingdom of The Netherlands (including Belgium and Luxembourg) was formed in 1814–1815. In 1830, the southern provinces (including over half of Luxembourg) proclaimed their independence of the Dutch, with final independence and neutrality gained in 1839.

Capital Bruxelles (Brussels).

Population 9 925 000 of which 97 per cent live in urban areas (10 per cent of the

This Flemish doll is 17.75 cm (7 inches), but 21.5 cm (8.5 inches) to the bottom of the skirt (this is a common trait in Belgian dolls). She wears a white lace head-dress with lace brim and flying panels each side. She wears a paisley shawl over her orange and tan jacket with lace at neck and sleeves, an orange and tan skirt with orange frill at the bottom and two bands of brown braid, and black shoes.

Bruxelles (Brussels) A plastic doll dressed in a white lace head-dress over blonde plaits, a white lace blouse, green corselet, red skirt with green bands and a band of white lace, and a lace apron with the Bruxelles crest and a gathered lace edging. The doll has a gold cross at her throat.

A 17.75-cm (7-inch) doll which is actually an 11.5-cm (4.5 inch) doll with long skirt. The doll wears a tall white head-dress with lace side puffs, a wide lace collar, orange dress with lace neck insert, and white decorated apron. She holds a brocade garland.

A 10-cm (4-inch) celluloid doll from the 1920s, wearing a white cap with wide front brim and flying lace panels; a gold cross; white lace blouse; mauve skirt with black band; and black apron with black/gold lace trim.

This plastic doll wears a red headscarf, white blouse with red trim and medallion at the neck, blue skirt trimmed in red with a lace border at the hem, and a white lace-edged apron with 'Souvenir Belgique' on it. On her back she carries a blue and white check basket.

Flanders This plastic doll (16 cm, 6.25 inches to hem) has a card reading 'ZANDRINE des FLANDRES, Le Minor Made in France.' She wears a white bonnet with wide lace brim; gold cross at the neck; white shawl with lace edging; white jacket with pleated peplum at the back; green satin brocade skirt; black apron with black lace edging; white undies.

urban population live within the metropolitan area of the capital. 55 per cent are Flemish (of Teutonic origin) and 33 per cent Walloons (French-Latin). Of the citizens of foreign birth (nearly 900 000) 31.8 per cent are Italian, 11.8 per cent French, 12 per cent Moroccan and 0.72 per cent Turkish.
Religion Christianity, with over 75 per cent Roman Catholic (8.72 million), 24 000 Protestants and 35 000 Jewish.
Language Official languages are French 32 per cent, Dutch (Flemish) 50 per cent, and German (the inhabitants of Wallonia, east of Liege), with the capital, Brussels, bilingual.

Bengal Asia

See Bangladesh for further information on the history, capital, population etc.

Bolivia (Republic of) South America

A land-locked country in the west of South America, Bolivia shares its borders with five other countries — to the north Peru and Brazil, and to the south Paraguay,

The all-clay 17-cm (6.75-inch) doll or figure on the left represents the God of Plenty, symbol of wealth and happiness. Hanging on a string around his neck are small parcels of 'food', and also a clay car, suitcase, shoes and so on. The 17.75-cm (7-inch) woman doll is made of cloth. She has black cloth hair, a flat white hat, white blouse, hand-woven cloak, and green woven skirt with red and yellow plaited trim. In her right hand she carries a spinning distaff. She wears black sandals. The 17.75-cm (7-inch) male doll has embroidered features and wears his hair in a single plait under a flat white hat. He has a green neckscarf over a white shirt, hand-woven vest, fawn trousers, black sandals, and a multicoloured cord at the side of his waist.

One of a series of International dolls by Madame Alexander, USA (1963-66). The plastic doll with bendable knees is dressed in a black hat, white jacket, black skirt, green undies. (Courtesy Audrey McMahon, New South Wales. Photograph: Shirleyanne McKay, New South Wales)

Argentina and Chile. It covers an area of approximately 1 098 580 square kilometres (424 052 square miles) which includes Lake Titicaca, the world's highest navigable body of water. Over 50 per cent of Bolivia is forested and less than 4 per cent is arable.

From the thirteenth to the sixteenth century the Incas ruled an empire which included Bolivia as well as parts of the countries that now surround it. With the Spanish conquest of the Incas, present-day Bolivia became Upper Peru in the Viceroyalty of Peru (1544-1824). Bolivia takes its name from Simon Bolivar (1783-1830), the national hero of many present-day South American countries.

The process of winning independence from Spain began in 1809, but was not successful until 1824. Later wars with Chile and Peru led to Bolivia becoming land locked.
Capital La Paz.
Population Approximately 7.3 million of which 49 per cent live in urban areas. 30 per cent are Quechua Indian, 25 per cent Aymara Indian, 30-35 per cent mestizos (mixed Indian and Spanish) and 5-10 per cent European (mainly of Spanish descent).
Language Spanish is the official language, but most Indians speak Aymara or Quechua; a composite of these three is also widely spoken.
Religion Roman Catholic 95 per cent with Baptist, Methodist, Baha'i and Jewish, as well as some traditional beliefs among the Indians.

Bosnia-Hercegovina Europe

Two land-locked provinces joined as one country cover a total area of approximately 51 129 square kilometres (19 736 square miles), depending where the borders are during the current turmoil in the area.

Under Justinian, the southwest of the country embraced Christianity. In 1463, Bosnia, the last major Serbian outpost in the Balkans, fell to the Ottoman Turks and became a tributary of Turkey. The country was annexed by Turkey in 1528, and Islam was introduced.

Under the Treaty of Berlin in 1878, after the Russo-Turkish war of 1877-78, Austria-Hungary was given the right to administer Bosnia and Hercegovina under nominal Turkish suzerainty.

In 1908 Austria announced the annexation of Bosnia-Hercegovina but England protested and demanded a conference on the issue. Austria refused, but offered a monetary compensation to the Sultan (Turkey). As England was not prepared to fight, Austria had its way. Serbia was exasperated and anti-Austrian propaganda, both inside and outside Austrian territory, eventually led to the outbreak of World War I.

At the end of World War I, in November 1918, the Serbian monarchy

Left This doll is dressed in a red pillbox hat with gold medallion trim, worn under a white headscarf. She has a white blouse, red bolero trimmed with yellow braid, black waistband, white trousers and red shoes with white ornamentation. *Right* The doll wears a cream head-dress, white blouse with lace cuffs and collar, small pink scarf, red skirt and black apron trimmed with yellow braid.

united Serbia and Montenegro with the former Austro-Hungarian territories of Slovenia, Dalmatia, Croatia, Bosnia, Hercegovina and Vojvodina to form the new Kingdom of Serbs, Croats and Slovenes. The country's name was changed to Yugoslavia in 1929.

Yugoslavia was overrun by German armies in April 1941, and the Germans created the Independent State of Croatia, incorporating into it much of Bosnia-Hercegovina. After World War II Bosnia-Hercegovina was once again part of Yugoslavia, but as a separate unit within the country. The Muslims, who make up the larger part of the population, were recognised as an ethnic group in 1969.

In 1991 Bosnia-Hercegovina indicated that it did not intend to remain in the Yugoslavian federation if Croatia and Slovenia seceded, and it has since become a country in its own right, although racked by civil war and with a dubious future.
Capital Sarajevo.
Population Approximately 4.1 million.
Religion Predominantly Mulsim.
Language Serbo-Croat; they mainly use the Latin alphabet.

Brazil (Federative Republic of) South America

Brazil has the fifth largest land area of any country in the world, an area of 8 511 965 square kilometres (3 288 585 square miles) situated in central and northeastern South America. With just over 7 per cent of the land arable, two-thirds of the area *was* forested (accounting for one-seventh of the earth's total forest area). Bounded on the northeast and east by the South Atlantic Ocean, Brazil shares its land borders with the following nations — Bolivia, Paraguay and Uruguay in the south, Peru in the west, and Colombia, Venezuela, Guyana, Surinam and French Guiana in the north.

The indigenous Indians initially welcomed the arrival of the Portuguese in 1500, who named the area Brazil after the much sought-after red dyewood *pau-brasil*. In 1533 Portugal divided the territory into twelve captaincies, hoping to consolidate its control against growing British, French and Spanish interest. With various periods of foreign rule and intervention from the Spanish (1580–1640) and the Dutch (1637–1654), and later the French invasion of Portugal in 1808, the final ties with the Iberian Peninsula were only cut when Brazil gained its independence in 1822. In 1889 the Republic of Brazil was proclaimed. A new capital city — Brasilia — was founded in 1960, and the whole city built from the ground up in three years.
Capital Brasilia.
Population 150.4 million of which 75 per cent live in urban areas (30 per cent of these live in the coastal strip). 53 per cent are of European extraction (Portuguese, Italian, Spanish and German), 22 per cent mulatto, 12 per cent mestizo, 11 per cent black and 0.8 per cent Japanese.
Religion Mainly Christianity; 89 per cent Roman Catholic, 6.6 per cent Protestant, 2.0 per cent Afro-American Spiritualist, 1.7 per cent Spiritualist, 0.3 per cent Buddhist, 0.2 per cent Jewish, and the Dahomeyan voodoo cult is active in some areas.
Language Portuguese is the official language, with over 120 Amerindian languages. German and Italian are second languages.

The 20-cm (8-inch) plastic doll on the left is actually a double-headed or 'Topsy-turvy' doll. The side showing represents 'Carnival', the other doll underneath is dressed in ordinary clothes. The Carnival doll wears a blue headscarf with a basket of fruit on top as well as large gold earrings, gold bracelets and a bead necklace. The dress has a lace bodice and a three-tiered green, yellow and blue skirt with lace trimming. A blue sash completes the outfit. Underneath, the doll wears a floral turban, fruit in a basket, gold earrings, necklace and bangle. The dress has a floral bodice and the skirt is trimmed with blue flowers. The small 19-cm (7.5-inch) doll has 'BRAZIL NAGO' on the back. Her yellow bandana is topped with a cane basket of fruit. She wears gold earrings, a gold necklace and bangles and a bead necklace. A deep lace collar is worn over a mauve, lemon and mustard skirt trimmed with silver lace. The doll wears red sandals.

Brides

Throughout the world, the costume worn by both brides and grooms is usually of great traditional significance, and varies greatly from country to country. While white is the colour normally worn by brides in modern western countries, in other areas this is not necessarily so, and in Japan the traditional colour is red.

Turkey These 19-cm (7.5-inch) painted plastic dolls represent a Turkish bridal couple. The female doll wears a red turban with green front trim, covered with a thin pink veil. Her red floral jacket is trimmed in green brocade. She wears a long white skirt and holds a 'plate' with candles in each hand. The male doll wears a tall white head-dress which flows down the back of the head and is trimmed in gold. He wears a striped shirt, and long red over-gown with gold and brown edging. His wide green waistband holds an antique pistol and a scimitar. He has white baggy breeches and black pointed-toe shoes. (Courtesy Vera Woodhead)

Korea Two pairs of Korean dolls in traditional costume. The pair on the left portray the traditional wedding outfits worn by bride and groom. The female doll on the right wears a tiny crown at the front of her forehead. Dolls similar to this portray a princess from Korea's history.

Hungary A pair of 21.5-cm (8.5-inch) cloth dolls with painted features, dressed in their wedding regalia. The female has a floral head-dress and fine veil. The dress is white brocade satin with short puff sleeves, trimmed in blue. Her skirt is finely pleated and has an embroidered blue braid halfway down the skirt and blue ribbon at the hem. Her apron is also finely pleated with blue ribbon trim and lace edging. Her petticoat is finely pleated as well, helping to hold out her skirt. She wears black shoes. The male doll has a black hat trimmed in red and white braid, white shirt with wide sleeves trimmed in red and green with red predominating. He wears full, finely pleated white trousers, black waistcoat with yellow trim, black richly decorated apron with long black fringing and black boots to complete his outfit.

Bangladesh A pair of cloth dolls depicting the traditional wedding attire of the country. The groom wears a turban with small bells on the end. He has a long white jacket with high collar and silver buttons, white trousers, and a long floral lei around his neck. The bride is dressed in red, and has a painted design on her forehead and a gold nose pin. She also wears jewellery at the neck and wrists. Her gown is embroidered and edged with gold trimming.

Norway These 21.5-cm (8.5-inch) dolls have resin heads and hands and cloth-covered wire-armature bodies. The female doll (bride) wears a tall gold crown with red interior on her long blonde hair. Her white blouse has lace at the neck, and the red sleeveless jacket has green trimming and an embroidered insert. Her waistband is braid over a red skirt with silver trimming and green hem. Her white apron has orange ribbons over it and she holds her virginity sampler in her right hand. The male doll (groom) wears a black hat, white shirt with lace trim and black bow tie. His waistcoat, with green front and white back, is trimmed in red. Black trousers and shoes finish his outfit.

Japan The doll wears traditional Japanese bridal costume: a wide white hat and a red and gold kimono.

Poland (Cracow) A pair of 13-cm (5-inch) plastic dolls in their wedding finery. The bride doll wears a red and green fringed head-dress with flowers on top. She has a white dress over which is worn a sheer lace apron. She wears a floral vest with lace streamers. The male doll wears a flat red hat with green, yellow and red streamers hanging from it. His heavy long off-white coat is trimmed in red. He wears a white shirt, red belt, and red and white striped trousers tucked into high black boots.

Philippines Bridal pair of cloth dolls. The bride doll is 21.5 cm (8.5 inches) tall and wears a white gown made from pineapple fibre. She wears a gold necklace, pearl earrings and carries a bouquet. Her sheer white veil is missing. Her black hair is coiled at the nape of her neck. The groom, who is 21 cm (8.25 inches) tall, wears a white self-striped shirt of pineapple fibre, with black trousers and shoes.

Morocco *Above* A bridal pair of 17.75-cm (7-inch) plastic dolls. The male doll is labelled 'Rich Berber wearing the Bedaya'. He has a red felt fez, white shirt with high collar, blue waistcoat with gold buttons and coloured ric-rac trim. Long white baggy pants and yellow pointed shoes complete his outfit. The female doll has a sheer orange veil with gold headband ornament and facial ornamentation, as well as fancy earrings. Her face veil is edged with lace and she wears a long brocade frock with gold braid on the bodice, neck and waists. Long full underpants and green felt shoes complete the ensemble. The doll is labelled 'Noble Berber girl in her wedding dress'. Both dolls are circa 1970s.

Brides of India These dolls were made in the workshop of Shankar's Doll Museum, Delhi, India, for the author as part of an exchange programme.

Manipur *Top centre* The Manipur bride wears a stiff bell-shaped skirt decorated with tiny mirrors and sequins. The shawl which covers her head is made of pineapple fibre. The doll's head-dress and richly embroidered skirt are red, and the ornamentation is in gold and silver with mirror work. Her *kurta* (blouse) is navy blue with white trim at the neck. Her shawl is edged in gold brade. The caste-mark on her forehead and the jewellery add to the effect.

Himachal Pradesh *Right* Himachal, in the foothills of the Himalaya, requires the bride to be well clad in a colourful skirt, a tight bandana-like scarf around her head and a huge nose ring, along with other jewellery such as bangles, necklaces and anklets. The doll wears a red scarf and tight-fitting jacket edged with gold. Her dark blue skirt is edged with a wide band of gold braid, and she has a series of necklaces and large looped bead earrings as well as small beads on her nose ring.

Delhi *Above* The Delhi bride wears the truly national costume as worn by the modern Indian woman today, except that her sari is richer, either of costly brocade or heavily embroidered with gold thread. The doll is dressed in a pink sari with a wide gold-embroidered and sequined edge. She wears many gold and red bracelets, a hair adornment and a long chain with a medallion on it. Her hands are richly painted with henna designs.

Kerala *Top left* The Kerala bride, keeping the hot climate of her southern-most state in mind, prefers a cool crisp two-piece cotton sari (*mund* and *neriyathu*) as her bridal attire. The purple mund is used as a petticoat, while the neriyathu is pale cream edged in gold, worn over it like a sari.

Assam Khasi bride *Left* From the hill country of northeast India, the Khasi bride wears the Christian bride's white gown adapted to the state in which she lives. It is in simple style heavily decorated with gold braid at the hem and side edge. She wears a ruff of white lace around the neck and similar lace cuffs. The doll's ensemble is finished off with two long necklaces.

Uttar Pradesh Muslim bride This bride wears a dress typical of the religion, a long flowing divided skirt with a short *kurta* or blouse draped over with a bordered *dupatta* or long stole. The doll's outfit is red with long fringing of gold on the dupatta and gold borders on the kurta and divided trousers.

Punjab bride and groom The bride wears a heavy red and gold *salwar-kameez* with a gold-bordered *dupatta* or shawl. Her red bangles are loaded down with silver and gold *kaliras* that her friends tie on as good luck charms. The male doll is dressed in white and gold with a very elaborate head-dress.

Jammu and Kashmir bride and bridegroom The people of Jammu and Kashmir wear uni-sex clothing. The *salwar* and *kurt* are loose roomy pyjamas and shirts which not only keep them warm but also allow free movement. The male doll (groom) wears a green turban adorned with a pink feather and medallion at centre front. He wears a black kurta with attached long cape edged in gold braid. Around his neck he wears a string of seed pods. His salwar is white and his shoes black. The female doll (bride) is dressed in a pink salwar and kurta painted to simulate embroidery, and the kurta has hand embroidery at the centre front, and also wide white cuffs. She wears a green headscarf with silver trim. She has silver medallions adorning the front of her hair, very large silver earrings, silver nose ring and silver necklace and many bangles.

Bulgaria (People's Republic of) Europe

Situated in eastern Europe with borders to Romania, Serbia (formerly part of Yugoslavia), Greece and the Black Sea, Bulgaria covers an area of 110 912 square kilometres (42 812 square miles) and is divided into 28 provinces or *okruzi*. The Danube Plain extends south from the Romanian border, making up about one-third of Bulgaria's total area. The Balkan Mountains cross central Bulgaria and the Rhodope Massif (highest point 2925 m, 9596 ft) divides Bulgaria from Greece. Thirty-five per cent of the land area is arable and 35 per cent forest and

On the baseplate of this doll is the word 'SOFIA'. The doll has a wooden ball head, painted features and a cloth body. He wears a white lambswool hat over leather hair; a white shirt with red and black embroidery down the sleeves and front, under a black waistcoat with red/orange/yellow yarn border; a wide red waistband with two white panels decorated with red, gold and black braid tucked under its black baggy breeches tucked into long white socks; and brown shoes with upturned toes. The doll holds a large bottle in his hands. (Courtesy Vera Woodhead, Queensland)

Four 17-cm (6.75-inch) dolls with wooden bead heads, wire armature bodies and painted felt hands. *From left* The male doll wears a black fur hat; white shirt with red, black and yellow painted decoration down the front and red-edged sleeves; red cummerbund; black cotton trousers with white painted decoration tucked into white socks laced with black; grey turned-up-toe shoes. The female doll has black plaits under a pink babushka. Her white blouse has painted decoration at the front opening. She wears a white underskirt edged with lace and brown thread, and over this a green skirt with white and orange wool threaded at the hemline; a red apron richly painted in stripes; pink wool stockings with brown bands; and beige turned-up-toe shoes. The second male is similar to the first except for beige trousers and shoes and brown lacing over his socks. The male doll on the right has a black velvet cap with back point; white shirt; red cummerbund with tasselled fringe; black breeches, with white ornamentation; white socks laced in black; grey turned-up-toe shoes; and carries a pipe and bag instrument.

woodland, with the highest population density in the Danube Basin area.

The Thracians were the earliest known inhabitants of present-day Bulgaria, migrating from the Eurasian Steppes around 3500 BC. During the third century BC they were subject to the Macedonians and then the Romans. The Bulgars, tribes of mixed Slav and Turkish origin, arrived in the area between the fifth and seventh centuries AD and by the seventh century a Bulgarian state had emerged. The Bulgarians embraced Christianity in 864, and an independent Bulgarian church was established in 1870. Bulgaria was an important power in the Balkans during most of the medieval period.

The country was overcome by Ottoman armies in the fourteenth century, Turkish domination lasting almost 500 years, and it wasn't until the late nineteenth century that Bulgarian culture was revived. In 1876 a Bulgarian uprising against the Turks was brutally suppressed, but after the Ottoman defeat in the Russo-Turkish war of 1877–78, a large Bulgarian state stretching from the Danube to the Aegean was established. Due to pressure from Great Britain and Austria this area was reduced in 1878. In 1908 Prince Ferdinand of Saxe-Coburg-Gotha declared independence, with himself as head of state. Bulgaria, forming a coalition with Serbia and Greece, almost drove the Turks from the Balkans in 1912. After World War I Bulgaria went through a period of political turbulence ending in dictatorship in 1934. It was neutral from 1939 to 1941, when it joined the Axis powers, and declared war on Germany in 1944 when the monarchy was abolished and the Red Army extended its control over the country. Bulgaria came under Soviet Union control and it wasn't until the 1990s that free multi-party elections were held.

Capital Sofia.

Population 8 995 000 of which 64 per cent live in urban areas. Over 85 per cent Bulgarian, with Turks 8.5 per cent (in the northeast and east), Gypsies 2.6 per cent, Macedonians 2.5 per cent, and smaller communities of Armenians, Romanians, Greeks, Russians and Tartars.

Religion 80–85 per cent Eastern (Bulgarian) Orthodox, approximately 60 000 Roman Catholic, 10 000 Pentecostal Protestant, about 13 per cent Muslim and 0.8 per cent Jewish.

Language Bulgarian — a member of the South Slavonic language family, related to Serbo-Croat, Slovene, Russian and Macedonian. The cyrillic alphabet is used. Greek, Turk and Albanian vocabularies have been assimilated and Romany (220 000) and Turkish (760 000) are also spoken.

Burma (Myanmar, Union of Myanmar) Asia

Situated in Southeast Asian, with borders to Bangladesh, India, China, Laos, Thailand and the Bay of Bengal, Burma covers an area of 676 577 square kilometres (261 159 square miles) under 14 administrative divisions. The majority of the population (75 per cent) lives in the central lowlands. The highest peak, Hkakabo Razi (5967 m, 19 577 ft), is located in the north on the Chinese border.

During the country's early history no one racial group was prominent, but in the eleventh century the Tibeto-Burmese, the most numerous, united the country under the founder of the Pagan dynasty, which continued to rule until the end of the thirteenth century. This era is popularly known as the country's Golden Age. In 1287 Kublai Khan's Mongol armies captured Pagan, and although Mongol control ended in 1303 the second

These two 25.5-cm (10-inch) cloth dolls were made to represent Burma by Bangkok Dolls in Thailand in the 1970s. The male doll wears a white scarf turban, white shirt, black waist-length jacket, check wrap-around sarong (skirt), with wide pleat at the front. He also has red sandals, a cord waistband, and a woven bag with tassels and a wide black strap. The female doll has an elaborate hairdo, piled on top to hang down the side, and caught at the neck with flowers. She wears earrings, a short white crop top covered by a waist-length long-sleeved jacket, a yellow brocade sarong, deep pink scarf around her neck, and gold sandals.

The dolls are dressed in gauzy clothing, with tiny shell bracelets and anklets. The hair is elaborately moulded as part of the doll. (Courtesy Gwenda Spencer, Queensland)

This pair of cloth dolls with well-painted features was made in Thailand by a well-known doll manufacturer to represent a couple from Cambodia. The female doll (24 cm, 9.5 inches) has black hair and wears earrings. The pink broderie top with gold and diamante buttons is worn over reddish-brown draped trousers. Her gold/black handbag matches her shoes and she has gold bangles on each wrist. The male doll has black hair and wears a hip-length white jacket with two flap pockets and two inset pockets below the waist. A mustard yellow and brown design brocade sash is worn at the waist. Blue draped trousers and black pointed shoes complete the outfit.

Kingdom was not founded until the sixteenth century, when the Toungoo dynasty reunited the country. However, continuous fighting with neighbouring countries caused the kingdom and dynasty to fall into decline. The third and final dynasty, Konbaung, arose in the eighteenth century, controlling all of the present country, much of northeast India and western Thailand.

In the 1700s Britain viewed Burma's expansion into India as a threat to its own plans and three Anglo-Burmese wars in 1824, 1852 and 1885 led to Britain incorporating the country into the British Empire as a province of India in 1886. In 1937 Burma was separated from India and given its own constitution and elected parliament. Following British withdrawal five years later, the country was occupied by Japan, and in 1943 declared war on Britain and the United States.

Britain re-occupied the country in 1945 and independence was granted in 1947, resulting in 1948 in an entirely independent nation known as the Union of Burma. Due to continued unrest, military rule has dominated from the 1960s until today.

Capital Rangoon (Yangoon).
Population (1990 estimate) 41.3 million of which 23 per cent live in urban areas. 68 per cent are Bam/Burman (of Tibeto-Chinese extraction), 2 per cent Chin, 9 per cent Shan, 7 per cent Karen, 3 per cent Chinese and 2 per cent Indian.
Religion 85 per cent adhere to Theravada (an ancient strain of Buddhism); Animist, Hindu, Muslim and Christian minorities make up the rest.
Language Burmese is the official language, but there are also 100 indigenous languages spoken in the country. English is the second language, taught from kindergarten.

Cambodia (State of) Asia

Bordered by Thailand, Laos, Vietnam, and the Gulf of Thailand, Cambodia is situated in the Indochinese Peninsula in Southeast Asia and covers an area of 181 035 square kilometres (69 880 square miles). It is divided into 18 provinces. Approximately 75 per cent of the total land area is fertile lowland surrounding Tonie Sap (Great Lake) and 75 per cent of the country is forested. The vast majority of the population is rurally employed in forestry, fishing and subsistence agriculture.

According to Khmer myth the state of Funan was founded in the first century AD on the site of present-day Cambodia. During the fourth and fifth centuries the culture was broadened by Indianisation and early in the ninth century the Angkor Empire was founded north of Tonie Sap. Angkor reached its zenith in the eleventh century, falling into decline after 1215. The conquest of Angkor in 1444 led to the re-establishment of the Khmer kingdom of Phnom Penh (at the site of the current capital).

French rule over Cambodia evolved

out of France's involvement in Vietnam. During the 1850s the French wanted to expand against other potential aggressors, mainly Britain and Thailand, so in 1862 the king of Cambodia was forced into accepting protectorate status for his kingdom, and again in 1884 to sign an agreement making Cambodia a full French colony.

Japan occupied Cambodia in late 1940, and after the Japanese surrendered in 1945 the French returned. In 1946 absolute monarchy was abolished. Cambodia became independent in November 1953, and the head of state attempted to preserve the country's neutrality during the Vietnam war. After a coup in 1970 the country was renamed the Khmer Republic, and the decade that followed brought ferocious political purges and genocide. It wasn't until the late 1980s and early 1990s that Cambodia demobilised 70 per cent of all armed forces and free elections were eventually held in 1993.

Capital Phnom Penh.

Population Estimated at between 6.6 and 7.8 million, of whom 85 per cent live in rural areas. At the last census 93 per cent were Khmer, 4 per cent Vietnamese and 3 per cent Chinese.

Religion In 1989 Buddhism was elevated to the national religion. In 1980, 88.4 per cent practised Theravada Buddhism, 2.4 per cent were Muslim and a small minority Roman Catholic.

Language Khmer is the official language, although French is widely understood. The written language is a script of Indian origin dating back to the seventh century.

Cameroon (Republic of) Africa

Fronting the Gulf of Guinea to the southwest, Cameroon borders on Nigeria (west and north), Lake Chad, Chad, the Central African Republic (east) and Congo, Gabon and Equatorial Guinea to the south. Covering an area of 475 439 square kilometres (183 519 square miles), Cameroon is divided into 10 provinces. Thirteen per cent of the country is arable, but only 2 per cent is under permanent cultivation, while about 54 per cent is forested.

Little is known of the early history of the country, except that a large number of ethnic groups, including Bantu-speaking tribes, migrated to the south before the first century BC.

The Portuguese sailed up the Wouri River in 1472, naming it Rio dos Camaroes, from which Cameroon got its name. By early in the seventeenth century, Portuguese, Dutch and English traders were competing for the lucrative export trade in slaves.

A small 5-cm (2-inch) bead and shell doll. The face is of green beads, with yellow around blue for the eyes and blue beads for the mouth and eyebrows. The main part of the doll is done in blue and yellow beads arranged in a check pattern. The doll wears a red and black 'apron'. (Courtesy Jenny Miller, Glenbrook, New South Wales)

Germany signed a treaty with the chiefs in July 1884, setting up the protectorate of Kamerun. British and French forces occupied Kamerun during World War I, and in 1922 it was made a mandate of the League of Nations. After World War II the western part of the country — North and South Cameroons — was administered by the British as part of Nigeria, while the western part was administered by France, as French Cameroon, and was treated as a French Equatorial territory.

After a United Nations plebiscite in October 1961 the North Cameroons became part of Nigeria, while the Southern Cameroons formed a federal state with the independent former French Cameroon, and on 2 June 1971 the United Republic of Cameroon was declared.

Capital Yaounde.

Population (1990) 11.1 million of which 42.4 per cent live in urban areas. Over 200 ethnic groups populate the country, with the Fang (the largest, 19.6 per cent) followed by the Bamum, Duala, Luanda, Bassa, Fulani, Tikar, Mandara, Maka, Chamba, Mbum, Haiwa, and 0.2 per cent French. Over 8500 refugees from Chad were in Cameroon in 1987, and the Pygmy-Babinda people inhabit the southern forests.

Religion 39 per cent still practise indigenous animist faiths, 21 per cent are Catholic, 18 per cent Protestant, and 21 per cent Muslim.

Language French and English are the official languages. In the north the people are predominantly Sudanic speaking, with Bantu spoken in the northwest and equatorial forest areas.

Canada North America

Covering 40 per cent of the North American continent, Canada is divided up into 10 provinces and two territories, whose combined area totals 9 976 140 square kilometres (3 850 790 square miles) with approximately 243 791 kilometres (151 394 miles) of coastline,

Inuit (Eskimo) These two dolls have all-leather bodies and their leather faces have painted features. The doll on the left has a black leather hood trimmed with white fur around the face. The long black jacket or dress is trimmed with white fur. White knee-length socks and brown shoes. The doll on the right has a dark brown hood trimmed with brown fur. The brown jacket has fur at the cuffs and bottom edge and the brown trousers also have brown fur cuffs. Black boots with tan leather soles.

Two hard plastic dolls dressed to represent varying aspects of Canada. The small tan-coloured doll on the left is fully dressed in fur hood, jacket and trousers to represent the Eskimo/Inuit people who live in the Arctic regions of Canada. The 28-cm (11-inch) doll on the right represents the Canadian Mounted Police in dress uniform. The doll wears a plastic hat, suede flocked to represent their specially styled hat, with tan leather band; red leather jacket with brown leather collar, belting and pistol holster, yellow buttons and cord; black leather jodhpurs with tan side stripes and brown leather boots.

Prince Edward Island A 'Reliable' (Canada) plastic doll with long black braids is dressed in tan suede leather with fringed collar and hem, and is ornamented with coloured beading on the dress and shoes (moccasins). The doll also has a beaded headband into which a red feather has been tucked. The doll is a souvenir of the Prince Edward Island province.

A 19-cm (7.5-inch) hard-plastic doll with sleeping eyes made by the Canadian firm Reliable (Pat. 1958). The doll is dressed as a Canadian Mountie and wears a plastic hat formed in the correct peak shape, and a red jacket with yellow and blue trim, small brass buttons and leather shoulder and waist belting. The black trousers have yellow stripes down the sides of the leg. Black leggings simulate boots.

making it the second largest country in the world.

The vast Canadian Shield (seldom more than 600 m, 1968 ft high) covering nearly 50 per cent of Canada, the St Lawrence-Great Lakes lowlands and the interior plains of Saskatchewan and Manitoba (extensions of the United States prairie land), the rugged terrain of Nova Scotia and New Brunswick and the Arctic Archipelago give Canada a great diversity of geographical features. Mt Logan (5951 m, 19 524 ft) in the Yukon Territory is Canada's highest peak. Over 35 per cent of Canada is forested, 5 per cent is arable and 80 per cent of the population live within 160 km (100 miles) of the United States border.

The first human inhabitants were mongoloid peoples from Asia who crossed a land and ice bridge (now the Bering Strait). Evidence has emerged that the Inuit people regularly transversed the European, Asian and American Arctic area. The first European settlers were Vikings who settled for a short while in Newfoundland in the eleventh century. Extensive European settlement did not begin until after the Italian navigator John Cabot (on behalf of Henry VII of England) landed at Newfoundland in 1497. The French explorer Jacques Cartier discovered and claimed the St Lawrence Basin for France in 1534.

From 1686 the French and English settlements clashed regularly as their fur trading activities overlapped. In 1754 the French and Indian War broke out in North America between Britain and France, resulting in a resounding defeat for the French. They were forced to relinquish the St Lawrence and Quebec settlements to Britain which then had control of the whole area.

During the American Revolution (1775–78) many royalists living in America sought refuge in Canada, and the ensuing strong anti-American sentiment led to America feeling threatened and an attempted American invasion of Canada in the War of 1812. At the end of the war most of the Canadian/United States border was confirmed, excepting the Canada/Maine border settled with a treaty in 1842, and the Oregon Treaty in 1846.

The Canadian colonies achieved effective self-government in 1848, and later became the Dominion of Canada. In 1982 Canada acquired the right to amend its constitution without seeking the approval of the British parliament.

Capital Ottawa.

Population (1990 estimate) 26.6 million of which 75.9 per cent live in urban areas. The 1986 census showed that 28 per cent were of mixed ethnic origin; 6.3 million of British extraction, 6.09 million of French extraction, 709 000 Italian, 420 000 Ukrainian, 897 000 German,

352 000 Dutch, 360 000 Chinese, and 1.5 per cent aboriginal people including the Metti, Dene, indigenous North American Indians and 25 000 Inuit.
Religion Roman Catholic 46.5 per cent, Protestant 41.2 per cent, Eastern Orthodox 1.5 per cent, Jewish 1.2 per cent, Muslim 0.4 per cent, Hindu 0.3 per cent and Sikh 0.3 per cent.
Language English and French are both official languages and bilingualism is officially encouraged. 62.7 per cent speak English and 25.4 per cent French, and 4 million speak both. Native languages are Cree (57 645), Ojibway (16 380), Eskimo/Inuktitut (21 000).

Canary Islands Atlantic Ocean

The Canary Islands are a group in the Atlantic Ocean situated off the coast of Morocco in northwest Africa. The larger islands are Teneriffe, Grand Canary, Palma, Gomera, Hierro, Fuerteventura, Lanzorti; with six others they cover an area of 9728 square kilometres (3800 square miles).

First colonised in the fifteenth century, the whole archipelago forms two of Spain's provinces.

Celebes (Sulawesi) Asia

See Indonesia for further information.
This peculiarly shaped island lying east of Borneo, was known as Celebes when it was one of the spice islands in what was the Dutch East Indies before World War II. When these islands became the nation of Indonesia the name was changed to Sulawesi. The island is made up of four large peninsulas, and thus has a long coastline and a number of natural harbours. One of the main products besides timber is nutmeg. The chief city is Macassar.

Ceylon See Sri Lanka.

Channel Islands Europe

Although actually British since 1066, with their own elected assembly, the Channel Islands are closer to France, in particular Jersey which is just off the French coast. The other main islands are Guernsey, Alderney, Sark and Herm, and together with Jersey have a combined area of 179 square kilometres (70 square miles). The mild climate makes the islands excellent for dairying and agriculture, particularly vegetables.

This doll has a Las Palmas tag (the main municipality on Grand Canary Island). She wears a blue head scarf, white earrings and gold chain and cross around the neck. The white cloth bodice has a lace panel down the front and a white sash at waist. The underskirt is orange with wide black braid edging. Over this is worn a blue ruched skirt with wide cotton lace edging. A length of this lace is also used as an apron.

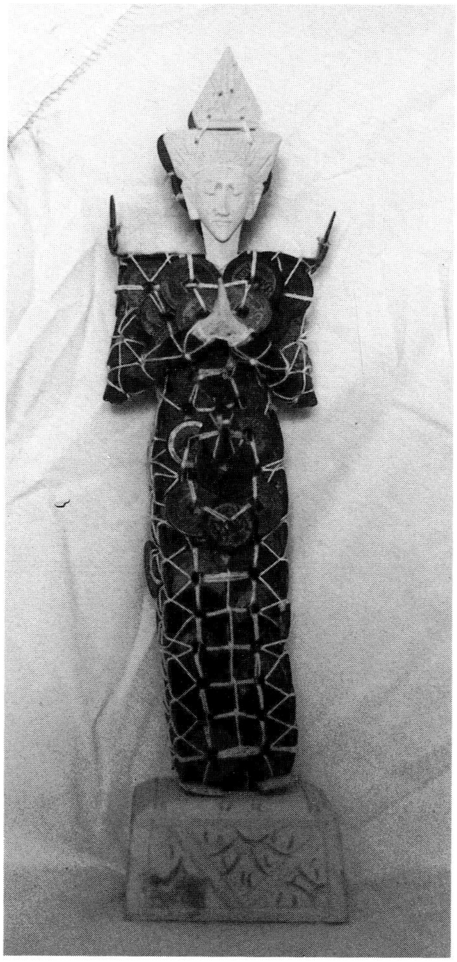

An unusual pre-1940 doll, with carved wooden head and washer-like coins cunningly lashed together to form the body shape.

Guernsey This 21.5-cm (8.5-inch) hard-plastic doll has brown hair covered by a black hood head-dress with gathered face and lower edge, and a black bow at the back. A black knitted shawl with knotted fringe edging is worn over a long black dress. A green and white check apron with white broderie hem gives a little colour. The undies are a red petticoat with white lace trim, a white flannel petticoat with white lace trim and lace-trimmed long trousers. The doll wears black shoes and carries a gold jug with 'Channel Islands' on it.

Jersey A 16.5-cm (6.5-inch) hard-plastic doll dressed to represent Jersey, the English island just off the French coast. She wears a large white bonnet with a wide, red and white check brim, slightly pleated to give fullness. A white blouse under a red bolero, a red and white check long skirt, and a long lace-edged apron complete the outfit. Underneath is a stiffened petticoat. The doll carries a gold jug with the Jersey crest and the words 'Channel Islands'

Chile (Republic of) South America

Chile covers a total area of 756 626 square kilometres (292 205 square miles) which stretches for 4350 kilometres (2710 miles) along the western (Pacific) seaboard of South America. With borders common to Peru, Bolivia and Argentina, the country is divided into 12 regions. Twenty-one per cent of all land is forested, with 7 per cent arable.

In 1535 the Spanish began their conquest of Chile but failed to subdue the Araucanian Indians or establish a settlement. Santiago was founded in 1541, but due to Araucanian resistance (which lasted until the nineteenth century) colonisation was only able to proceed slowly.

Civil war erupted in 1829–30 between powerful families and regional and ideological groups. A constitution was drawn up between 1831 and 1841 strengthening central government control.

Right This cloth doll with pressed mask face represents an Araucanian Indian. She wears a blue head-dress with multicoloured ribbons, black blouse with silver trim, black shawl with fringed yellow trim, and a mustard and black skirt. *Left* This rancher or cowboy doll with composition head and cloth hands wears a brown hat, brown shirt with fringed tartan yoke, and brown trousers and chaps.

During the War of the Pacific (1879–83) Chile seized lucrative Peruvian and Bolivian nitrate regions, greatly enhancing the country's power and revenue. In 1973 a coup ended a 46-year era of constitutional government in Chile. After what was in fact a dictatorship, a 1981 constitution guaranteed elections in 1989.

Capital Gran Santiago.
Population (1990) 13.1 million with 83.6 per cent living in urban areas. 92 per cent of the population are mestizo (mixed European/Spanish and Indian descent), with 7 per cent Amerindian.
Religion 80 per cent Roman Catholic, 6 per cent Protestant.
Language Spanish is the official language.

China (People's Republic of) Asia

The third largest country in the world, China covers an area of 9 596 961 square kilometres (3 704 427 square miles) and has the greatest number of international frontiers in the world — 13. China comprises 23 provinces, five autonomous regions and three municipalities under governmental jurisdiction. The country's topography includes Mt Everest, the vast Tarim basin, the Gobi Desert, and the Yangtze (Ch'ang Chiang) and Huang Ho (Yellow) Rivers. Ten per cent of all land

These two grandparent dolls made for export before World War II depict elderly people, who were especially revered in China. The male doll has composition arms and feet and a beautifully modelled composition head with painted features, but his long moustache is missing. He wears a black silk brocade skull cap and a queue (pigtail: a sign of submission to the Emperor) and a reminder of the hair style and hats imposed on all Chinese men by the conquering Manchus in 1644. These were worn until the collapse of the Manchu dynasty in 1912. The doll wears a pale blue jacket over a long dark blue tunic. Pale blue trousers and red shoes finish the outfit. The female doll also has a finely modelled face, and as with her companion the pierced nostrils add to the realism. On the back of her composition head is moulded a small bun, typical of older married Chinese women before 1911. The gold painted hair decoration shows that her husband is still alive (silver denotes a widow). She wears a black jacket over a dark blue skirt.

is arable, 5 per cent irrigated and 14 per cent forested.

According to Chinese legend, China's first dynasty, Xia, ruled from around the twenty-first to the sixteenth century BC. Recorded history began with the Shang dynasty (sixteenth to eleventh centuries BC). The Shang were overthrown by the Zhou. Confucianism and Taoism both date from this period. By 800 BC the power of the Zhou kings had waned, but the Chinese regard this period, which ended in 221 BC, as their classical age.

A Qin dynasty prince proclaimed himself China's first emperor in 221 BC, and although short lived the dynasty laid the foundation of a centralised

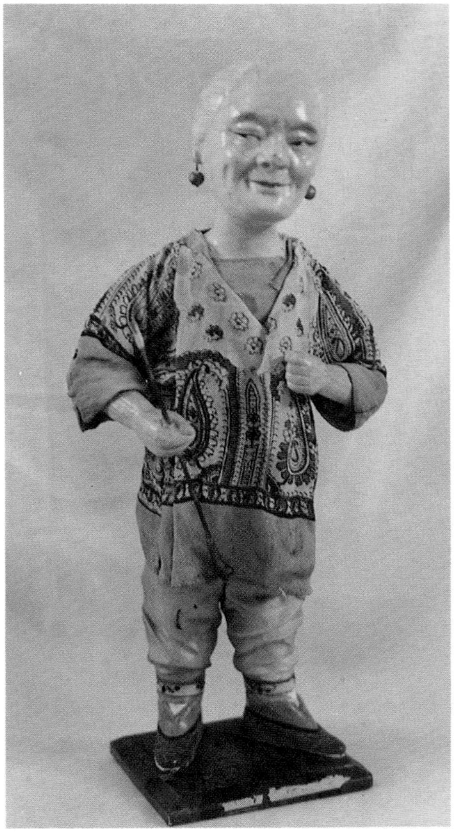

A Chinese lady with opium pipe dating from the 1920s to 1930s (31.75 cm, 12.5 inches). Probably made for export, this doll has composition head, hands and feet, with a body of straw and paper. Her shoes are moulded as part of her legs and painted blue and orange. Used widely in China at the time opium was not looked upon as the dangerous drug it is today.

A pair of pre-1940s composition-headed dolls with beautiful detail in their faces depict a male and female farmer. The male doll wears the traditional reed/straw outfit to protect him from the rain. His wide coolie-shaped hat, also made of straw/reeds, is missing. He has bare feet for walking in rice paddies. The female doll is dressed in shades of grey, with a turned-back-brim hat, bodice/blouse trimmed in red, grey trousers tight at the ankles (a custom of northern China) and a net or scarf over her left shoulder. Her feet appear much smaller than the man's, representing the tradition of binding feet still being practised in parts of China early this century.

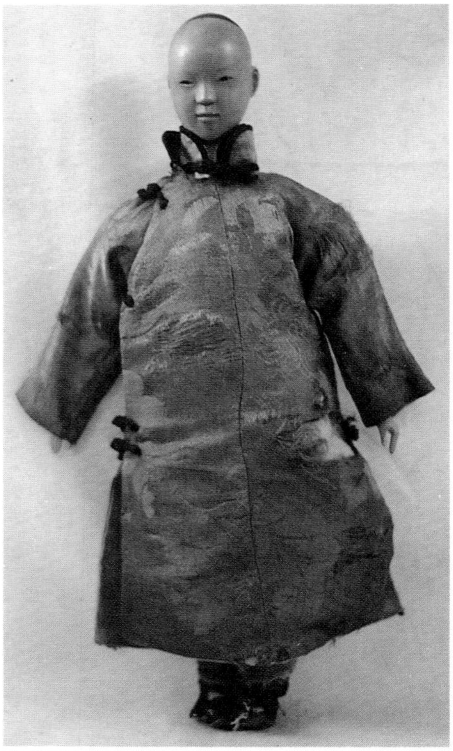

A 'Door of Hope Mission' doll, circa 1912. This 29-cm (11.5-inch) doll with features delicately carved in wood has a cloth body and finely detailed hands also in wood. It is a 'benefit doll' made at the Door of Hope Mission, established in Shanghai in 1901 for abandoned children rescued from the streets. The dolls were made to raise funds and teach the children a craft or livelihood. Each doll is authentically dressed in Chinese costume. This doll wears a long navy blue brocade tunic with high collar edged in black, padded undergarments and small black satin shoes.

bureaucracy by abolishing the feudal state.

The Han dynasty (206 BC–220 AD) at its zenith stretched from Korea to Xinjiang and south to present day Vietnam, and it was through Xinjiang trade lines that Buddhism entered China. One of China's great dynasties with regard to art and literature, the Han dynasty came to an end amidst sacking and pillage. Feudalism reappeared and in succeeding centuries numerous ruling groups and states battled for dominance. China was finally reunified under the Sui dynasty (581–681) and Tang dynasty (618–906), which culturally was an era of achievement. The ninth century saw China's borders shrink; Manchuria was lost, and Tibet and Thailand both threatened to invade. From 875 rebellion swept the country. The Sung dynasty (960–1279) restored order, but by 1223 the Mongols under Genghis Khan controlled most of China north of the Yellow (Huang Ho) River, and in 1260 Kublai Khan declared himself universal sovereign, with Beijing designed as capital. The Mongols crossed the Yangtze in 1273 and the Yuang or Mongol dynasty officially dates from 1279. By about 1300 the empire stretched from Kiev to the Persian Gulf and from Burma to Korea.

Chinese rule was restored in 1386 with the beginning of the Ming dynasty. Then early in the fifteenth century the Europeans began testing their strength, including Portugal, Spain, England and The Netherlands. The Manchu dynasty (1644–1911) took over with its capital at Beijing, and under the Manchus the empire reached its greatest territorial extent and achieved a period of peace. China traded with the Spanish, Japanese, Indians, Arabs, Portuguese, Dutch and English. During this time Europeans introduced and imported opium into China. China banned opium in 1800, and the burning of a large consignment led to the first opium war with Britain. The trade was not finally banned until 1911 by the British parliament. By the middle of the nineteenth century there were a number of serious rebellions caused by dissatisfaction with the Manchu rulers from the north, and millions died.

In 1855 China lost a war with Japan and ceded Korea, Taiwan and the Pescadores to the Japanese empire. Then the Boxer Rebellion of 1900 attempted to expel all foreigners, but this was suppressed, mainly by the British. Opposition to the Manchu finally led to the 1911 Chinese Rebellion and in 1912 China became a republic, although from 1916 to 1919 contending warlords conducted a civil war.

Then in 1931 Japan occupied Manchuria, and the famed Long March (1934–35) was undertaken by the Communists (CCP). They and the

This small doll with composition head, hands and cloth body, represents a young child. The doll has two tufts of hair on the head and wears an embroidered red satin top and dark green satin trousers with braid trim. The red shoes and white socks are painted on the composition legs.

A papier-mâché Chinese 'nodding' doll. The painted head and body are separate pieces resting on special pins so that they move if the doll is touched.

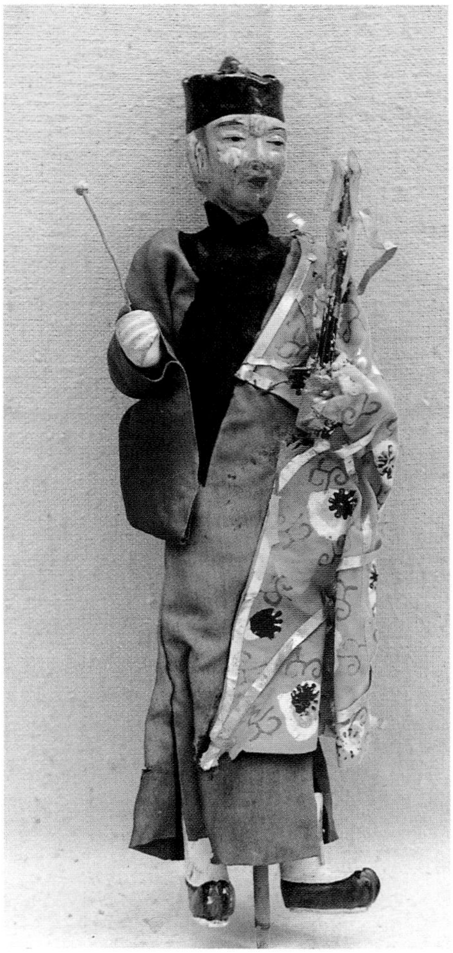

A pre-World War II Chinese doll (24 cm, 9.5 inches) with composition head and lower limbs and a cloth-over-wire body. A black hat is moulded as part of head. The doll wears a long blue tunic trimmed with black and a yellow drape over the shoulder. He carries rods in the left hand and a knobbed rod in the right. Yellow trousers and blue shoes complete the outfit.

Nationalists (KMT) joined forces to fight Japan, which had launched a full-scale invasion of China in 1937. In 1943 the Allies relinquished their privileges of extra-territoriality in China to encourage the Nationalists (KMT) not to make peace with Japan. After the Japanese surrender many of the Nationalists defected to the Communists and on 1 October 1949 the People's Republic of China was formally established with its capital at Beijing.

In 1951 Tibet was re-annexed and became a so-called autonomous region. Taiwan, the Pescadores, Quemoy and Matsu were left in the hands of the KMT. China signed a 30-year Treaty of Friendship with the USSR in 1951, but by 1960 Soviet technicians were withdrawn. Then

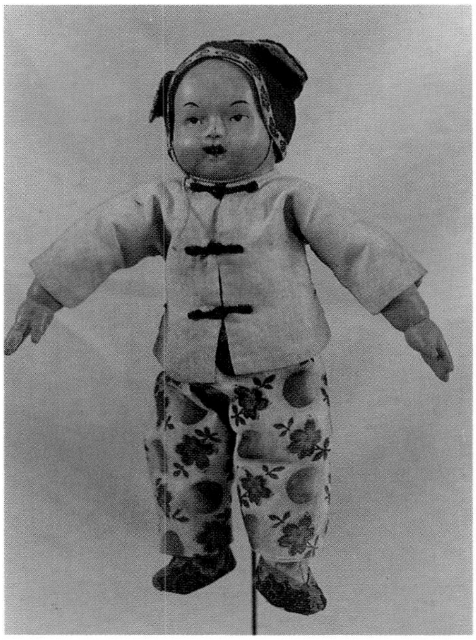

This pre-World War II Chinese child doll (25.5 cm, 10 inches) has composition head and arms, and a jointed cloth body. He wears a blue cap, frogged light blue jacket, floral pants and red cloth shoes trimmed in green.

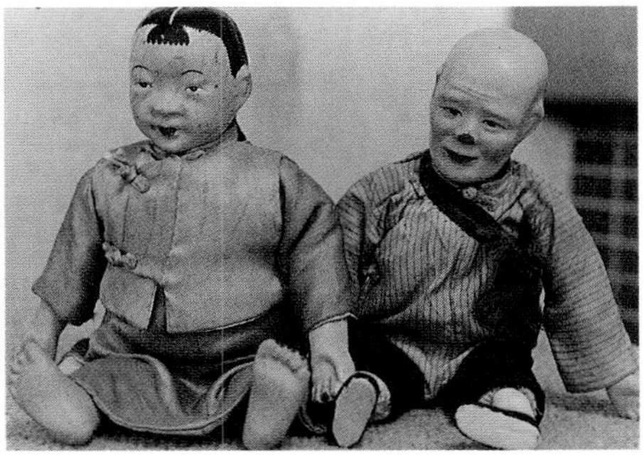

An elderly Chinese couple with composition head and limbs, and cloth body. The woman has painted hair with a long queue at the back, and a short silk jacket and skirt. The man is bald, with striped jacket, green sash, black trousers and shoes.

after the death in 1976 of both the chairman of the party and the premier of the state council, fierce power struggles ensued. Following intensified demonstrations, seen by those in power as a dangerous mix of turmoil and rebellion, in June 1989 troops took control of central Beijing by force, killing many unarmed civilians. Martial law was lifted in January 1990.

Capital Beijing (Peking).

Population 1,133 million, of which 36.6 per cent live in urban areas. 93 per cent are Han Chinese, 1.33 per cent Chuang, 0.72 per cent Hui, 0.59 per cent Uighur, 0.54 per cent Yi, 0.50 per cent Miao, 0.43

A pair of felt dolls by Italian firm Lenci dressed in felt to represent a coolie pulling a rickshaw complete with customer. The female doll is dressed in a long green felt jacket with orange trim and motifs on the sleeves and front, and long orange felt trousers. She has yellow felt feathers in her black hair. The male doll wears a white felt hat, with his black hair in a pigtail. He has a yellow felt jacket with red and blue trim, and blue felt trousers with red and yellow trim. Both dolls have black felt shoes with red felt soles and yellow stitching. The rickshaw is made of thin cane. (Private collection, Sydney)

Two 30.5-cm (12-inch) dolls with composition head and arms on cloth bodies (circa 1930–50). These beautifully detailed dolls represent two of the provinces of China. The doll on the left has long plaits covered with a black embroidered skull cap with bead fringing at the forehead. She wears a light mustard silk bodice with high collar and black cuffs, and over this a long maroon tunic edged with braid. Tight blue trousers and ankle boots finish the outfit. The doll on the right has a flat blue head-dress tied under the chin. She wears a blue overblouse with a short navy vest-like garment over the top. Her skirt is red edged with orange and blue bands; black shoes.

Opera characters. In the past all characters were played by men in traditional Chinese opera. The doll on the left is 26 cm (10.25 inches) and has four blue and gold pennants at his back and black and gold design streamers emerging from his hat. The large collar is royal blue, and red and gold panels cover the doll's sides, front, back and upper arms. He also wears a pale blue painted frontpiece, royal blue panel at the back trimmed in green, brown trousers and black boots. The doll on the right is smaller at 25 cm (9.75 inches). The green and gold collar is edged in red and has deep white fringing. A pink sash and ten pink and green, alternating braid panels, serve as a kind of skirt. The doll also wears a green over red front panel, plum trousers and red shoes.

Two 26.5-cm (10.5-inch) composite dolls. The male doll has a green undershirt, long deep cream brocade robe with green trim at front edge and on the sleeves. Around his waist he wears a cord from which hangs a short sword. The female doll has a high hairdo trimmed with flowers. She wears a long dark pink gown with cream collar edged in green, yellow cuffs and long projecting cream cuffs. She also wears a cream waist-sash, with a floating brocade sash and fine orange cords. (Courtesy J. Miller, New South Wales)

Modern vinyl Chinese dolls 16.5 cm (6.5 inches) tall in provincial costume. The doll on the left has moulded hair in braids around the head, a fawn shirt, red patterned wrap-around skirt, green waistband, blue socks/pants and red shoes. The middle doll has moulded hair, a painted white headband, green jacket with pink sleeves, black apron, pink trousers, and blue shoes. The doll on the right has black hair in two braids, a mauve blouse with black front, green trousers and red shoes.

Three modern versions of Chinese provincial costumes. The dolls are hard plastic and strung with rubber. The doll on the left has a yellow scarf, navy jacket with wide green embroidered green, navy trousers and pink shoes. The middle doll wears a blue hat, light blue jacket with blue and red trim, deep purple skirt and blue shoes. The doll on the right wears a pink blouse, blue tunic, striped apron, pink trousers and black shoes.

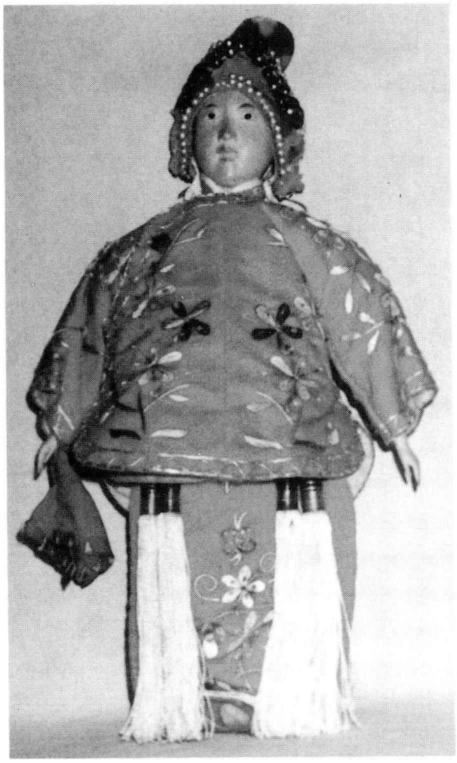

A 'Door of Hope' carved wooden doll dressed in traditional Chinese bridal costume of red, with white tassels. The doll is even holding her red handkerchief, a very important part of her wedding regalia. (Courtesy Audrey McMahon, New South Wales. Photograph: Shirleyanne McKay)

per cent Manchu, 0.39 per cent Tibetan, 0.34 per cent Mongolian.

Language 4 including Sino-Tibetan (of which Mandarin Chinese forms the basis for modern Standard Chinese) plus Altau, Indo-European, Austro-Asiatic.

Religion Officially atheist. The predominant religious philosophies are Confucianism, Buddhism and Taoism. Ancestor worship is uniformly practised. There are also 7 million Christians (3 million of whom are Roman Catholics). Islam reached China in 651 AD and there are 16 million adherents.

Colombia (Republic of) South America

Situated in the northwest of South America, with coastline to the Caribbean Sea and the Pacific Ocean, which are separated by its land border with Panama, Colombia also borders on Ecuador, Peru, Brazil and Venezuela. Divided into 32 departments, the country covers an area of 1 141 748 square kilometres (440 715

A pair of 19-cm (7.5-inch) plastic dolls dressed to represent the 'rancheros' who own land and raise cattle. The dolls have been painted with flat paint to give a more natural look. The female doll wears a finely woven straw hat turned up at the sides, with black band and edge and tied under the chin, over long hair tied at the nape of the neck, and large gold earrings. She also wears a white long-sleeve blouse under a leather waistcoat, a leather belt, black skirt, white undies and brown leather boots. The male doll wears a similar straw hat, white cotton shirt, black neckerchief, black leather belt, white flannel trousers tucked into black leather boots, and holds a rope lariat in his hands.

square miles). The Andes mountains separate the densely forested and sparsely populated lowlands east of the Pacific from the northwestern Caribbean coastal plain. Approximately 90 per cent of the population live in the Andean valleys and on the Cordillera plateau, of which 49 per cent is forested and a further 5 per cent arable land on the highland slopes of the Magdalena Basin.

The poorly organised Indians of the mountain region posed no threat to the main Spanish conquest from 1525, and Colombia was incorporated into the vice-royalty of Peru from 1544 until 1739 when Bogota (the present capital) became the centre of a new viceroyalty comprising present-day Colombia, Ecuador, Venezuela and Panama, and named New Granada. Gold had been worked by the early Indians (the Chibeha) and the area of New Granada was one of the world's

Clay-look over hard plastic 19-cm (7.5-inch) dolls. The female doll has a multicoloured head-dress worn over long black hair tied at the back. The arms are decorated with navy dots and a red design. She wears a gold and white brocade bra and coloured grass skirt with brocade top; single gold strap shoes. The male doll has a feather head-dress on his long black hair and wears a seed necklace. He has red dot and navy stripe painting on his arms; brown trousers fringed at the sides and with fine fur fringing at the waist; a red arrow quiver with three arrows at his back.

leading gold exporters until eclipsed by the nineteenth-century gold rushes in Australia and California.

Independence from Spain was finally achieved through the activities of Simon Bolivar in 1819, and an uneasy union with Venezuela and Ecuador ended in all three countries going their own way in 1830. Panama remained part of Colombia until 1903.

Capital Santa Fe de Bogota (Bogota).

Population 32 million of which 67.2 per cent live in urban areas. 58 per cent are mestizo, 20 per cent white, 14 per cent mulatto, 4 per cent black, 3 per cent mixed black-Indian and 1 per cent Indian.

Religion 95 per cent Roman Catholic, with a small minority of Episcopalians and other evangelists, approximately 25 000 Jewish and some traditional beliefs among the indigenous populations.

Language Castilian Spanish is the official language, but 180 indigenous Indian languages and dialects survive.

Colombia Flat paint over hard plastic 15.25-cm (6-inch) dolls. The female doll has long plaited black hair with a red headband, and gold earrings. She wears a navy blouse with white spots and lace decoration at the front and waist and a mauve pleated skirt with a wide band of velvet at the hem; a purple shawl edged with knotted fringe; white pleated cotton petticoat trimmed with coarse lace and white pants; blue and green sandals. She carries a woven basket containing flowers. The male doll has a painted moustache and wears a grey felt fedora with brown band on his short black hair. He wears a white cotton shirt, grey trousers, black sleeveless over-tunic with sides folded back to the inside, and white and red striped sandals with cork sole.

The 15.25-cm (6-inch) stump doll was bought at Expo 88, and is made of tapa cloth with black cloth hair tied at the back with raffia flowers, painted features, a seed necklace, tapa blouse and red/purple raffia skirt. The 26.5-cm (10.5-inch) stump doll has black hair tied at the back, tapa bodice of coconut fibre, woven body, and a painted and decorated tapa skirt covered with a pink/green/natural raffia skirt.

Capital Avarau.
Population (1989 estimate) 18 092 with the majority of Polynesian descent.
Religion Christianity (the Cook Islands Christian Church).
Language English.

Cornwall *Left* A 19-cm (7.5-inch) clay/wire/cloth doll called 'Cornish Pastie'. The card with the doll states:

Pastry rolled out like a pate
Piled with turmet tates and mate
Doubled up and baked like fate
That's a 'Cornish Pastie'.

The doll wears a white mob-cap, floral green/white dress with green cuffs. Her white apron has green straps. She is holding a plate with a Cornish pastie on it. *Middle* A plastic doll whose card reads 'West Country Dolls Hand-made in Cornwall TREGONGON'. Many women and girls were once employed in the work of 'spalling' or breaking up rocks in the tin mines with long-handled hammers. This doll is dressed in a white bonnet, mauve frock and white apron with lace trim. She holds a cane basket containing her hammer. *Right* A 7.5-cm (3-inch) plastic/cloth 'Cornish Pisky', one of the wee folk. The doll wears a tall conical red cap, and red outfit with green many-pointed collar and green cuffs.

Cook Islands Pacific Ocean

Situated in the South Pacific Ocean, the Cook Islands consist of low coral atolls in the north and hilly volcanic islands to the south. First settled between 500 and 800 AD, the islands were found by Spanish navigators in 1595, and Captain James Cook (England) explored them between 1773 and 1777.

British missionaries arrived in 1821 and took control of the islands, destroying the traditional culture. Britain declared the islands a protectorate in 1888 and they were annexed to New Zealand in 1901. In August 1965 the islands became a self-governing territory in free association with New Zealand, which had the responsibility for foreign relations and defence.

In January 1986 the Cook Islands declared themselves a neutral country.

Cornwall (English county)

Cornwall is an English county in the extreme southwest of Great Britain taking in an area of 3474 square kilometres (1357 square miles). It has long been famous for its tin mines, which may even have been familiar to the early Phoenician traders.

The county's early inhabitants were Celts, who also settled in Scotland, Wales, Ireland and parts of France. Of special archaeological interest, Cornwall's stone cromechs are among the most famous in Europe.

Côte d'Ivoire (Republic of Côte d'Ivoire), Ivory Coast Africa

Covering an area of 322 463 square kilometres (124 471 square miles) divided into 26 departments, Côte d'Ivoire on the Guinea coast has borders common to Liberia, Guinea, Mali, Burkina Faso and Ghana.

By the sixteenth century the area was occupied by a large number of ethnic groups divided into local kingdoms, such as the Kru from Liberia and the Voltaic tribes from the Upper Volta. The Mande from Guinea and Mali and the Baule from Ghana migrated to the area in the eighteenth and nineteenth centuries.

The area's first European contact, in 1637, was with French missionaries, to be followed by the Portuguese and Spanish who later established trading posts for exporting slaves, in competition with the French and British.

From 1840 until 1900 France established protectorates over the various kingdoms in the coastal areas, with the

Côte d'Ivoire A 13-cm (5-inch) plastic doll with a small doll in a pouch formed by a shawl. On the doll's head is a woven cane basket containing fruit, sitting on a dark cloth turban. The doll wears a short red dress over a long straight skirt. Her dark shawl is draped around her body. She also wears a gold chain necklace. (Courtesy J. Miller, New South Wales)

combined territories becoming a colony in 1893. The French pushed northwards from 1893, supressing several revolts and incursions by surrounding tribes. The Ivory Coast became a member of the Federation of French West Africa in 1904, with the capital at Dakar (now in Senegal).

After World War II the inhabitants of the Ivory Coast became eligible for French citizenship. Then in September 1958 the French president organised a referendum allowing French colonies in Africa to choose either immediate independence or membership within a French community; in August 1960 the Ivory Coast became independent, to be known as Côte d'Ivoire.

Africa's largest church was consecrated in 1990 in Côte d'Ivoire's new capital Yamoussoukro.

Capital Yamoussoukro (Abidjan was the old capital).

Population 11.6 million, with 47 per cent living in urban areas. The population consists of Akan 41 per cent, Kru 18 per cent, Voltaic 16 per cent, Malinke 15 per cent, Southern Mande 10 per cent, about 2 million foreign Africans, 40 000 French and 25 000 Lebanese.

Religion Traditional beliefs 44 per cent, Christian 32 per cent, Muslim 24 per cent.

Language French is the official language, but many African languages are spoken.

Crete (province of Greece) Europe

Situated to the south of Greece, the island province of Crete is 240 kilometres (150 miles) long and varies in width from 16 to 56 kilometres (10 to 35 miles), with an area of 8192 square kilometres (3200 square miles).

Crete, the seat of one of the world's earliest civilisations, has been occupied over the centuries by Greeks, Romans, Turks, Venetians and again by the Turks. It was the centre of frequent rebellion over the centuries owing to the tension between Turkey and Greece, but after a brief war in the late 1800s the European powers declared the island autonomous in 1897. In 1912 Cretan members sat in the Greek parliament, and the island was formally annexed to Greece.

Many of the costumes worn in this island province are quite distinct from those of Greece.

Three lovely epoxy plastic dolls dressed in Cretan costume. The doll on the left is dressed in a black skull cap with tiny tassels extending from the brim. He wears a white shirt, black waistcoat trimmed down the front with red, black trousers and a red waist sash, white painted boots. *Middle* The female doll wears a white headscarf, white blouse with lace skull cap and is dressed in a maroon jacket with yellow braid decoration, maroon skirt, white trousers with black decoration at the knees, and black shoes. The three dolls were made by the World Crafts Council. (Courtesy the Greek Pavilion, Expo 88)

Croatia Europe

Situated in southeastern Europe, the country is bordered by Slovenia, Hungary, Bosnia-Hercegovina and the Adriatic Sea.

Croatia was an independent country from 1102 until 1849, when it became part of the large Hungarian empire. Until 1918 it remained under Austro-Hungarian domination, but at the end of World War

A 19-cm (7.5-inch) plastic doll marked 'Hrvatska Posavina' (an area south of Zagreb). The doll has long black braids under a red and white, lace-edged woven cap, held by a gold filigree tiara with pearl decorations. Her white bodice has red stitching and a braid collar and is decorated with a medallion necklace. The red/white woven sleeves feature lace cuffs. The white skirt has a red/white woven band near the hem and white lace at the hem. She wears a red/white woven apron edged in red/white lace, and red shoes. (Courtesy Vera Woodhead, Queensland)

A pair of 23-cm (9-inch) vinyl dolls marked 'Prigorije'. The female doll wears a red and white spotted babushka and apron, white blouse, red neck scarf with red/white/blue ribbon, large white apron with braid trim, white skirt, white stockings with red bows at the knees and leather moccasins on her feet. The male doll wears a navy hat with red/white/blue band, white overshirt with braid down the front, blue waistcoat with red/white/blue braid trim, white trousers and black boots.

Left Plastic dolls dressed in the correct costume of the Slavonia region by Maria Böhm. The male doll is dressed in a blue hat with red/white/blue band, white shirt, navy vest with collar trimmed in red, red/white/blue waistband, and white trousers. The female doll has her hair done in the elaborate style worn by the women of the area, achieved by using a mixture of sugar and water to stiffen the hair and hold the shape. She wears a white dress trimmed with lace, a hand-embroidered shawl, and pink brocade apron. The photo above shows the beautifully detailed pleated back to the dress and the back of the hairdo.

'Zagorje' cloth doll wears a red floral babushka, white blouse with red braid trim at cuffs and front and a red/white/blue ribbon at the neck. She has a white skirt with red braid decoration, red floral apron tucked through a braid waistband, and wears white stockings and brown moccasins.

I was merged with Bosnia-Hercegovina, Serbia, Montenegro, Slovenia and Macedonia to form the new country of Yugoslavia. Croatia became nominally independent under German supervision during World War II, to become part of Yugoslavia again in 1944. In 1991 Croatia seceded from Yugoslavia and became an independent country after a brief and brutal civil war.

Capital Zagreb.
Religion Mainly Roman Catholic.
Population Mainly Croats, but some other ethnic groups.
Language Croatian and Serbo-Croatian, with English and German widely understood. The Latin alphabet is used.

Cuba (Republic of) North America

Just 217 kilometres (135 miles) south of the tip of the American state of Florida in the Caribbean Sea, Cuba, the main island, along with smaller isles and cays, has an area of 115 704 square kilometres (44 662 square miles) divided into 14 provinces and the densely populated capital La Hababa (Havana). Three mountain regions cover 25 per cent of the country with the lowlands and basin

A pair of 21.5-cm (8.5-inch) cloth dolls with embroidered features (1920–30). The male doll has a black hat with tag at the back, purple satin jacket with gold/black braid around the shoulders, white shirt, black tie, cream silk vest, orange silk cumberband, purple satin knee-length breeches, with gold/black decoration at the knees, white socks, and black shoes. The female doll has black hair with a cardboard comb, a rose at her ear, and a red stone necklace. She wears a yellow blouse, pink silk skirt, red/black/gold brocade shawl with red fringing, and high-heeled boots. She carries a painted paper fan.

This 19-cm (7.5-inch) plastic doll has black hair covered with a yellow and mauve scarf turban style, a lilac bodice with full gathered sleeves of sheer white, lemon and mauve, and a pink sash. The skirt is draped to the back, in pink with black edging, lemon and mauve. The doll wears black shoes.

Painted cloth face 16.5-cm (6.5-inch) dolls with wire armature, cloth wrapped, and plastic lower arms. The male doll has a black head-dress, and wears a white shirt under a red checked jacket, black cummerbund, black baggy trousers, black long knitted socks and black shoes. The female doll wears a yellow headscarf over black plaits, white underdress edged with red, long striped over-jacket open at the sides below the waist and edged with navy blue ric-rac. She has a yellow waistband, long white pantaloons edged with red, and black shoes.

making up the other 75 per cent which supports the local agriculture.

Cuba was first inhabited by Ciboney Indians who were displaced by the Arawak Indians from Haiti. Columbus's first expedition in 1492 brought the first Europeans to Cuba, and he claimed the area for Spain. From 1511 the island was settled and colonised, but the main Spanish impetus moved to Central and South America. Havana became a strategic link in the Mexico-Spain trade route.

Although Havana was captured by the British for 10 months in 1762 it was returned to Spain, remaining under Spanish rule until 1864. Then, after a 10-year war, a peace treaty was signed in 1878. Slavery was finally abolished in 1886. Another war in 1895 reversed the situation and Spanish troops reimposed order. Due to the blowing up of the USS *Maine* in Havana harbour, the United States declared war on Spain. Cuba was captured and placed under military government until an independent government could be formed. The United States left the island in 1902 but kept military bases there. Cuba prospered during World War I due to its sugar production. For many years Cuba has been ruled by dictators and this is still the case in 1994.

Capital La Hababa (Havana).

Population 10.6 million, with 70.8 per cent living in urban areas. At the last census 66 per cent were white (mainly of Spanish extraction), 21.9 per cent mulatto and 12 per cent black.

Religion 40 per cent are Roman Catholic (but not all practising communicants), 3.3 per cent Protestant, and 1.6 per cent Afro-Spiritist.

Language The official language is Spanish, with a little English spoken.

Cyprus (Republic of) (Greek and Turkish) Europe

The third largest island in the Mediterranean Sea, Cyprus is located 80 kilometres (49.7 miles) south of Turkey, and has an area of 9251 square kilometres (3572 square miles) divided into six districts. Nearly half the total surface is arable and 18 per cent is forested.

Settled at least from 6000 BC, Cyrpus later became part of the Persian empire and later part of Alexander the Great's empire in the fourth century BC, coming under Roman rule in 58 BC, and finally passing on to the Byzantine Empire in 395 AD. Held at the end of the Third Crusade (1189–92) by Richard the Lionheart of England, it was ruled by the French feudal system until annexed by Venice in 1489. The Ottoman Turk conquest in 1571 led to three centuries of Muslim rule, when the island's Greek population was supplemented by Turks.

In 1878 Cyprus came under the protection of Britain, and both Greece and Turkey recognised British sovereignty in 1923, the island becoming a Crown Colony in 1925. Demands by Greek Cypriots for Cyprus to become allied to Greece and from Turkish Cypriots for union with Turkey led to unrest on the island from 1931, but it was not until 1959

Two cloth dolls bought at the Cyprus pavilion at Expo 88 in Brisbane, made by Cyprotoys, Nicosia. The 33-cm (13-inch) cloth girl doll is dressed in a red woven dress with yellow/black stripes and white apron, and long white pants. She wears a black chiffon scarf over her black wool plaited hair, and has two gold medallions on a thin necklace. The male doll is actually a printed cloth doll with a tag reading 'Cyprus Folk Costume'. He has printed brown hair, with black hair band; red brown vest, white shirt, black cumberbund, baggy pants and black boots, all printed on fabric.

that Britain, Greece and Turkey reached an agreement for Cyprus to become an independent republic within the British Commonwealth. This agreement quickly foundered and in 1968 the Turkish Cypriots set up an autonomous administration in the northern 40 per cent of the island, while the southern part of Cyprus became a haven for Greek Cypriots.
Capital Nicosia (on the border separating the two parts of Cyprus).
Population 700 000 of which 63.6 live in urban areas. 77.1 per cent are Greek Cypriot, 18 per cent Turkish Cypriot, with Armenian, Latin and Maronite minorities making up another 5 per cent.
Religion Greek Cypriots are predominantly Orthodox Christian. Turkish Cypriots are mostly Sunni Muslim.
Language Both Greek (81 per cent) and Turkish (19 per cent) are official languages, with English widely understood.

Czech Republic Europe

Formerly part of Czechoslovakia (an amalgamation of two republics — the Czech and Slovak Republics from 1918, and also part of Bohemia), it became a separate nation in 1993. It is a landlocked country in central Europe bordered by Germany, Poland, Slovakia and Austria.

Traces of human settlement date back to the fourth millennium BC, and the earliest known inhabitants were the Celtic Boii, supplanted at the beginning of the Christian era by Germanic Marcomani. A cohesive Czech state emerged in Bohemia and Moravia between the tenth and twelfth centuries when an influx of German settlers began.

A Czech monarch was crowned Holy Roman Emperor in 1346. Then the Austrian Catholic Hapsburg dynasty acceded to the thrones of the Czechlands and Hungary in 1526. A national revival began in the late eighteenth century and by the nineteenth century was marked by bitter competition between Czech and German national movements. With the collapse of the Hapsburg Empire in 1918, the independent republic of Czechoslovakia was formed with a coalition government from the previous Czechlands and Slovakia. Many Slovaks and Germans resented Czech domination. The depression of the 30s affected the German areas (the Sudetenland) which, with the acquiescence of Britain and France, were ceded to Germany in 1938. In March 1939 Germany occupied the Czechlands which then became the Protectorate of Bohemia Moravia.

With the end of World War II general elections were held in May 1946 and the Communists emerged as the strongest political grouping, remaining in power until the end of 1989 when a new coalition

This 31.75-cm (12.5-inch) doll has composition head, cloth limbs and body. She is dressed in a red babushka, white blouse with square collar edged in black lace and embroidered front, black apron, and red skirt, with red brocade bands from a red waistband. Black sewn boots complete a colourful outfit. (Courtesy Jo Harvey, Noosa, Queensland)

This Czech man doll is 20 cm (8 inches) tall. He wears a navy hat with red crown and flower trim; white shirt with blue/white brocade trim; navy jacket with blue/red/yellow trim featuring red tassels; navy trousers with blue trim; and black boots.

A 28-cm (11-inch) vinyl doll with blonde hair covered by a red babushka. She wears a white blouse with full sleeves and black/white edging on the sleeves and square collar; red brocade sleeveless jacket with red brocade ribbon down the front and on the waistband; red wrap-around pleated skirt with two red brocade bands, black apron edged with white lace; and black boots. Triangular label reads 'DRUZSTVO UMFLECKE YYROBY'.

government was sworn in. In 1990 the first free election in four decades was held. The return of democracy also renewed separatist sentiments amongst the Slovaks and in 1991 the Czechs said they would not hinder the Slovaks if they wanted to secede. In 1993 Czechoslovakia became two nations once again — the Czech Republic and Slovakia.

Capital Praha (Prague).

Population Mainly of Czech origin, with some Slovaks, Hungarians, Poles and Gypsies.

Religion Roman Catholic, with Czech Brethren, Reformed Christians and approximately 6000 Jews (in Prague).

Language Czech, with some Hungarian spoken. The Roman alphabet is used.

Czechoslovakia See Czech Republic or Slovakia.

Dance

Dancing involves graceful and rhythmical motions of the limbs and body, often telling a story, and normally with a musical accompaniment. The art and expression of the dance have been instrumental in preserving many regional costumes now used only for celebrations and festive or religious occasions.

Costuming for the dance ranges from hand-painted designs on the bodies of Australian Aboriginals preparing for a corroboree, to the flamboyant and colourful dresses worn by Spanish dancers, the ornate dress of India, and the colourful costume of Scottish Highlanders.

Sri Lanka These three dolls are made of cloth. *Left* This 25.5-cm (10-inch) doll depicting a woman dancer has a high black hairdo trimmed with gold and beads, as well as earrings and a gold necklace. She wears a white cropped blouse with red trim, short pleated gathered overskirt with floating side panels, also red trimmed. Her long red waist decoration is trimmed with beads. Her long white skirt is specially pleated at the front and back to cover long draped trousers. The middle doll (25 cm, 9.75 inches) represents a drummer who accompanies the dancers. He wears a white turban with red trim and bead decoration. His wide red neck band is trimmed with beads and he wears red bangles at the shoulders and wrists. He wears a red waistband over white trousers formed from one piece of cloth and with gathers at the ankles. A long horizontal drum hangs from his waist. The 25-cm (9.75-inch) doll on the right represents a male dancer. He wears a metal head-dress over a red bandana; a bead necklace around the neck; decorative breastplate; red bangles at the shoulders and wrists; and a wide red belt with front ornamentation of beads and tassels and a plain red panel at the back. He is dressed in a two-tiered gathered overskirt with floating side panels trimmed in red, over pleated trousers formed by a red band from front waist to back.

Lithuania Two small dolls dressed to represent a Lithuanian dance. The girl doll is dressed in a white blouse and pink over red check skirt with red-embroidered white apron. She wears a green cord around her blonde hair. The boy doll is dressed in a straw hat with red band, white shirt with yellow bow at the neck, green sleeveless coat and striped trousers. Both dolls have wooden shoes. (Courtesy J. Krukelis, Brisbane)

Russia A lovely French bisque, leather-bodied lady doll dressed in the costume worn by peasant to middle class Russians for dancing a quadrille (square dance) in the nineteenth century. The doll wears a fine white blouse with braid trim at the cuffs and a bead necklace. Her pinafore is red with pompon braid around the scoop neckline and white and black pompon braid around the hem. Her hailspot muslin apron is richly trimmed with red/white/blue braid and lace. (Private collection, Sydney)

South Korea Fan Dance, 1988. The 24-cm (9.5-inch) doll is made from cloth and wire. She wears a red and gold crown on the front of her black hair, which is plaited and tied with red ribbon. Her multi-striped blouse is white edged and trimmed with a bow with long ends at the middle front. The doll wears a full white skirt with gold decorations over white trousers. She carries two multicoloured fans with red/gold trim and white feather edging. Graceful movements by the dancers are enhanced by the fans forming intricate patterns during the dance.

South Pacific Islands These two brown celluloid dolls balanced by springs on metal legs wobble (dance) in the breeze. They give an impression of what doll manufacturers thought of islanders. The doll on the left wears only a grass skirt. The doll on the right has a moulded headband and necklace painted blue. She wears a long grass skirt to cover the simple mechanism.

Spain Flamenco dancers. *Woman* This 30.5-cm (12-inch) plastic doll wears a black mantilla with a red rose. Her black dress, patterned with red roses has gold edging to each of the flounces. She carries a white fan. *Man* A 25.5-cm (10-inch) plastic doll, he wears a flat black hat, white shirt, short black jacket with gold trim and yellow tassels at the waist, and a wide red cummerbund over black trousers.

Scotland *Left* A 14.5-cm (5.75-inch) hard-plastic doll dressed as a country dancer. She wears a long tartan cloak with a thistle brooch at the neck, white blouse, and tartan skirt with shoulder straps. *Centre left* A 16-cm (6.25-inch) hard-plastic doll dressed as a Scottish dancer in a black bonnet with a red toori on top. He wears a red plaid held by a cairngorm (brooch). His black jacket is worn over a white lace jabot and lace cuffs. He has a red tartan kilt, sporran and white spats. *Centre right* A 16-cm (6.25-inch) hard-plastic doll dressed in a black beret, black jacket, blue tartan plaid and kilt. She has white lace jabot and cuffs, white spats. *Right* A 19-cm (7.5-inch) vinyl doll dressed as a Scottish country dancer in a long white dress with red tartan plaid held by a cairngorm at the shoulder.

Thailand Present-day classical Thai dance-drama *(Lakorn Ram)* dates from the late Ayudhya period some three hundred years ago, and reached its height in the early 1800s. Most Thai classical dance-dramas have a prince as the hero and a beautiful princess as the heroine. These two dolls of cloth over wire are typical of such dancers. Dressed in tall gold bejewelled helmets, with their elaborate red costumes enhanced with gold trimmings, they are very striking dolls.

India Clay modelled dolls by Shankars Doll Museum workshop, Delhi, India. The doll on the left represents the dance *Odissi* from Orissa state where the legendary Sun Temple of Konark is situated. The doll's hair is done in a bun surrounded by white feather-like halo. She wears a fawn sari edged with maroon, with a maroon shoulder drape finished as a pleated front drape from the waist. She wears plenty of stylised silver jewellery at the neck, ears and hands and small bells hang from her waistband. The middle doll represents the *Matra* (pitcher) dance from the desert state of Rajasthan. This dance is a long swirl of movement, with the skirts billowing rhythmically as the girls take their backward and forward steps, moving round in circles with their brass pitchers balancing on their waists. Their animated faces peep from behind their heavy tie-dyed veils draped over their head and falling down to the skirt, covering their *cholis* (blouse). The beauty of the final gestures made by the hands holding the veil and skirt in turns is enhanced by the intricate henna patterns adorning the palms and backs of their hands. The bangles jingle along with the gentle tinkle of their anklets. The doll wears a magenta and white striped veil over a purple cholis and skirt edged with gold and silver braid. She holds her pitcher at her waist. The doll on the right represents the dance *Kuchipudi* from Andhra Pradesh state, originally performed only by men, even the female roles. The costume is a silk-like sari worn tucked between the legs to allow free movement. A rich apron of pleats falls in front. The doll has a long black plait interwoven with simulated flowers. Her white sari has a maroon and gold edging. She wears simulated jewellery: a gold waist belt, choker, hair adornments and bangles, and a 'precious' stone nose decoration.

Denmark (Kingdom of) Europe

Part of Scandinavia, Denmark consists of the Jutland Peninsula (in the north central part of Europe) and the islands of Sjaelland, Funen, Lolland and Falster, as well as 480 smaller islands, giving a total area of 43 080 square kilometres (16 629 square miles). Denmark also has two self-governing dependencies, Greenland and the Faroe Islands. Sixty-one per cent of the country of Denmark is arable with 12 per cent forest or woodland.

Plastic dolls (17 cm, 6.5 inches). *From left* **Hedebo** This male doll with blond hair wears a long red cap with gold ornament at the point, red shirt with white lace front, red/white striped jacket with gold buttons, and green pants. **Hedebo** A female doll with blond plaits wearing a black bonnet with white broderie facing and yellow back, green dress with orange trim, red-check shawl edged with lace, and red check apron. (Married women wore a red skirt and black hat.) **Amager** A male doll with blond hair wearing a black top hat, yellow shirt, black jacket with gold trim, and black trousers. **Amager** A female doll with blond plaits wearing a black bonnet with red lining and edged with black lace, black dress with lace trim, black shawl with red braid trim, and blue apron with red braid trim. Amager is an island famous for its market gardens and Kastrup airport. It is connected to Copenhagen by three bridges.

Plastic dolls (17 cm, 6.5 inches). *From left* **Copenhagen** A female doll with blond plaits wearing a red hat, red dress with two black lace ruffles and white lace cuffs, black muff and cape, and black shoes. **Copenhagen** This male doll wears a red top hat with white bow at the side, white shirt with lace trim, red cut-away jacket, red and black striped pants, and black shoes. **Rosnaes** A female doll with blond plaits wearing a black cap with pink bow at the back and lace-edged braid brim, black blouse with lace cuffs, black waistcoat with green trim, blue/green/maroon/white striped skirt, and white apron with lace edge and braid ribbon sashes. **Rosnaes** This male doll with blond hair wears a red cap, green jumper, red coat slit at the middle back from the waist down and with gold buttons, and yellow trousers.

Left A 16.5-cm (6.5-inch) plastic doll with blond hair, red bonnet with white lace frill and flower trim (denoting the doll represents a single woman), red dress with white collar and cuffs, and blue cape with lace edge. *Right* A 20-cm (8-inch) plastic doll with blond plaits wears a black peaked bonnet with braid trim and red ribbons, black embroidered shawl crossed over at the back and edged with black lace, black over-bodice, sash and skirt, red pleated apron with black trim, black shoes and check petticoat.

Cloth dolls with painted faces. *From left* The woman holding a baby (15 cm, 6 inches) wears a turban-type hat of dark plaid, dark plaid shawl, blue floral blouse, red waistcoat and skirt, blue/white striped apron, black slip, blue stockings, and black shoes. The baby wears a red helmet with lace trim, blue blouse, red skirt, and blue/white apron. The fisherman (18.5 cm, 7.25 inches) with a yarn beard wears a black sou'wester, grey knitted sweater with black design, brown trousers, and high black boots. He holds a fish in his left hand. The fisherwoman (16 cm, 6.25 inches) wears a white scarf with lace edging, blue/white striped blouse, black waistcoat, green skirt with red trim, red check apron with large pocket (for fish), red slip, black stockings, and black shoes with silver buckles.

Present-day Denmark (although settled since the Neolithic age) first entered recorded history in the fifth century AD when its seafaring warriors, particularly the Angles of Jutland, invaded other lands, notably what is present-day England. In their own land the Angles were replaced by the Dan people from southern Sweden, and united in the tenth century by Gorm the Old, who founded the Danish monarchy, they became Christian. Anglo-Saxon England bore the brunt of the Danish expansion, which by the early eleventh century had united the whole of Scandinavia and England under Cnut the Great, but this empire disintegrated after his death. In the twelfth century, Denmark reasserted its Scandinavian ascendency and in 1397 Queen Margrethe of Denmark became ruler of both Norway and Sweden (including Finland).

Danish dominance waned with the election of Gustavus I to the Swedish throne in 1523, and after protracted struggles between the two countries the Danes were driven out of Sweden by

Vinyl dolls (30 cm, 11.75 inches). *Left* AMAGER-KIRKE (on label). Red peaked hat, yellow braid on brim, black lace edge. Black bodice, white lace cuffs. Black pleated skirt, red hem band. Black shawl, worn peak at front, yellow trim. Red pleated apron with bands of black lace. A Bible (prayer book) hangs from the waist. White undies. *Right* MOR DANMARK (on label). Actually a costume composed from characteristic Danish costumes, made in Denmark's colours of red and white. Red hat, yellow braid on crown and brim, lace edging. Red bodice and pleated skirt, lace trim, yellow braid band. White pleated apron, lace trim. White shawl with lace edge, red ribbon trim.

1645. In 1660 absolute monarchy was established in Denmark, and Norway remained Danish. Throughout the eighteenth century Denmark remained neutral, and it was only when the British navy destroyed a Danish fleet at Copenhagen that Denmark allied itself to France, to later share its defeat in the Napoleonic wars. This led to Norway being transferred to the Swedish crown, although Iceland, Greenland and the Faroes remained under Danish sovereignty.

In 1864 Denmark was forced to cede its two southern provinces of Schleswig and Holstein and in 1871 they passed into the new German Reich, with Schleswig voting to return to Denmark in 1920.

Despite reaffirming its neutrality at the outbreak of war in 1939, Denmark was occupied by Germany without bloodshed, with Germany in complete control by 1943.

In 1944 Iceland declared its independence.

After the defeat of Germany in 1945 Denmark returned to normal and in 1948 the Faroes were granted home rule, followed by Greenland in 1979.

Denmark became a member of the EEC, along with Britain and Ireland, in 1973.

Capital Copenhagen (Kobenhavn).

Population 5 119 000 of which 84.3 per cent live in urban areas. 95 per cent were born in Denmark, the rest in other Scandinavian countries, Germany, the rest of Europe, with a small minority of Asians.

Greenland population (1988) 54 524 of whom an estimated 42 000 are Inuit (Eskimo).

Faroe Islands population (1988) 46 352.

Religion 90.6 per cent Evangelical Lutheran (National Church) with other Protestant denominations and approximately 28 000 Roman Catholics and 3000 Jewish.

Language Deriving from Old Scandinavian, the Danish language is closely related to Norwegian and Swedish, with a German influence in the south of Jutland. Faroese and Greenlandic are spoken in the relevant dependencies.

Djibouti (Republic of) Africa

Djibouti, a small country situated on the coast of the Horn of Africa, has an area of 23 310 square kilometres (8938 square miles). Eighty-nine per cent of the terrain is desert with less than 1 per cent arable land.

Djibouti has been inhabited for thousands of years despite the heat and aridity, and Somali and Afar nomadic pastoralists have contested for space through the years.

France negotiated for part of the country in the north in 1861, but by 1880 had moved its administration to Djibouti, which became the capital of French Somaliland in 1892. The port of Djibouti was an important bunkering station for the Suez Canal.

When the predominant Somali community wanted independence, a referendum was held in March 1967, with the decision that the country retain its association with France. After a decade of contesting this decision, the country became independent in June 1977.

Capital Djibouti.

Population 400 000, with 75 per cent living in urban areas. 60 per cent of the population are Somali, concentrated in the south, with 35 per cent Afar, concentrated in the north and west. 5 per cent are French, Arab, Ethiopian and Italian.

Religion Sunni Muslim 94 per cent, and 6 per cent Christian.

Language Arabic is the official language with French, Somali and Afar widely spoken.

The doll's tag reads 'Artisan femme Djibouti'. This is a French black plastic doll with small baby held by a check shawl. She wears a red head-dress with white bead decoration/earrings, necklace and bangle, and a fawn top over a long skirt of the same colour. Her long stole/shawl is a green background check. (Courtesy Jenny Miller, New South Wales)

Dominica (Commonwealth of) West Indies

Situated in the Windward Islands group of the West Indies, the volcanic island of Dominica is approximately 47 kilometres (29 miles) long by 26 kilometres (16 miles) wide. Although the rich soil supports dense tropical vegetation over 41 per cent of the island, only 9 per cent of the land is arable.

Dominica was first inhabited by Arawak Indians, later displaced by the South American Caribs, who firmly

Man This brown cloth doll with painted features is standing on a plaited straw base. A straw hat is perched on his head. A red floral shirt, blue cummerbund, and orange trousers complete his costume. *Woman* She has a brown cloth torso, straw cone lower half, and painted features. She wears a red turban, floral bodice, full overskirt with red background, and full gathered white underskirt.

resisted attempts at European settlement until the mid-eighteenth century. First colonised by the French, Dominica was seized by the British in 1759. African slaves were used until the abolition of the slave trade early in the nineteenth century. The island gained full internal autonomy in 1967, and was granted full independence to become a republic on 3 November 1978.
Capital Roseau.
Population (1990 estimate) 100 000 of which 91 per cent are black, 6 per cent mixed race, 1.5 per cent Amerindian (including 500 Caribs) and 0.5 per cent white.
Religion Predominantly Christian, of which 80 per cent are Roman Catholic.
Language The official language is English, although a local French patois is also used.

East Germany See Germany.

Ecuador (Republic of) South America

The country of Ecuador straddles the Equator on the northwestern coast of South America, with an area of 283 561 square kilometres (109 455 square miles) including the Galapagos Islands, and is divided into 20 provinces. The Andean Sierras traverse the country north to south, with the world's highest active volcano, Cotopaxi (5896 m, 19 344 ft) found in this highland area. Sixty per cent of the area is forested, consisting largely of lowland rainforest, and only 9 per cent is arable. Of the population 49 per cent inhabit the lowland area, 47 per cent the Sierras and 3 per cent the Oriente (alluvial forest plains in the east).

The highlands surrounding Quito have been settled by Indian tribes for thousands of years, with the Incas the latest and most sophisticated. After the execution of the Inca emperor by the Spanish in 1533, the Spanish refounded the city of Quito on its present site in 1534. The ensuing colonial system endured for 300 years — mainly under the viceroyalty of Peru (1544–1824).

The coastal city of Guayaquil wished for free trade, and with outside assistance from Argentina and Venezuela secured its independence in 1822, in which a neutral Quito was not included. This step reinforced antagonism between the coastal and highland regions which still endures. Ecuador gained its full independence in 1830, but in the years to 1895, 21 different governments and juntas occupied the presidency 34 times, establishing a tradition of turbulent politics which has continued into this century.
Capital Quito.
Population (1990) 10.7 million of which

Wooden heads, wire and thread bodies. *From left* Woman (21.5 cm, 8.5 inches). Woven straw hat, black braids. Green blouse, green woven skirt with embroidered red and yellow trim. White stole (shawl). Basket of flowers. Man (23 cm, 9 inches). Woven straw top hat, black hair, white shirt, woven red serape with yellow/blue trim. Basket of flowers. Black trousers with yellow cuffs. Woman (24 cm, 9.5 inches) and baby. Wooden hands and feet. Tall woven straw hat with blue band, black plaits. Yellow jacket with green cuffs. Green woven skirt with embroidery trim. Red woven slip. White stole with crochet and fringe ends. The doll holds a baby (11.5 cm, 4.5 inches) with black hair. White hood, red band; yellow embroidered blanket, blue trim. The woven cloth is hand made on simple looms.

Vinyl dolls (28 cm, 11 inches). *Left* Black/white scarf head-dress, gold bead earrings, gold bead necklace. Single brown plait, wrapped in red/white/blue braid. White blouse, lace trim, gold braid trim on sleeves and bodice. Black wrap-around skirt, white hem trim. Red/white/blue waistband. Black sandals. *Right* Dark brown hair, red/brown/white braided plait. Red bead earrings, necklace, and bangle. Red shawl, green trim. Black wrap-around skirt, yellow and red embroidered trim at hem. White blouse, braid cuffs. Green apron, red trim. Red braid sandals.

Dolls woven of straw are a tradition of the Otabolin Indians. *From left* Woman (13 cm, 5 inches). Woven straw. Bodice and skirt red. Red/black woven straw shawl with fringe. Woman (15 cm, 6 inches). Clay and wire. Straw hat, plaits, yellow blouse, green skirt with pink and beige band trim, white stole. The doll carries flowers and woven hats. Man (14 cm, 5.5 inches). Woven straw. Jacket of coloured straw. Trousers of finely woven red and black straw. He carries a straw lariat.

52.8 per cent live in urban areas. Indian 25 per cent, mestizo 55 per cent, Spanish 10 per cent, African 10 per cent.
Religion No official religion, although Roman Catholic is the most prevalent of the Christian religions.
Language Spanish is the official language, although English is taught and understood. The principal Indian language is Quechua.

Egypt (Arab Republic of) Africa

The country of Egypt is situated in the northeast of Africa and occupies an area of 1 001 449 square kilometres (386 559 square miles) divided into 25 governorates. Ninety-nine per cent of the population lives in the fertile Nile valley and delta, although this represents only 3 per cent of the country's total area. Over 90 per cent of the rest of the country is barren desert.

Around 5000 BC a predynastic culture, using domestic animals and able to support craftsmen, developed. Two kingdoms arose in the Nile valley and delta and were unified under one pharaoh around 3000 BC. During the following 3000 years, Egypt was ruled by 30 family dynasties and it was during this time that the pyramids and other great architectural works were built and trade was expanded into Asia.

This doll was made when Egypt was joined with Syria in the United Arab Republic. The doll and camel are made of leather. This doll wears a white head-dress, black shawl, white robe, and has a rod in his right hand. The camel has a red/green saddle cloth with yellow fringing.

Cloth dolls (20 cm, 8 inches) with firmly stuffed body, hardened head and painted face. Made in Cairo. *Man* Beige knitted skull cap, cream undergown, blue cotton overgown with thin navy braid edging. Long white shawl. Black scuff-type shoes. *Woman* Long black voile veil edged at front of head with yellow and red beads, over blue head-dress. Long hair in plaits. Yellow undergown. Dark pink, white-spotted overgown with drop waist, gathered skirt, purple trim. Beaded necklace with coin. Both veiled and unveiled women are seen in the streets of Cairo. Similar dolls are sold at the Egyptian Museum in Cairo.

Persian kings ruled from 525 to 404 BC with Alexander the Great conquering the state in 332 BC. He and his successors continued the traditions of pharaonic rule until the death of the last ruler, Cleopatra, in 30 BC.

When Egypt became part of the Roman Empire, it was exposed to different cultural traditions, including Christianity. The Muslim Arab conquest in 632 AD led to Arabic becoming the official language by the eighth century. Cairo, founded in 969, became a centre of cultural and intellectual life, as well as the focus of east-west trade. Saladin (1171–1193) attempted to drive Christianity from the eastern Mediterranean and imposed Sunnism on Egypt.

In the thirteenth century the Mamelukes (originally slave soldiers) rebelled and set up the finest regional army, making Egypt a Sunni Muslim stronghold. They ruled until the Ottomans seized Cairo in 1517. The Turks ruled until 1914 although their control was only nominal after Napoleon's occupation (1798–1801).

The Suez Canal opened on 17 November 1869, owned jointly by Egypt and France, but due to financial problems Khedive Ismail was forced to sell his shares to Britain, and to accept dual British and French control of the country's budget. Due to a variety of circumstances Britain was the dominant force in Egypt from 1883 to 1907, but without a formal British colonial authority it remained nominally under Ottoman rule. Britain declared Egypt a protectorate in 1914.

Nationalism grew after World War I, and although Britain was unwilling to give up control of the country, and in particular the Suez Canal, Egypt achieved limited independence in February 1922. With the creation of the state of Israel in 1948 serious rioting occurred in Cairo, culminating in the forced abdication of King Farouk and the proclaiming of the Republic on 18 June 1953.

Two 15-cm (6-inch) hard-plastic dolls commercially dressed to 'represent' Egypt. *Left* This doll is dressed in traditional early costume. Black straight hair, gold band with jewel ornament. Wide white collar, yellow trim. Long red gown, yellow waist cord. *Right* A male doll dressed in traditional Arab costume as a sheikh. White burnous with gold and black band. White undershirt and trousers. Long black robe with yellow trim on sleeves, yellow braid fringe down front edges. Painted shoes.

In 1956 the Suez Canal Company was nationalised and in 1958 Egypt joined Syria, establishing the United Arab Republic, although Syria withdrew three years later. On 1 September 1971 the country changed its name to the Arab Republic of Egypt.
Capital Cairo (El Qahira).
Population (1990) 54.7 million of which nearly 49 per cent live in urban areas. The majority of the population in the Nile delta is Hamito-Semitic (90 per cent). Other include Bedouins, Arabs and Berbers (desert dwellers) and the Arab-Negro Nubians (Upper Nile valley).
Religion An estimated 90 per cent are Muslim, predominantly Sunni, with approximately 7 per cent (2 million) Coptic Christian and another million Christians of different sects, and about 1634 Jewish.
Language Arabic is the official language but several distinct dialects are spoken by various desert dwellers.

Eire See Ireland.

England (Great Britain) Europe

Although England is part of Great Britain (or Britain), it is often seen as a separate entity, particularly by its people, and as different from the other regions that make up the United Kingdom — Scotland, Wales and Northern Ireland. England has an area of 130 240 square kilometres (50 875 square miles).

Typical souvenir dolls portraying regiments of Royal Guards, available all over London. These are 1960s hard-plastic dolls.

Left The wire/cloth doll with wooden head represents John Bull. *Right* This plastic doll is a souvenir from HMS *Victory*, Nelson's ship, at Portsmouth.

As early as 250 000–100 000 BC early hunters, including Neanderthals, crossed the ice bridge then joining England to Europe, and from 1000 BC the tribal structure of Iron Age Britain was formed. Around 400 BC Celts (from Gaul in France) settled in Yorkshire, and the Belgae (from Picardy) had settled in Kent by the end of the second century BC.

When the Romans occupied Britain in AD 43 they found Celts in possession, and although England continued to be a Roman province for nearly 400 years, no attempt appears to have been made to subdue its northern neighbour, except for the building of Hadrian's Wall around 122 AD. Towns flourished and Christianity was introduced around 300 AD. After the Roman evacuation in AD 410, Britain was left open to invasion, not only by the Picts (from Scotland) but by tribes from North Germany and Denmark, with first the Jutes, followed by the Angles and Saxons, driving the Celts north into Scotland, west into Wales and southwest into Cornwall. The process of reconverting England to Christianity began again at the end of the sixth century.

Due to the development of small separate kingdoms throughout England, the foundation of the English monarchy was not laid until the banding together of three kingdoms, with Egbert King of Wessex crowned in 827 (regarded now as the first King of England). The Danes invaded once again, only to be defeated by Alfred the Great in 878, but Danish invasion began again in greater force at the end of the tenth century.

Then in 1066 William (the Conqueror), Duke of Normandy, was crowned king of England, and the Normans (from France) crowded across the Channel in his wake to play their role in a modified feudal system. Royal power went relatively unchecked, until King John, who managed to alienate nearly every class of his subjects, including priests and barons, was forced to sign the Magna Carta in 1215. King Edward I (1272–1307) summoned a complete and model parliament in 1295, and so began the struggle between parliament and the royal prerogative which continued over the next three centuries, with immense and far-reaching effect.

Wars, revolts and the plague led to the end of serfdom in the 1300s, and merchant and craft guilds emerged in the 1400s, increasing the wealth of England. During Henry VIII's reign, the British Navy was founded, and with the defeat of the Spanish Armada during Elizabeth I's reign, the country was established as a great power, and a leader in exploration and maritime enterprise.

Left Yeoman, 14-cm (5.5-inch) hard-plastic doll by Rogarth, Wales, UK. Black felt hat, braid trim. Red jacket, black and gold trim. Red trousers, red stockings, black shoes with buckles. *Centre* English policeman or 'Bobby', 17.75 cm (7 inches) hard plastic. Helmet with badge. White shirt, navy tie, jacket and trousers, black shoes. *Right* 'William Shakespeare', 18.5 cm (7.25 inches), hard plastic. White neck ruff, blue jacket, with black trim, blue knee breeches, white stockings, black shoes, grey cloak. The doll holds a scroll in the left hand.

When James VI of Scotland became James I of England in 1603, a new era began. Then England became a republic in 1649 under Oliver Cromwell, who attempted to reorganise the shattered constitution. After the Restoration of the monarchy, the unpopular James II was replaced by William III of Orange, who was invited to take the throne in 1688, and in February 1689 the Bill of Rights was accepted. Henceforth, despite an attempt by George II to gain constitutional power in the late 1700s, the monarchy lost its supreme importance, and the fortunes of the country were no longer dependent on the caprice of the monarch.

In the early 1800s, almost at the same time as the French Revolution, England evolved from a mainly agricultural country into an industrial one, and with the reign of Victoria (1837–1901) became an important industrial power.

Capital London (also of Great Britain).
Population 47.5 million.
Religion The established church, the (Anglican) Church of England; as well as Methodist, Baptist and Roman Catholic.
Language English is the official language, but other languages such as Chinese, Gujarati, Bengali, Punjabi, Urdu, Hindi, Arabic, Turkish, Greek, Spanish and Japanese are also spoken by a substantial number.

Estonia (Estonian Republic) Europe

Situated on the eastern shore of the Baltic Sea, Estonia is the most northern of the Baltic States with borders to Latvia, Russia and the Gulf of Finland. It covers an area of 45 000 square kilometres (17 370 square miles).

The country that is now Estonia was part of Sweden until 1721, and then part of Russia until late in World War I. The country had struggled for autonomy from 1905, and in May 1918 the claim was recognised by Britain, France and Italy. After the Treaty of Tartu in 1920 Russia finally recognised Estonia's independence, and in 1921 recognition became general.

In 1939 the Soviet Union annexed Estonia along with Latvia and Lithuania, and it became another republic in the USSR.

Unofficial nationalist agitation for greater autonomy began to emerge in these three Baltic republics in the late 1980s, and by October 1988 all three had established independence movements.

Plastic doll (27 cm, 10.75 inches). High white head-dress ornamented in red, blue, gold. Blond hair in rolls. White blouse, red cuffs with yellow design. Blue design collar and front. Finely pleated lime-green/mid-green/white skirt, blue and lemon braid at hemline. Red apron with design in yellow, black waistband. White painted stockings, black shoes.

Lithuania was the first to declare itself an independent state in March 1990. Estonia, following a similar course, passed legislation allowing its young men to avoid service in the Red Army, and by May 1990 had declared itself the Estonian Republic. In March 1991 the Estonian parliament declared that the republic was entering a transition period to independence, to become fully independent in 1991.

Capital Tallinn.
Population 1.6 million. Estonian 64.7 per cent, Russian 27.9 per cent, Ukrainian 2.5 per cent, Byelorussian 1.6 per cent, Finnish 1.2 per cent.
Religion Freedom of worship since 1990. Mainly Lutheran.
Language Russian and Finno-Ugric.

Ethiopia (People's Democratic Republic of) Africa

Located on the Horn of Africa, Ethiopia, formerly known as Abyssinia, is divided into 15 regions, which cover an area of 1 221 900 square kilometres (471 653 square miles). Twenty-nine per cent of the total area is forested and 12 per cent arable, mainly the fertile alluvial silts of the Blue Nile and the rich basaltic loams of the highlands.

Hominid remains have been found in Ethiopia dating back 1.5 million years. In 719 BC Shebek (or Sabaco) led an immense army into Egypt where he established an Ethiopian dynasty. From the sixth century BC to the first century

These cloth dolls (here 28 cm, 11 inches) are produced in various workshops sponsored by the Ethiopian Tourist Trading Corp. which tries to promote development of Ethiopian handcrafts as an industry. *Man* Black hair. Long white shirt with splits at side. Lightweight white shawl draped over shoulder. White trousers, brown sandals. *Woman* Black hair. Sheer white dress, braid trim at hem. Sheer white shawl with braid trim, white underdress, knee-length panties, brown sandals.

Cloth dolls with hardened heads and painted faces. *Left* 24 cm (9.5 inches). Black hair. Long white jacket with splits at side, black stitching trim. White lightweight draped shawl, green and yellow lining. White trousers with black stitching trim. Black shoes. *Right* 25.5 cm (10 inches), Shoa-Tigre region. Black hair, shaved in design and tufted at nape of neck. Long white robe with blue/green/ yellow embroidered cord around waist and Coptic cross at waist; green/yellow/ tan trim at cuff and on shawl. Lightweight white shawl draped over head, crossed over at back and front. White trousers, black shoes.

AD northern Ethiopia was under the influence of Arabia. However an independent kingdom, formed in the second century AD and centred on Aksum, flourished until the ninth century. Christianity was adopted as the state religion in the fourth century.

In 1523 Ethiopia was devastated by a Muslim invasion, repelled only with the assistance of a small Portuguese contingent in 1543. Links with Portugal led to a union of the Ethiopian Coptic Church with Rome, but this union was revoked in 1610. With Gondar becoming the centre of power in 1632, although isolated, the Ethiopian empire flourished.

In 1889 the Ethiopian ruler pushed the borders of his empire south and eastward, doubling its size. However this move brought Ethiopia into contact with European colonial powers (Italy in Eritrea and Somalia, France in Djibouti, Britain in northern Somalia). After the defeat of an invasion of Tigray by Italy, the various colonial powers reluctantly recognised Ethiopia's independence.

In 1936 Italy conquered and occupied Ethiopia, but was driven out in 1941. The feudal system remained, although a government, constitution, parliament, cabinet, education system and a modernised army were formed by the Emperor Haile Selassie. When Haile Selassie was deposed in September 1974 Ethiopia became a socialist state, fighting on and off with its neighbours until 1988, and involved in a long civil war until May 1991.

Unrest remained in the former Italian colony of Eritrea, which had been administered by Britain until September 1952, and was united with Ethiopia in November 1962. Within the next few years Eritrea is likely to become a separate nation.

Capital Addis Ababa.

Population (1990) 51 million of which 10.6 per cent live in urban areas. The Amhara are the dominant ethnic group, with Tigrayans sharing the Amhara's Hamito-Semitic origins. Others are Oromos (Gallas) and Somalis in the southeast and Afars in the northeast.

Religion 40–45 per cent are Muslim and 35–40 per cent Christian (predominantly Ethiopian Orthodox). Animist beliefs still flourish in the deep south (5–15 per cent). The Ethiopian Jews (Falashas) have mainly gone to Israel.

Language Amharic is the official language, although there are over 100 provincial languages. English is commercially used and understood.

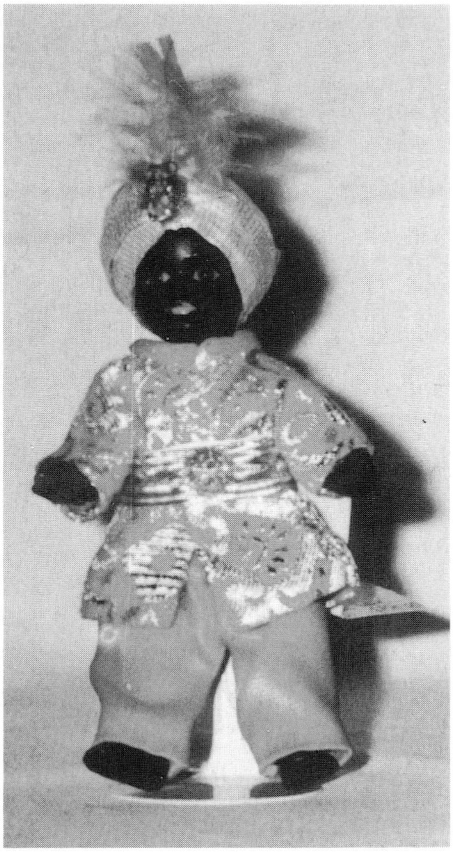

This lovely bisque-headed Nubian doll, possibly by Kestner, wears a gold turban decorated with a blue feather. He has a richly decorated red brocade jacket, gold waistband, red trousers. (Courtesy Audrey McMahon, New South Wales. Photograph: Shirleyanne McKay, New South Wales)

Fiji (Republic of) Pacific Ocean

Situated south of the Equator in the southern Pacific Ocean, approximately 1770 kilometres (1099 miles) northeast of Sydney, Australia, is the archipelago of Fiji. Consisting of approximately 332 islands and 500 islets, Fiji has a total area of 18 333 square kilometres (7077 square miles). The International Date Line makes a bend to accommodate the country's position. Seventy per cent of the population live on the largest of the islands, Vitu Levu, with another 20 per cent on Vanua Levu.

The archipelago forming the nation of Fiji has been inhabited by the Melanesians for over 3000 years. The Dutch started the era of European exploration in 1643, and

Hard-plastic 25.5-cm (10-inch) dolls made in Australia by Pedigree and dressed in authentic tapa cloth and woven fibre in Fiji to represent a Fijian wedding pair. On the left is the bride, on the right the groom. The bride has a tapa cloth bodice and two-tiered skirt with fibre adornment at the neck and waist. The groom wears a tapa cloth skirt (lap lap) with short loops and long strands on the belt. Beige straw around the bodice is tied at the back. Fibre loops decorate the neck. He holds a straw emblem in his right hand.

Plastic dolls. *Left* This 27-cm (10.5-inch) doll representing a Fijian of Indian origin was dressed in her green taffeta sari in Fiji. Black hair, caste mark on forehead, jewel in nose, earrings and necklace. *Right* A 30.5-cm (12-inch) doll made in England. The wrist tag reads 'Authentic Fiji Dolls'. Seed and shell necklace, red cotton bodice, tapa cloth two-tiered skirt, red sandals, brown waistband.

Hard-plastic 15-cm (6-inch) dolls made in Hong Kong and dressed for the tourist trade. *Left* Bandsman with red tunic, white shoulder strap and belt, white skirt (lap lap). *Middle* Female doll with bead necklace, blue bodice, grass skirt over red cloth underskirt. *Right* Policeman with navy tunic, white shoulder strap and belt (red undersash), white skirt (lap lap).

Rubber dolls (14 cm, 5.5 inches). *Girl* Short blond hair, red headband. White blouse, green decorated collar, black sleeveless bodice. Red/black/yellow striped skirt. White apron, green trim. White painted socks. Black shoes. *Boy* Black cap. White long-sleeved shirt, stand-up collar. Red sleeveless double-breasted lapelled jacket with simulated buttons. Yellow knee breeches. Red painted hose, black shoes.

'Trad' Troll Dolls (1960–70) with fibre heads, fur material over wire bodies, wire tails with fur tips, leather hands and feet. *Left* 'Hemmi'. Fur hair, yellow bodice, blue skirt with red outlines of Hemmi-like figures. *Right* 'Hiski' (labelled on tail). Fur hair, blue eyes. Yellow/blue/white figured jacket, orange pants.

it was resumed by the British in the last quarter of the eighteenth century. The early years of the nineteenth century witnessed the settlement of traders and missionaries and intense tribal wars, until the establishment of Fiji as a British crown colony in 1874. From 1879 until 1916, Indians entered Fiji to work the sugar estates.

Although European settlers secured political representation in the Legislative Council in 1904 and Indians in 1929, other major constitutional changes did not occur until the 1960s, when universal adult franchise was introduced and political parties established. On 10 October 1970 Fiji became a constitutional monarchy within the Commonwealth, and the first general election was held in 1972.

Then on 6 October 1987, after two coups engineered by Colonel Rabuka, Fiji was declared a republic and suspended from the Commonwealth. Full civilian rule was not achieved until January 1990.
Capital Suva.
Population (1990) 800 000 of which 38.7 per cent live in urban areas. Indian 48 per cent, Fijian (Melanesian-Polynesian origin) 46 per cent and other races including European, Chinese and other Pacific Islanders 6 per cent.
Religion 53 per cent Christian, 38 per cent Hindu with minority groups of Muslims, Sikhs and Confucians.
Language English is the official language, although Fijian in a variety of dialects, including Bavan, is spoken, as is Hindustani by the Indian-Fijian population.

Finland (Republic of) Europe

A northern European country with more than one-third of its land within the Arctic Circle, Finland is divided into 12 provinces and has an area of 338 145 square kilometres (130 524 square miles). Predominantly a low-lying country, Finland has 65 per cent of its land under cultivation and over 50 per cent of its population live within the five southern provinces.

Inhabited from 8000 BC, Finland was first settled by tribes from Asia. From the first century AD the Lapps were pushed north by the Finns. Viking penetration from around AD 800 was followed by English and Swedish missionaries who introduced Christianity in the eleventh and twelfth centuries, amid competition between Sweden, Novgorod, the Teutonic Knights and Denmark for control of the Gulf of Sweden. From 1323, due to increasing Swedish dominance, Finland became part of Sweden for almost 500 years. It became a grand duchy in 1581. After being defeated by Peter the Great of Russia in 1721, Sweden was forced to cede extensive territories in the Gulf of Finland to Russia, and the annexation of Finland was confirmed in 1815.

Turned-wood dolls (17.5 cm, 7 inches) stamped 'Made in Finland' underneath and painted to represent costume. *Girl* Blond hair with red band, white blouse, black laced bodice, white apron, multi-striped skirt. *Boy* Blond hair, white shirt, red/yellow/blue/black striped double-breasted jacket, black trousers, red socks, black shoes.

Rubber dolls (20 cm, 8 inches). *Left* Brown hair, red headband. White blouse with wide collar, lace edge. Silver necklace. Red vest. Red woven skirt with green/black/red stripes. Red/white striped apron. (The doll's legs have melted.) *Right* Blue cap, crocheted edge. Blond plaits, white blouse, figured shawl, blue double-breasted vest. Blue woven skirt with black/yellow/red/white stripes. White apron.

Plastic doll (14 cm, 5.5 inches). White stocking cap with braces. Red jacket, white lapels. White socks, black shoes.

As a grand duchy within the Russian Empire, Finland enjoyed considerable autonomy. In 1863 Finnish became an official language alongside Swedish. World War I and the Russian Revolution presented an historic opportunity and Finland declared its independence in 1917, with a republic declared in July 1919.

Finland was invaded by Russia in November 1939, and after two defeats by Russia finally entered into peace negotiations in August 1944. In the 1947 Treaty of Paris Finland lost its access to the Artic Ocean, but by 1948 it had signed a friendship treaty with the Soviet Union and was soon able to develop an increasingly prosperous market economy.

Capital Helsinki.

Population (1990) 5 million, of which 61.8 per cent live in urban areas. The Lapp population is between 2000 and 4500, and there are an estimated 5500 gypsies concentrated in the southern regions.

Language Two official languages — Finnish and Swedish — with Lappish a separate branch of Finno-Ugric.

Religion 88.9 per cent Lutheran National Church, 1 per cent Greek Orthodox Church of Finland, 16 700 Jehovah's Witnesses, 13 192 Evangelical Free Church, 1309 Jewish, 926 Muslim.

France (French Republic) Europe

France, the largest central European state, borders on Belgium, Luxembourg, Germany, Switzerland, Italy, Spain, Andorra, the Mediterranean Sea, Atlantic Ocean and English Channel. It has an area of 547 020 square kilometres (211 150 square miles), and consists of 95 metropolitan departments, including the Mediterranean island of Corsica, as well as four overseas departments, two *collectivités territoriales* and four overseas territories. Approximately 60 per cent of the land area is fertile and agriculturally useful, with another 30 per cent forested.

Because the boundaries of France have changed a great many times during its history, what is now modern France is not necessarily equivalent to what is known as

Santons Well-modelled and painted clay dolls representing French villagers of another era. Dressed in well-designed clothes, they were often used as part of the Christmas nativity display in French churches. (Private collection, Townsville)

Bretagne (Brittany) Fisherman. A pre-World War II cloth doll with cloth face sculpted and painted by E. Ravca. The tag at the back reads 'Original Ravca'. The sewn tag on the jacket 'Made in France'. The doll wears a black beret and has a white beard, multicoloured scarf, brown jacket and trousers, brown sabots. He carries a net over the right shoulder and a lantern. (Private collection, Queensland)

the Frankish Kingdom or the Napoleonic Empire.

Site of some of the earliest prehistoric remains in Europe, France entered the Neolithic Age in the fourth millennium BC. The foundation of Marseilles as a Greek colony about 600 BC is the start of France's recorded history. When Caesar conquered Gaul (France) in 57–52 BC and incorporated it into the Roman Empire, he found three disunited tribes — the Belgae, Celts and Aquitanians. Then in 486 Clovis, King of the Franks, defeated the last Roman governor and was converted to Christianity; his dynasty was to rule France until 751. Although

Alsace Lorraine Celluloid, 'Altkirk' dolls bought in 1976. *Woman* 14 cm, 5.5 inches. Black shawl hat with tricolour on left. Blond plaits. White lace blouse. Green brocade shawl. Red skirt, gold braid trim. Black apron with painted design, red waistband sash. White undies, black shoes. *Man* 12.75 cm (5 inches). Straight-sided beige velvet hat with red top. White shirt, wide collar. Black bow tie. Red waistcoat with gold buttons. Black jacket with gold buttons. Black trousers, wooden sabots.

Gendarme. Cloth doll (24 cm, 9.5 inches). Black képi with white band, white shirt. Black tie, jacket and trousers. White webbing and cuffs. **Paris, Ile de France** Cancan dancer. Peticollin celluloid (13 cm, 5.25 inches). Gathered black lace headpiece. Blond hair. Yellow dress, black lace trim. Tiered lace slip, black stockings, yellow garters. Sailor. Peticollin celluloid (19.5 cm, 7.75 inches). Hat with red pompon, 'MARINE NATIONALE' on band. Navy jacket, white collar. Navy trousers, white duffle bag.

Auvergne, Provence French celluloid doll. Hat with white lace edging. White blouse, lace and black bow trim. Yellow figured dress trimmed at hem with black ribbon. Matching shawl trimmed with black lace. Black apron, edged with lace.

Calais Clay and cloth dolls (bought 1976), representing Calais fisherfolk sitting on a wooden bench. *Woman* Elaborately pleated lace-trimmed hat. Grey hair. Black jacket over black blouse (lace collar). White shawl with fringe. Black brocade skirt. White/blue apron. Long panties, black stockings, brown shoes. Cross on chain at neck. She holds a fish on a board in the left hand, a knife in the right. *Man* Navy peaked hat, grey beard and hair, carved pipe in mouth. Blue/white striped sweater/shirt. Navy breeches, black boots. He is mending a fishing net.

Côte d'Azur, Cannes/Nice Peticollin celluloid. The doll wears a straw hat with embroidered trim, white blouse with lace trim. She has a yellow scarf/shawl with black lace trim. She wears a cross at her neck, and has a red/white striped skirt with black trim, red apron with gold trim, white socks and red shoes.

repeatedly attacked by barbarians from the north in the early years, the Frankish Empire expanded into what is now Italy, Hungary, the Czech Republic and Germany, reaching its zenith under Charlemagne who was crowned Holy Roman Emperor in 800 AD. German-speaking Franconia separated from what was to become France in 843. Due to fighting between the feudal lords, Hugh Capet was elected king in 987, and this dynasty lasted until 1328. This was a time of prosperity and civilisation flourished:

Alsace Lorraine French moulded celluloid. The dolls' clothes are moulded as part of their body and then painted to represent material. *Male doll* Black hat, jacket, trousers and ribbon tie. White shirt, red vest. *Female doll* Black scarf hat, white blouse, striped bodice with black front, red skirt, green apron with pink flowers, white stockings, black shoes. (Courtesy G. Liebers)

Celluloid dolls. *Left* This 16.5-cm (6.5-inch) doll wears a straw hat with black ribbon ties over a lace cap, and a cross on a chain. She has a white blouse with lace trim, red shawl with lace edging, green taffeta skirt with red trim, red embroidered apron with gold edging. *Right* **Pont Aven, Brittany** The doll wears a high hat of white lace on a blue base with blue ribbon trim. She has a wide white pleated collar, a cross on a chain, black bodice with 'v' insert featuring braid trim, black skirt with gold and braid trim, blue apron with gold trim and lace edging.

Two bisque-headed, jointed-body dolls by the French dollmakers SFBJ (1900–1930). The dolls are dressed in fully original French provincial costumes. The boy wears a black hat and black jacket with gold trim, blue embroidered shirt, yellow waistband, navy trousers with yellow trim and long blue-grey cuffs. The girl doll wears a lace cap, white bodice with lace collar, black jacket with gold trim, cream skirt with braid trim and red apron with gold and lace trim. (Courtesy Audrey McMahon, Sydney)

Left The 15-cm (6-inch) celluloid doll wears a lace mob-cap with green ribbon trim, paisley shawl, tomato red dress with lace collar, white brocade apron trimmed with lace. *Centre* **Provence** This 16.5-cm (6.5-inch) plastic doll is dressed in a straw hat over a lace mob-cap, red shawl with black lace edging, white blouse with lace at the front and lace cuffs, a gold cross at the neck, patterned lemon skirt with black band, black apron with a painted floral design and lace edging. *Right* A 17.75-cm (7-inch) doll, **Porticcio** by Poupées Maguy. She wears a red head scarf pinned with a gold cross, red dress with black lace trim at neck and sleeves, black shawl with lace edging, black lace-edged apron with 'Porticcio' painted on it.

Left The 15-cm (6-inch) plastic doll wears a gold cap, black bodice edged with white lace, black shawl with red/black braid trim, red skirt with black braid trim, black apron embroidered with golden flower design. *Centre* **Perigord** The 12.75-cm (5-inch) plastic doll wears a tall puffed hat edged with flat white lace and braid, blue bodice, blue paisley shawl edged in lace, white waist-sash, blue skirt with gold braid trim. On her red apron edged with white lace and decorated with a braid band is the word 'Perigord'. *Right* A 12.75-cm (5-inch) plastic doll wearing the 'Bigoudenne' costume from the region of Penmarch, Saint Guenole and environs. She wears the tall white lace hat famous in the region, black bodice trimmed in yellow and orange, navy skirt with orange/yellow trim and white apron trimmed with an orange/yellow band.

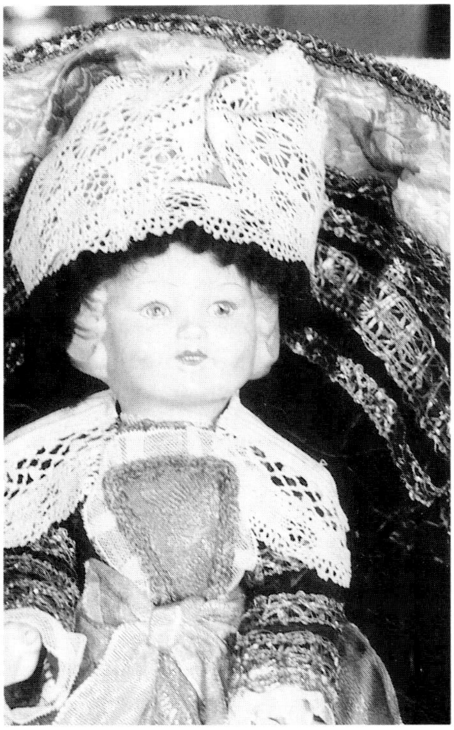

A lovely 25.5-cm (10-inch) composition doll with moulded hair and painted eyes, and dressed in detailed French regional costume. Part of her elaborately decorated skirt can be seen behind her lace head-dress. (Private collection, Kempsey, New South Wales)

Bretagne A white bisque-headed doll with yellow painted hair, dressed in the costume of a fishwife. She wears a lace-edged head-dress, and russet jacket and shirt with a black shawl. (Private collection)

towns grew, universities were established and cathedrals built.

The crown passed to the house of Valois in the 1300s, at which time half of France belonged to Edward III of England. The English were eventually driven out of France, except Calais (which was recaptured in 1558). From 1494 over a period of 100 years, various wars continued to strengthen and centralise the crown's powers, until Henry IV, first of the Bourbon kings, brought the country out of the wars, and increased France's international standing. Further wars followed in the 1700s, including French support for America during their War of Independence against Britain (1776–83). France suffered a series of financial disasters which eventually led to the storming of the Bastille on 14 July 1789, and the capturing of the royal family as hostages. On 20 April 1792 the French Revolutionary Wars began, and in September the monarchy was abolished and France became a republic.

Napoleon Bonaparte toppled the Directory (parliament) in 1804, making himself emperor of the French. Although leading successful campaigns abroad, he

Provincial costume of the late 1800s. This white china-headed doll with cloth body wears a red dress, navy jacket with fine white stripe, and white apron with red band.

was forced to abdicate in April 1814 when the Prussians captured Paris. Constitutional monarchy was restored, but a 'citizen king' was installed in 1830, only to fall in 1848. Napoleon's nephew, Emperor Napoleon III, was crowned in 1851, but after he was captured in the Franco-Prussian War (1870–71) the Third Republic began in September 1870.

In 1875 a republican constitution was adopted. The years before World War I were marked by the expansion of France into Africa and Asia, particularly Indo-China. After World War I Alsace-Lorraine was returned to France. After declaring war against Germany in September 1939, France was overrun by June 1940 and occupied until liberated in 1944.

After World War II, France became one of the five great powers in the newly formed United Nations.

Capital Paris.

Population (1990) 56.4 million, with 74 per cent living in urban areas. At the 1982 census there were 1.47 per cent Algerian, 1.4 per cent Portuguese, 0.79 per cent Moroccan, 0.61 per cent Italian and 0.59 per cent Spanish living in France.

Religion Christianity is the dominant religion with approximately 42.35 million Roman Catholics and 850 000 Protestants. Other groups include 2.5 million Muslims.

Language French is spoken by 93.4 per cent, German by 2.3 per cent, Breton 1.0 per cent, Catalan 0.4 per cent, Arabic 2.6 per cent, and 2.9 per cent are wholly or partially bilingual in Occitan (the old language of the south).

French Polynesia (Tahiti) Pacific Ocean

French Polynesia, formerly known as Tahiti, consists of five archipelagoes with a total area of 3941 square kilometres (1521 square miles).

First settled about 2000 years ago, the islands had their first contact with Europeans in 1767. The London Missionary Society, from their base in Tahiti, quickly converted the islanders to Christianity. French colonisation began in 1842, and in 1957 the islands became a French overseas territory. Autonomy, particularly in regard to economic matters, was extended in 1977 and again in 1984.

Capital Papeete.

Population (1989) 196 246, mainly of Polynesian descent.

Tahiti This 29-cm (11.5-inch) plastic doll is jointed so she can move her hips to simulate the hula. She has a red floral headband over long dark hair, red floral lei. She wears a red bodice with coloured trim and red tassels, long white fringing skirt. She holds white tassels in each hand.

Religion Christianity, both Protestant and Roman Catholic.

Language French is the official language; Tahitian is also spoken.

Georgia (Republic of) Europe/Asia Minor

Bordered by the Russian Federation to the north, Armenia and Azerbaijan to the southeast, Turkey to the south and the Black Sea to the west, Georgia covers an area of 70 000 square kilometres (27 020 square miles). Once part of the Ottoman (Turkish) Empire, Georgia was an independent nation until annexed by Russia in 1801. It regained its independence in 1918 after World War I, but this was short lived as it became one of the three countries (with Armenia and Azerbaijan) that made up the Transcaucasion Federation of Soviet Republics in 1922.

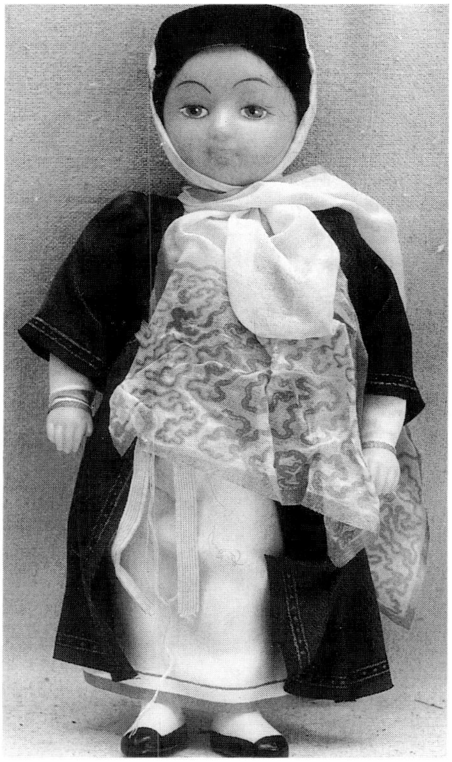

Plastic head and limbs, cloth body (26.5 cm, 10.5 inches). The doll wears a black pillbox hat; sheer headscarf, ornamented and edged with gold over her single black plait; a long ankle-length cream gown with gold trim at hem and cuffs; ankle length green coat with gold trim at front, hem and cuffs and a golden yellow waist sash; black shoes.

This was dissolved in 1936, and the three constituent countries became the Armenian Soviet Socialist Republic, Azerbaijan SSR and Georgian SSR. Georgia became independent again in 1991 and its 1918 flag was raised once again.

Capital Tbilisi.

Population 5.3 million; 68.8 per cent Georgian, 9 per cent Armenian, 7 per cent Russian, 5 per cent Azerbaijani, 3 per cent Ossetian and 1.7 per cent Abkhazian.

Germany (Federal Republic of) Europe

Germany is situated in central Europe with borders to Denmark, The Netherlands, Belgium, Luxemburg, France, Switzerland, Austria, the Czech Republic and Poland. It has an area of 357 039 square kilometres (137 818 square miles) which includes coastal access to the North and Baltic Seas. Thirty per cent of the land is arable; 30 per cent is forested.

Original Schmider Trachten dolls (21.5 cm, 8.5 inches). *Left* 'Bärbel aus Gutach im Schwarzwald'. The doll wears a beaded crown, tied under the chin with red ribbon; white blouse with puff sleeves; pink shawl edged in black feathered braid. Her navy skirt has white and gold braid trimming; a deep maroon apron is edged in lace. The doll has white painted stockings and black shoes. *Right* 'Conny Berlin Spreewald'. The doll has a tall blue head-dress edged in white lace that hangs in a peak at the back. Her dress bodice is black with white sleeves, and her skirt red with braid and lace trim and black velvet ribbon band. She wears a white lace shawl and apron and has white painted stockings and black shoes.

These three (20-cm, 8-inch) dolls are made of a celluloid-like plastic. The doll on the left is dressed in a white shirt with red double-breasted jacket, black bow tie, short black trousers, white painted socks and black shoes. The middle doll represents the **Black Forest** area, and wears a flat black hat with red band. He is dressed in a white shirt, red double-breasted jacket with gold buttons and simulated watch and chain, black bow tie, black breeches with red sashes on top of white stockings and black shoes. His long black jacket has red lapels and front edging and brass button trim. The right-hand doll is dressed in a white cap with lace edging; blue frock and puff sleeves, black ribbon trim on the skirt and black lacing on the bodice. Her small white shawl and apron are trimmed with lace, and she has white socks, black shoes.

Bavaria Celluloid doll (15 cm, 6 inches). She wears a tall green hat with a long feather falling to one side, white blouse, short waistcoat with gold button trim, and green skirt trimmed with red braid. Her white apron is trimmed with red and white lace. A short shawl or collar trimmed with red embroidery is attached to the bodice with flowers. She has white stockings and black shoes. Outfits similar to this are worn by women attending the Oktoberfest in Munich. (Courtesy Hilary Dunford)

Germany's recorded history dates to AD 9 when the Cherusci, a Germanic tribe, defeated three Roman legions. Then in the fourth and fifth centuries AD West Germanic tribes overran Roman Gaul (France) and adjoining regions, establishing the Frankish Empire, which reached its peak under Charlemagne (768–814), crowned Holy Roman Emperor in 800.

German-speaking Franconia separated from what was to become France in 843. By the end of 1190 (after a succession of kings and a dispute with the pope) Germany fragmented into a host of semi-sovereign states. The Teutonic Knights (a Christian military order) expanded eastward among the Slav people, firmly establishing a virtual monopoly of Baltic and North Sea trade by the thirteenth century.

For 600 years from 1273 German history was tied to the Austrian Hapsburg dynasty, which had a virtual monopoly of German and imperial titles from 1438. In the sixteenth century a long period of religious wars between the Catholic system and followers of the Protestant doctrines of Martin Luther ensued, culminating in the Thirty Years War (1618–48) and the wholesale devastation of Germany, with territories in the east and north ceded to France and Sweden.

By the end of the seventeenth century, German states such as Prussia-Brandenburg, Saxony, Bavaria and Hanover had emerged as considerable powers in their own right. But, although Frederick the Great of Prussia finally triumphed over Austria in 1763 and both states gained territory from the first division of Poland (1772), they were defeated by Napoleon Bonaparte who forced the merger of a number of small principalities into 16 larger states bound together by the Rhenish League in 1806. The Holy Roman Empire ceased to exist when Austria's emperor renounced the title. A new German Confederation was created in 1814–15 under the nominal leadership of Austria.

Germany was mainly unaffected by the unrest in Europe in 1830, except for the continual rivalry between Germany and the Austrian emperor. In 1862 Bismarck warded off further intervention, taking over the Danish provinces of Schleswig and Holstein in 1864, defeating Austria in 1866 forcing the Hapsburgs to vacate the German arena, and routing Napoleon III and bombarding Paris. The southern German states opted to join the new German Empire in 1871, with Berlin as the capital. France ceded Alsace and Lorraine to Germany in 1871. By the 1890s Germany had acquired colonies in Africa and the Pacific.

Rivalry between France and Germany and also England and Germany simmered from the 1890s with a series of incidents antagonising both France and England. This culminated in World War I, with Germany first declaring war on Russia and France, then Britain by violating Belgian neutrality. After suffering a general retreat, Germany signed an armistice in November 1918, and a republic was declared. In 1919 it was

Hard-plastic dolls (13 cm, 5.25 inches) representing **Gent, Luneburger Heide, Zillertalerin, Hamburg** and **Bueckeburg.** *Far left* The doll has a white lace cap trimmed in black over her hair plaited in a bun. Her dress has a wide brown band at the hem. A white figured shawl edged with pink fringing is tucked under a black waist-sash. She has white stockings and black shoes. *Left* The doll wears a wide straw hat over hair plaited and arranged at the back of her head. She wears a white blouse, green vest, black skirt with coloured braid trim and lace at hem, blue apron, white stockings and black shoes. *Centre left* The boy doll is dressed in a green Tyrolean hat with white feather trim, white shirt and green bow tie. His grey jacket has green lapels and buttons. His grey shorts, representing lederhosen, have a bow at the side. He wears white socks and black shoes. *Centre right* The doll has hair plaited over the ears under a high black hat with red peak and black ribbon trim. Over her golden bodice she wears a red shawl with braid edging. She has a blue skirt with pale blue and lace trim, green apron trimmed in gold, white stockings and black shoes. The doll is marked 'Gura Ochsenfurt'. *Right* The doll has hair plaited over the ears under a flat-topped square hat edged with braid. Her red dress is trimmed with white and gold braid and is edged with lace. Her white shawl is lace edged, and the yellow apron is trimmed with black lace. She wears white stockings and black shoes. *Far right* The doll has hair plaited over the ears under a tall black hat trimmed in front with yellow. Her black bodice has a square neckline edged in green braid, with the same braid at the cuffs. The bodice has a pink crossover insert. The green skirt is edged with an orange trim from the inside. Pink apron, white stockings and black shoes.

forced to surrender all colonies and to return Alsace-Lorraine to France.

The world depression brought mass unemployment to Germany, and with increasing political turmoil, Hindenburg reluctantly appointed Hitler chancellor in 1933. Hitler's ideas were at first thought to be of benefit to the people, but by 1938 German forces had marched into Austria, incorporating it into the Reich, had annexed the whole of Czechoslovakia by March 1939, and later that year Germany invaded Poland causing France and Britain to declare war.

Left The doll wears a flat black hat trimmed with white braid. She has a white braid frill around the neck of her wine-coloured frock, lace trim at hem. The apron is of a small pink floral design with large bow and lace trim at hem. *Centre* This doll is celluloid and has a lace-edged cap on top of moulded hair. She wears a white blouse under a blue bodice and skirt. Over the shoulders and around the skirt are red/yellow/navy striped ribbons. She has a multi-striped apron of orange/red/black/blue/white, and black shoes. *Right* The doll wears a green hat with cord trim. Her white blouse is covered by a check shawl. She has a red skirt trimmed in gold and a blue apron.

Left Celluloid doll (20 cm, 8 inches). This female doll is dressed in the **Black Forest** regional costume. Her straw hat has large red pompons on the crown covered by black net. She wears a white blouse under a black bodice trimmed at the neck with red and gold bands. Her black skirt has a wide braid band at the hem. She wears a dark green brocade apron with white lace trim, white socks and black shoes. *Centre* A 9-cm (3.5-inch) plastic doll representing **Munich** is dressed in a dark monk's habit with yellow trim. A monk is the emblem of Munich. The doll was bought in Munich in 1976. *Right* A cloth doll representing H. Zille, a famous Berlin artist, complete with identification, sent from Germany in the 1980s. The doll wears a large-brimmed flat-top black hat, white shirt, red tie, brown coat with wide cape collar, black trousers and shoes.

Hard-plastic dolls (14 cm, 5.5 inches) bought at St Goar on the Rhine, in 1976, and representing the **Rhine** region. The male doll wears a green hat with white cord band, white shirt, black bow tie, red waistcoat, green sleeveless jacket with gold buttons, grey trousers and black shoes. The female doll has autumn leaves in her hair, gold braid at the neck. She wears a square-necked white blouse, black vest with gold cord, green skirt trimmed with red. White lace apron, white stockings and black shoes.

After defeating Poland, Germany had occupied Denmark and Norway by May 1940, followed by France and Holland by June 1940. Italy joined Germany, and after the attack on Pearl Harbour by the Japanese in December 1941, Germany declared war on the United States. Germany's unconditional surrender was signed in France in May 1945 and the defeated country was placed under a four-power occupational regime with Britain, French, United States and Russian zones. Berlin was also divided into a Soviet sector and three western sectors under joint four-power control.

German territory to the east of the Oder-Neisse was given to Poland. The Soviet Union took northern East Prussia. Because the Soviet Union vigorously opposed many of the changes proposed by the Western Allies for Germany, a serious rift emerged between west and east, ending with the division of Germany into two states — the Federal Republic of Germany (a free-market democracy aligned with the West) and the German Democratic Republic (a Communist-ruled state within the Soviet bloc).

An antique bisque-headed doll dressed in traditional German costume. The doll wears a straw hat on top of a red scarf. She has a white blouse under her black velvet bodice with jewellery trim. Her red and black striped skirt has a maroon waistband or sash.

Federal Republic of Germany Bonn was chosen as the capital in May 1949, and the country achieved full sovereignty in May 1955. In 1961 the infamous Berlin Wall was erected by the GDR, effectively separating West Berlin from the Soviet sector; it was already separated from the rest of West Germany by surrounding East German territory. The Federal Republic made a rapid economic recovery with the help of the Western Allies.

German Democratic Republic Proclaimed in October 1949, the GDR, often referred to as East Germany, was immediately recognised by the Soviet Union, becoming a founding member of the Warsaw Pact in May 1955. In 1974 the GDR was described as an inseparable part of the socialist community, and in 1975 both the GDR and FRG signed an act in which the existing borders of all

German plastic play dolls (30.5 cm, 12 inches) representing **Bavaria**. The girl is dressed in a green hat, white blouse, and multicoloured shawl. She wears a black corselet with brass studs over her red skirt trimmed in green. Her apron has lace trimming at the hem edge. The boy wears a green hat, check shirt, grey felt *lederhosen* (pants) with black braces.

European states were declared inviolable. Then, in 1987, for the very first time, a GDR leader paid an official visit to Bonn, the capital of the FRG.

Although reforms had been instituted in the Soviet Union after 1985, East Germany refused to concede that such reforms might be applicable to them. Suddenly an irreversible movement for unification occurred in both Germanys and on 9 November 1989 the GDR lifted travel and emigration restrictions. Within hours thousands of jubilant West and East Germans converged on the Berlin Wall, and symbolically the wall ceased to exist, allowing families and friends to be reunited after nearly 30 years of separation. On 18 March 1990 the GDR held the first free election of the Volkskammer (parliament).

Unification In August 1990 the Volkskammer acceded to the FDR, signing the Unification Treaty on 31 October. In October the Big Four formally agreed to pass all responsibility over to Germany. Full sovereignty and unification were achieved and celebrated in early October, with five new states — Brandenburg, Mecklenburg-Western Pomerania, Saxony, Saxony-Anhalt and Thuringai — added to the FRG. A reunited Germany held its first free national elections since 1933 on 2 December 1990.

Capital Berlin.

Population 78.5 million. Of the 4.7 million foreigners in reunited Germany, 1.48 million are Turks, 597 600 Yugoslavs, 544 400 Italians, 279 900 Greeks, 110 000 Sorbs (Slavs), 0.3 per cent Spanish, 0.2 per cent Dutch.

Religion Germany is predominantly Christian — Protestant (Lutheran Reformed, Lutheran and Reformed, Baptist, Methodist, Nemonites and Lutheran Free Church) and Roman Catholic; there are also 1.4 million Muslims and approximately 37 000 Jews.

Language German is the official language. Turkish, Greek, Italian, Dutch, Spanish and English are also spoken, plus three major regional dialects — Upper German (Allemanic), Central German (Franconian) and Low German (Plattdeutsch). In eastern Germany Saxon is still in common use, and the Sorbian minority retain their own language.

Ghana (Republic of)

Situated on the section of Africa once known as the Gold Coast, Ghana has common borders with Côte d'Ivoire,

A 30.5-cm (12-inch) 'Ashanti' fertility doll. The black-painted wooden male doll has carved features and an incised midriff showing a square with slanted lines. This type of doll is called an *akuaba* and is carried by a woman who hopes to have a beautiful child just like the carving. (Courtesy Sherry Morgan, Clearwater, Florida. Photograph: J. Maxson)

This 17.75-cm (7-inch) brown plastic doll wears a red head-dress, yellow/orange floral peplumed jacket over gathered skirt, long yellow/orange floral shawl draped over the shoulder, red shoes.

A cloth doll wearing a yellow scarf (turban) on her head; gold earrings, necklace and bangles; a brown figured dress with separate wrap-around skirt. (Courtesy J. Miller, New South Wales)

Burkina Faso and Togo, and to the south is the Gulf of Guinea (Atlantic Ocean). Divided into nine regions, the total land area is 238 686 square kilometres (92 133 square miles). Approximately 11 per cent of the country is cultivated and one-third is covered by evergreen and semi-deciduous tropical forest.

Named after the Ghana Empire, which ruled in western Sudan from the eighth to the twelfth centuries, modern Ghana is situated to the southeast of the old empire. In the thirteenth century the coastal states were settled by the Akan, followed by Mande traders from the north in the fourteenth century, and Hausa merchants searching for kola nuts in the sixteenth.

The Ashanti (Twi-speaking Akan) established an empire in the forest belt in the seventeenth century and traded slaves first with the Portuguese and later with the British, Dutch and Danish. When Britain abolished the slave trade in 1807 there was fighting, and the Ashanti defeated Britain in 1824. In 1874 Britain captured the Ashanti capital and the Gold Coast colony was founded in the southern portion of the Ashanti Empire, but it was not until 1901 that the remainder of the empire was absorbed into the colony.

In 1947 the move towards autonomy began and on 6 March 1957 the Gold Coast became independent, merging with former British Togoland to form Ghana. In 1960 Ghana became a republic.
Capital Accra.
Population (1990) 15 million, of which 31.3 per cent live in urban areas. Akan 44 per cent (southwest), Mole-Dagbani 11 per cent (north), Ewe 13 per cent, Ga 8 per cent (around Accra), and Fante (on the coast.)
Religion Christianity 52 per cent, Muslim 13 per cent, traditional animist customs and beliefs 30 per cent.
Language English is the official language. Akan is spoken by the Ashanti; and Fante, Mole-Dagbani and Ewe are also spoken.

Gold Coast (Africa) See Ghana.

Great Britain See England, Scotland and Wales.

Greece (Hellenic Republic) Europe

Situated in southeast Europe, Greece occupies the southernmost part of the Balkan Peninsula and includes over 1400 islands in the Ionian and Aegean Seas, with a total area of 131 990 square kilometres (50 961 square miles). The majority of the people live on the mainland, with one-third of the population in Greater Athens. Approximately 30 per cent of the land is arable, with 22 per cent forested.

Dolls with cloth heads, plastic/cloth hands, wire armature bodies. *Left* The 23-cm (9-inch) Greek Orthodox archbishop wears a tall head-piece, long black robe, white stockings, black shoes. He has a gold cross on a long chain and holds a staff topped by a blue stone. *Right* This 18-cm (7-inch) doll portrays a Greek Orthodox priest. He wears a tall round hat with a flat top, black gown with a wide gold brocade band down the front and black shoes. He holds a crucifix in the right hand.

These 28-cm (11-inch) dolls have cloth heads, plastic arms and torso, wire and cloth bodies. *Left* the *Evzone* (palace guard) dates to the war of liberation from the Turks. He wears a red velvet cap with black tassel, white wide-sleeved shirt, blue velvet waistcoat with white/silver/yellow trim, a very full pleated skirt over an underskirt, white stockings decorated with black cord and tassels at the knees, black shoes with large blue pompons on the toes. *Right* The female doll is dressed in a costume based on clothing worn at the court of Queen Amalia. She wears a coiled cloth band around the head, lace mantle (stole), white lace jabot, red jacket with multi-coloured edging, long lace and net cuffs. Her long skirt is trimmed with a wide band consisting of lace, ric-rac and braid, and there is a gold braid band at the hem. Over this she wears a net, lace and braid apron.

A peasant girl doll made of carton or papier mâché. She is dressed in a tall red hat folded to one side with a long tassel falling from the point, and a red jacket with coffee lace at the neck and cuffs. Her skirt of navy blue is trimmed with braid and she has a white apron embroidered and edged with lace.

Rhodes shepherd. According to Greek mythology Rhodes was where the sun god Apollo married the nymph Rodas, and that is the reason why Rhodes has the most sunshine of the Greek islands. The doll wears a grey skull cap under his hooded grey cloak, which is trimmed with black ric-rac. He has a white shirt and black waistcoat with a red waistband. He wears a short white skirt, white stockings with black cord decoration at the knees and black pointed-toe shoes called *tsaruchia*. He carries a shepherd's staff in his right hand.

Europe's earliest advanced civilisation — the Minoan — flourished in Crete from 2300 BC to about 1400 BC, overlapped by the Mycenaean civilisation on the mainland. The invasion of tribes from Asia Minor ushered in the Greek dark ages, with Greece fragmented into hundreds of little states, each with its own separate government, the largest of which was Athens.

Two invasions by kings of Persia in 491 BC and in 480–479 BC were driven back, and the golden age of classical Greece began, laying down the intellectual foundations of Western civilisation. The Athenians created an empire but were toppled by the Spartans in 404 BC, later beaten themselves in 338 BC. Alexander the Great conquered the Persian Empire around 331 BC. Greece was subjugated by the Romans in the second century BC, and became part of the Byzantine Empire (founded AD 395).

Disputes between Constantinople and the Church of Rome in 1054 led to the Greek Orthodox Church regarding itself as the spiritual embodiment of the empire. The Byzantine empire gradually succumbed to the Ottoman Turks: Constantinople in 1453, followed by Greece in 1456. Many of the populated Greek islands in the Aegean Sea held out much longer, but eventually all of the eastern Mediterranean Greek world came under Muslim Turkish rule.

Championed by many important British and French, as well as a Russian regime, the Greeks finally overcame the Ottoman Empire, and Greek independence was declared on 25 March 1821. Constitutional rule was implemented in 1843. The Ionian Islands, a British protectorate since 1815, were ceded back to Greece in 1863, followed by the acquisition from Turkey of Thessaly in 1881, and southern Epirus, Crete and the eastern Aegean Islands after the Balkan Wars (1912–13).

In 1917, Greece entered World War I on the Allied side against Turkey. In 1923 under the Treaty of Lausanne, Greece accepted British rule in Cyprus, Italy's acquisition of the Dodecanese Islands and a Turkish presence in Anatolia. A republic was declared in May 1924, with the monarchy restored in November 1935, followed by a dictatorship from 1936.

Greece repelled an attempted invasion by Italy in 1940, only to be overrun by

A series of Greek dolls dressed in various male attire representing from left to right: shepherd, priest, evzone, archbishop, shepherd, and a man from Crete. (Courtesy the Greek Pavilion, Expo 88)

A series of Greek dolls dressed to represent various village, peasant and island costumes. *Left* The doll wears a blue headscarf, check blouse, mustard skirt with black apron trimmed in red and blue and carries a load of wood on her back. *Inner left* The doll wears a red headscarf, white blouse, red vest, black skirt trimmed with braid and lace. *Middle* The doll wears a check headscarf and check trousers, white blouse and grey waistband. *Inner right* The doll wears a blue headscarf, orange bodice and skirt trimmed with black, paisley overtunic with medallion trim and blue scarf around the waist. *Right* The doll wears a yellow headscarf, green bodice, woollen check skirt, black apron with yellow and red trim, and a heavy white jacket trimmed in black. In her left hand she carries a distaff for spinning wool. (Courtesy the Greek Pavilion, Expo 88)

Traditional costumes of no specific region, referred to as 'Pan Hellenic'. *Left* This 23-cm (9-inch) cloth doll has black hair worn in buns at the side of her head, under her gold and orange head-dress. She wears a blue dress with red bands on the bodice and yellow, red, blue bands on the skirt. Her long blue coat has braid edging and decorative banding of red and blue. A red waistband is worn over the coat. *Centre* A 28-cm (11-inch) doll of cloth and plastic wearing a lace head shawl, with a red blouse trimmed at the neckline with medallions and lace. Her blue skirt is banded with gold and lace, and her red apron has black lace edging, and is trimmed with black lace and gold braid. *Right* A 25.5-cm (10-inch) doll of cloth and plastic dressed in a red cap with yellow tassel, red blouse with lace at the front and lace cuffs with gold trim. Her blue skirt has lace and braid trimming at the hem, and around the waist is a multi-coloured braid waistband.

Island costume. This 24-cm (9.5-inch) cloth doll wears a red headscarf, white blouse, black bolero trimmed with red and white braid. Around the waist she wears a gold braid sash. Her black skirt has red and white braid bands and white lace at the hem.

German forces in 1941, and was not liberated until 1944. The monarchy was restored in 1946, and lasted through several upsets until 1973. Under the 1947 Paris peace treaty, the Dodecanese Islands were returned to Greece.

A republic was proclaimed by the military regime of June 1973. Voting in December 1974 was against the restoration of the monarchy, and a new constitution declared a presidential parliamentary republic in June 1975. In 1987 Greece formally ended a state of war with Albania which had technically existed since 1940.

Capital Athens (Athinai).
Population 10.25 million, 61 per cent living in urban areas. Greek 97.7 per cent, Macedonian 1.5 per cent, Turkish 1.3 per cent, with 1 per cent Albanian, Slav or Vlach.
Religion 98 per cent adhere to the Greek Orthodox Church, 47 759 Roman Catholic, 5000 Jews and 1.3 per cent Muslim.
Language Greek is the official language, comprising two branches — the predominant Demotiki (the spoken and written language) and Katharevousa (classical Greek). English, German and French are widely understood.

Greenland Arctic Ocean

A large island in the Arctic Ocean, Greenland has an area of 2 175 600 square kilometres (839 782 square miles) of which 341 700 square kilometres (131 896 square miles) are icefree. Settlement is confined to the narrow rocky coast area.

Norwegian Vikings began to settle Greenland late in the tenth century, with Norwegian sovereignty confirmed in 1262, but the island came under Danish rule in 1397. By the late fifteenth century contact was lost, and it appears the settlement died out. Danish missionaries and settlers re-established a colony from 1721, and although disputed several times Greenland remained under Danish

Cloth and skin dolls. *Left* The male doll has black hair in a tall topknot banded with red. He wears a red coat with black fur cuffs over braid, red/white/blue beaded collar/cape. Black fur trousers with braid trim are worn with a wide braid belt, and red knee boots with white trim. *Right* The female doll has a baby in the hood of her fur jacket. She has black hair with red trim, white blouse under a red jacket, and her fur overjacket is trimmed with red braid and white beads. She wears dark grey fur trousers with braid trim and red knee boots with white trim. (Courtesy Vera Woodhead)

This 17.75-cm (7-inch) plastic doll has a tall black hairdo and wears a red jumper (sweater) with white trim, a green/white/red neck scarf, wide braid waistband and green leather trousers. She wears red boots with yellow trim and braid at the top, and her wide shoulder shawl/cape is decorated with braid and pompon trim.

control. Internal autonomy was achieved in May 1979.
Capital Nuuk (Godthab).
Population (1989) 55 415.
Religion Christianity — Evangelical Lutheran.
Language Eskimo dialects and Danish.

Grenada (State of) The Caribbean

One hundred and forty-five kilometres (90 miles) northeast of Trinidad, in the eastern Caribbean, is Grenada, the southernmost island of the Windward group. The total land area, divided into

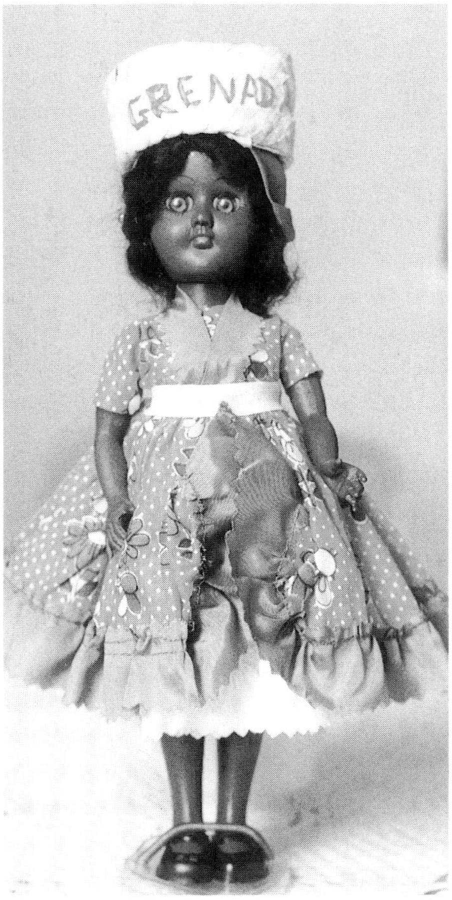

This 17.75-cm (7-inch) brown plastic doll is wearing a woven straw basket on her head with 'GRENADA' stitched on. Her red cotton, white pin spot, floral dress has green taffeta trim and frill.

six parishes, is only 344 square kilometres (132.8 square miles) and this includes the Southern Grenadines, a crescent of islands stretching northwest from Grenada to St Vincent.

Named Conception, after Columbus first discovered the island in 1498, Grenada's earliest inhabitants were the Arawak Indians who were later displaced by the Caribs from South America.

London merchants tried to settle the island in 1609, but were forced to abandon the plan in the face of harassment by the Caribs. The Caribs were eliminated by the French in the 1650s, and the island remained French until captured in 1762 by the British, who imported slave labour until the abolition of slavery in 1834.

Grenada gained full internal self-government in 1967, and attained independence from Britain in February 1974.
Capital St George's.
Population 100 000, with 25 per cent living in urban areas. 84 per cent are of black African descent, 12 per cent mulatto (mixed origin), 3 per cent East Indian, 1 per cent white.
Religion Christian — 64 per cent Roman Catholic, with the remainder Anglican, Methodist, Presbyterian and Baptist.
Language English is the official language, although a French-African patois is also spoken.

Guatemala (Republic of) Central America

Located in the Central American isthmus between the Pacific Ocean and the Caribbean Sea, Guatemala is bordered by Mexico to the north, with Belize to the west, and Honduras and El Salvador to the south. The country is divided into 22 departments, with 12 per cent of the land arable and 40 per cent forested. Guatemala has an area of 108 889 square kilometres (42 031 square miles).

Guatemala's contemporary Indians can be traced back to the Maya-Quiche nation (1500 BC to 1500 AD), one of the richest civilisations ever known, but which had almost vanished when the Spanish

Jointed cloth dolls (24 cm, 9.5 inches). The girl has a woven cane basket on her head, black yarn hair in two plaits, black button eyes and earrings. She wears a white overblouse with embroidery around the neck and sleeves, woven gathered skirt and brown sandals. The boy has a woven straw hat set back on his black hair, button eyes, red check shirt with blue trim around the front edges, grey tweed trousers, woven houndstooth apron tied on with a red sash, brown sandals.

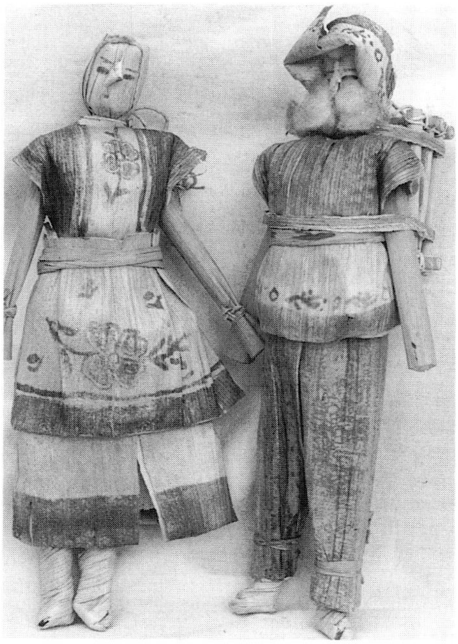

A pair of dolls with corn leaf bodies and clothing painted to give details (24 cm, 9.5 inches). The woman's headscarf and overdress are painted with flowers and border. The skirt has a painted hem. The man has a cottonwool beard, and turned-back hat with hand-painted brim. His overshirt has painted trim and he wears purple trousers. He has an elaborate wood and cane backpack.

arrived in the 1520s. Although Guatemala's mineral reserves were the poorest in the region, the country became the political heart of Spanish rule in Central America. Known from 1549 as the Kingdom of Guatemala, the country declared independence from Spain in 1821.

Following a period of liberal rule (1871–1885) the country entered a 22-year dictatorship, followed by successive coups (many of them military) right through to the 1980s. Guatemala finally abandoned its long-standing claims to Belize, which gained its independence from Britain in September 1981. In 1991, with its second consecutive elected civilian president about to take over, Guatemala looked forward to better years ahead.

Capital Guatemala City.

Population 9.2 million, of which 32 per cent live in urban areas. 56 per cent are Ladino (of mixed Hispanic-Indian descent), 44 per cent are Indian of Maya descent, and there are also small white and black minorities.

Religion 75 per cent are Roman Catholic, approximately 25 per cent Protestant, and some Indians still practise Mayan religious customs and beliefs.

Dolls with cloth heads and paper-wound armature. *Left* This 22-cm (8.5-inch) doll has a straw basket on her head, black hair with an interwoven yarn halo, and a woven check blouse with wide scarf which holds the baby on her back. The baby has a woven head-dress and clothes. The mother wears a red woven skirt with cord waistband, and paper undies. *Right* The 20-cm (7.75-inch) doll has a woven scarf (turban) on her head, orange/white woven bodice with pink cotton sleeves, black short trousers (or skirt) decorated with yellow stitching and embroidery. She wears a green cord waist-sash *(faja)*, yellow cord scarf at the neck and holds a sheaf in the left arm. Traditional Guatemalan Indian dress has colourful patterns and designs often using natural dyes.

Language Spanish is the official language, although 40 per cent speak one of the 20 indigenous Indian dialects.

Haiti (Republic of)
The Caribbean

Situated in the Caribbean about 1000 kilometres (621 miles) southeast of Florida, Haiti occupies the western third of the seismically active island of Hispaniola (the other two-third section is the Dominican Republic), and includes a number of small West Indian islets. Haiti is divided into nine departments with a total area of 27 750 square kilometres (10 712 square miles). About 33 per cent of the land is arable with 4 per cent forested.

Dolls with clay head, brown cloth body (25.5 cm, 10 inches). The female doll wears a red scarf, blue-grey dress with white lace trim on bodice, red sash. The male doll wears a woven straw hat with wide turned-up brim; blue-grey overshirt with large pockets at the front under a red poncho-type shawl; navy trousers.

The Taino Arawak Indians are the first known inhabitants. The island was discovered in 1492 by Columbus who named it Hispaniola and claimed it for Spain, with European settlers arriving soon after.

By 1697 the presence of French settlers in the western third of the island was recognised by Spain, and the island was ceded to France. First known as Saint-Domingue, the territory's agriculture, based on the use of African slave labour on the plantations, proved highly profitable.

The French Revolution, followed by a slave rebellion in 1791, led to 13 years of war, only resolved in 1804 with the declaration of the world's first independent black republic. The first president was assasinated in 1806, but a succession of others followed. France recognised Haiti's independence in 1825, and from 1822 to 1844 Haiti occupied the eastern portion of Hispaniola (now the Dominican Republic).

Growing instability early in twentieth century prompted United States intervention, and US Marines administered Haiti from 1915 until 1934. From 1946 until 1957 there were various coups, with a one-party system operating until free presidential elections were held in 1990.

Capital Port-au-Prince.
Population (1990) 6.5 million, of which 28.9 per cent live in urban areas. 95 per cent are descended from the African slave population, 5 per cent are mulatto or European.
Religion 75–80 per cent Roman Catholic, although this is often merged with the folk religion Voodoo; 10 per cent Protestant.
Language Although French is the official language it is spoken by only 10 per cent. The Haitian French-African creole is universally understood (90 per cent French in origin, 10 per cent African), but not by other French creole-speaking inhabitants of the Caribbean.

Hawaii See United States of America.

Honduras (Republic of) Central America

Covering an area of 112 088 square kilometres (43 266 square miles), Honduras is the second-largest country on the Central American isthmus. Included in the area are the Bay Islands in the Caribbean and a further 288 islands off the Pacific coast. Honduras shares borders with El Salvador and Guatemala to the west and Nicaragua to the south. Over 75 per cent of its area is mountainous terrain, while only 14 per cent is arable and 34 per cent forested.

Indian sites have been found dating back to 1700–1600 BC and the Mayan people (AD 250–900) flourished in what is now Honduras, only to decline when the Spanish invaded early in the sixteenth century. Along with four other Central American countries, Honduras gained its independence from Spain in 1821.

From late in the nineteenth century, the export of fruit, mainly bananas, has been the country's main source of income; and because of the varying prices associated with the fruit trade, Honduras has had a tendency to be politically unstable.

Capital Tegucigalpa.
Population (1990) 5.1 million, of which 40.7 per cent live in urban areas. 90 per cent are mestizo (mixed Indian and European), 7 per cent Indian (including black Carib), 2 per cent black, 1 per cent white.
Religion 97 per cent Roman Catholic, with a small minority Episcopal and Baptist.
Language Spanish is the official language.

A simply jointed wooden doll with drawn features (26 cm, 10.25 inches). On her head she carries a woven cane basket containing fruit. Her hair falls in long sisal plaits. A red/white shawl is held together with a centaro Honduras coin. She wears a bright yellow blouse trimmed at the neck with blue/white over a floral skirt with pinked waistband; white apron with green ties.

A number of Indian dialects are also spoken, and an English Creole in the Islas de la Bahia.

Hong Kong (Crown Colony of) Asia

Lying just off the southwest coast of mainland China is the island of Hong Kong. The territory of Hong Kong, 1072 square kilometres (414 square miles), consists of Hong Kong island and adjacent islands (just under 80 square kilometres (31 square miles), Kowloon (a peninsula on mainland China, 10.6 square kilometres (4 square miles), and the New Territories north of Kowloon with adjacent island (approximately 980 square kilometres, 378 square miles).

Left A 25.5-cm (10-inch) cloth doll wearing a woven straw coolie hat. He has a plaited wool topknot, embroidered features, navy jacket with frogged front, black trousers and shoes. Marked 'Made in Hong Kong (Ada Lum)'. *Centre* A 29-cm (11.5-inch) vinyl doll sold as a souvenir of Hong Kong in the 1970s. The female doll has black hair in a plait, a red jacket frogged at the side, blue trousers, white socks and red shoes. A waist tag reads 'Made in China'. *Right* A 29-cm (11.5-inch) cloth doll, 'Amah'. She has black yarn hair in a single plait, embroidered features, a blue/white striped jacket frogged at the side, black trousers, white bib apron with gold/white/red/green braid. A round tag reads 'Chinese Doll Amah (1207) handmade in Hong Kong'. An *amah* was a nursemaid who looked after children.

Inhabited in prehistoric times, probably by people from northern China, and from the second century BC by Cantonese, the island now known as Hong Kong had no recognised name before 1841. By the end of the eighteenth century Britain was the principal European trading partner with China, and in the 1820s Hong Kong had become a shelter for opium-carrying ships. The anchorage at Aberdeen was known to sailors as Heung Kong, whose Chinese characters may be translated as either 'fragrant streams' or 'fragrant harbour'.

The Chinese tried to ban the import of opium, which eventually led to war with Britain in 1839–42. As the victorious British required a free port, a treaty was signed in 1842 ceding Hong Kong island in perpetuity to the British crown. In 1860 and 1898 Britain secured a perpetual lease on the Kowloon Peninsula and a 99-year lease on the New Territories.

During the twentieth century Hong Kong has become an important centre for refugees — after the revolutions in China of 1911 and 1940 and the Sino-Japanese War in 1937, and the 1980s exodus of refugees from Vietnam.

The Japanese invaded Hong Kong in 1941 and occupation lasted until 1945.

Plans for self-government were mooted after World War II, but these were abandoned. Eventually, talks between Britain and China about the future of Hong Kong started in 1982, leading to an agreement in 1985 that on 1 July 1997 China will regain sovereignty over Hong Kong, with its present economic and social systems remaining unchanged for 50 years afterward.
Capital Victoria.
Population 5.7 million; 98 per cent Chinese (59 per cent born in Hong Kong, 37 per cent in China) and 2 per cent other, including Europeans.
Religion Majority Buddhist, with a large Taoist and Confucianist element. 10 per cent Christian, and some Muslim, Hindu, Sikh and Jewish communities.
Language English and Chinese are the official languages, with most Chinese speaking Cantonese, although Mandarin is widely understood.

Hungary (Republic of) Europe

A land-locked country in the Carpathian Basin of Central Europe, Hungary borders on Austria to the west, Slovakia to the north, Ukraine and Romania to the east, Serbia, Croatia and Slovenia to the south. Hungary is divided into 19 counties and 8 cities with county status, and has an area of 93 030 square kilometres (35 910 square miles). Fifty-four per cent of this land is arable and 18 per cent forested, with an estimated 25 per cent of the population living in metropolitan Budapest.

The Carpathian Basin, irrigated by the Danube, lay on the frontiers of the Roman provinces before invasions by the Huns and Avars between the fourth and sixth centuries AD. The area was settled by Finno-Ugrian Magyars moving west from the middle Volga between eighth and tenth centuries, with a dynasty founded by Prince Arpad in 904 AD lasting through until 1301. A descendant, St Stephen, completed Hungary's conversion to Christianity and became first king of Hungary in AD 1000. During its first 200 years, the Hungarian Kingdom (which included present day Slovakia, Trans-Carpathian Ukraine,

Cloth dolls (16 cm, 6.25 inches). The male doll has a tall black hat with brocade band, black hair, white shirt with embroidered collar and lace cuffs, black waistcoat with yellow trim, red scarf with long fringe at the front waist, fully pleated long white trousers. A heavy white overcoat trimmed with red is worn loose over the shoulders and held at the front with red ties. Black boots. The female doll wears a head-dress, scarf with large blue/green/red pompons, floral bodice with flared peplum and braid corselet, finely pleated skirt with black braid band and blue braid at the hemline. A black apron richly embroidered in blue and yellow has a long black fringe. She holds a lace hankie in her right hand, and wears short black boots. The tag reads 'Hungary Co-op'.

A 1930s doll with composition head and arms, cloth body. She wears a white head-dress with blue ribbon insert trim. Her red floral bodice has a lace collar and white sleeves. She has a white cotton and lace apron over a dark skirt and wears black boots. (Private collection, Brisbane)

Cloth dolls (17.75 cm, 7 inches). *Left* 'Kazari' on the tag. The doll wears a white/yellow head-dress with red crown and streamers; white blouse; red shawl with yellow/pink fringing and lace trim on the neck edge; red pleated skirt with a blue band at the hem; white lace-edged apron; red boots. *Right* 'Rimo Cibaba' on the tag. The doll wears a red floral crown head-dress; white cap with blue trim and red ribbon streamers; white blouse under a red shawl with coloured fringe; red skirt featuring a blue band near the hem; white stockings; red boots. (Courtesy Vera Woodhead, Queensland)

A 16.5-cm (6.5-inch) plastic doll labelled 'Boldogi'. This female doll wears a coloured cap with blue band and lace edging; fawn bodice with blue collar, and lace-edged pink frill; red pleated skirt with yellow band, blue braid and lace trim; embroidered apron with lace and embroidery trim. *Right* A 17-cm (6.75-inch) male cloth doll wearing a black hat with blue headband; white shirt with embroidery down the front; black sleeveless jacket with beaded trim; long black apron with embroidery trim and silver fringe; black trousers and boots. (Courtesy Vera Woodhead, Queensland)

A pair of composition-headed dolls with cloth bodies from the 1930s. The woman wears a white blouse, red waistcoat, red floral skirt with an orange hem band. Her sheer white apron is lace edged and she has red shoes. On her head she has a floral headband. The male doll has a red hat, white shirt, red sleeveless jacket, white trousers, embroidered navy apron and brown boots (damaged). (Private collection, Brisbane)

Transylvania and most of the northern part of what was Yugoslavia) successfully resisted Byzantine, German and Turkish encroachments. But recurring internal strife between feudal lords finally led to central Hungary being seized by the Turks while western Hungary submitted to the Austrian Hapsburgs. In a treaty in 1699 the Hapsburgs finally expelled the Turks from Hungary thus reuniting the country, but the Magyar people found themselves in the minority.

Magyar national culture revived early in nineteenth century, with the Hungarian Diet (parliament) demanding equality between Hungary and Austria in 1861. The new capital, Budapest, became a major centre of European culture. Hungary supported the expansionist foreign policy of Austria-Hungary's ally Germany, and consequently shared in the defeat of World War I. Czech, Serb and Romanian forces occupied all but the purely Magyar heartland, and an independent Hungary was reduced to a mere 93 000 square kilometres with a population of 8 million.

A Soviet Republic was established in March 1919, to be overthrown when Romanian troups entered Budapest in October 1919. Further internal problems moved Hungary into the orbit of Nazi Germany, and it was rewarded in 1938, 1940 and again after joining with the Axis against Russia in 1941, with Czech, Yugoslavian and Romanian territories which had formerly belonged to Hungary. Germany occupied Hungary in March 1944, with the last German forces leaving in April 1945.

Early in 1946 the monarchy was abolished and a republic established. In the mid 1980s Hungary turned its back on over 40 years of communism and in 1990 free and multi-party elections were held. Finally in July 1991 the commander of Soviet forces left Hungary, officially ending a 47-year military presence.

Capital Budapest.

Population (1990) 10.6 million, with 56.8 per cent living in urban areas. 95 per cent Hungarian (Magyar), 2.3 per cent German, 1 per cent Slovak, 0.25 per cent Romanian, 0.9 per cent Southern Slavic, and between 500 000 and 700 000 Gypsies.

Religion 67.5 per cent Catholic (Latin or Byzantine), 20 per cent Calvinist, 5 per cent Lutheran, and a variety of Orthodox, as well as Muslims and Jews.

Language 98 per cent speak Hungarian Magyar (a member of the Finno-Ugric branch of the Uralic language family). Most of the Gypsy population speaks Romany.

Iceland (Republic of) North Atlantic

Eight hundred kilometres (497 miles) north of Scotland, 900 kilometres (559 miles) west of Norway and 300 kilometres (186 miles) southeast of Greenland in the North Atlantic is the volcanic island of Iceland. Divided into eight regions, Iceland has an area of 103 000 square kilometres (39 758 square miles) with glaciers covering 10 per cent of its surface area. Only 1 per cent of the land is arable, but nearly 25 per cent is suitable for grazing.

Iceland was settled by the Vikings, mainly of Norwegian origin (with a touch of Celtic), in the later part of the ninth century AD. It established its own parliament in 930, the first in the modern world. Christianised around 1000, it enjoyed a literary golden age, culminating in the sagas of the twelfth and thirteenth centuries.

Left A 16.5-cm (6.5-inch) hard-plastic doll. The tag reads 'Island Sondag national doll Made in Denmark'. The doll has a black bonnet with a long tassel trimmed with wide gold braid and yellow braid around the face, white blouse with lace at the front and cuffs, black jacket with white fur collar, black waist band, black skirt under a maroon apron. *Right* A 14-cm (5.5-inch) cloth 'stump' doll made in Iceland. She has a black cap with tassel at the side, blond sisal looped plaits. The black bodice has a white bow at the neck. The black skirt forms part of the body (filled with small stones) under a black/fawn patterned apron. The doll holds white yarn, wooden knitting needles and knitting. Circa 1970s.

Iceland declared allegiance to Norway in 1262, and when the union of Norwegian and Danish crowns was confirmed in 1397, Iceland came under Danish sovereignty. At the end of the Napoleonic Wars in 1814, Iceland remained Danish when Norway was transferred to Sweden.

An awakening of national feeling led to limited home rule in 1874 and full sovereignty in 1918, although Iceland remained under the Danish crown. Because Denmark was under German control during World War II Iceland was occupied by British and American troops. Iceland finally declared itself an independent republic in 1944.

Capital Reykjavik.

Population (1990) 300 000, of which 89.7 per cent live in urban areas. 96.9 per cent are native Icelandic, with minorities of Danish, American, British, Norwegian and German citizens.

Religion 95 per cent Evangelical Lutheran, with other Protestant denominations and about 2000 Roman Catholics.

Language Icelandic (Islensk), part of the West Scandinavian branch of North Germanic languages related to Norwegian and Faroese.

India (Republic of) Asia

See also Pakistan if the doll is from before 1946.

The seventh largest country in the world, India is situated in southern Asia. It is divided into 25 states and 7 union territories with a total area of 3 166 289 square kilometres (1 222 396 square miles). Fifty-five per cent of the land is arable with 23 per cent forested, mainly on the lower slopes of the Himalaya and areas which have not been cleared for rice growing in the coastal regions.

Numerous sites of human settlement may be found in India dating back to approximately 40 000 BC. Tribal people of the Aryan language group from central Asia settled in the Ganges Valley during the second millennium BC, laying the foundations of Indian culture, especially Sanskrit, Hinduism and the caste system.

Turkish invaders from Afghanistan

Gujarat family. Gujarat is a state on the west coast of India. In Porbandar, Gujarat, once a princely domain, the founder of the Indian nation, Mahatma Gandhi, was born. Peasants and shepherds roam the entire state, the men distinguished by their many-fold turbans of flame red, fancy shoes with upturned toes and gold earrings. Their finely cut white *kedivas* (shirts) and *dhotis* contribute to their elegant appearance. The male doll wears a russet waistband. The female doll is dressed in a green *kurta*, black skirt with red braid at the hem, and a wine shawl covers her head. On her hip she carries a baby dressed in a yellow cap decorated with mirror embroidery and a jacket similar to the father's.

Left **'Maharashtra** man and woman'. The man wears a white dhoti, long black coat and white turban. A white cotton or silk shawl is draped from back to front over the shoulder. The woman wears an 8.5-metre dark-coloured sari with woven borders and pallav in rich greens/blues and maroons. The *mangalsutra* around her neck and the green bangles are essential for married women. She wears a vermillion dot on her forehead with a black crescent mark beneath. *Right* **Bihar** man and woman. Men from Bihar wear simple sober dress. The doll wears a white dhoti, with a white kurta or shirt, a dark beige button-through waistcoat, and a dark *topi* or cap on the head. The female doll wears a simple red cotton sari with a cotton blouse. The red *pallav* is drawn over the right shoulder to the front and then thrown over the left shoulder. She wears silver anklets and bracelets. Bihar women sometimes wear silver chains drawn across the forehead.

Left **Tripura** man and woman. The female doll wears a one-piece knee-length purple/blue/maroon dress with a multitude of bead necklaces. The bare-chested male doll wears a short white dhoti and a number of bead necklaces. *Right* **Tamilnadu** man and woman. The female doll wears her cerise sari drawn between the legs from front to back and tucked in at the back. She wears nose pins in each nostril and gold bangles and necklaces. The male doll depicting a Brahmin wears a white dhoti with the sacred thread and scarf across his chest. His head is half shaven and the long strands at the back are tied up in a knot. Caste marks decorate his forehead, chest and arms.

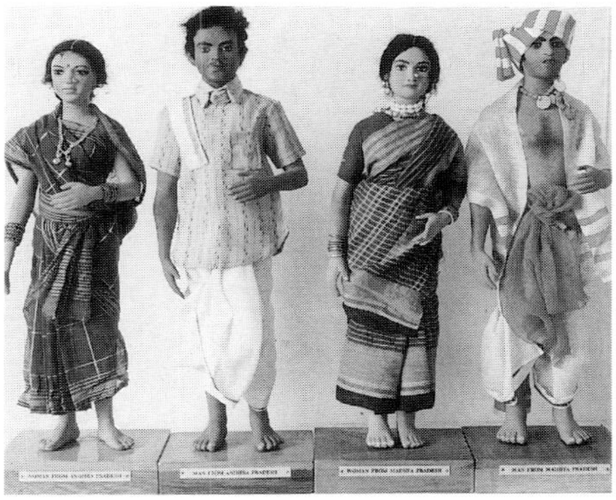

Left **Andhra Pradesh** man and woman. The Andhra Pradesh woman because of the heat in her state wears a simple blue cotton sari without a blouse. Her long hair is knotted in a bun on the side of the head, just behind the ear. The male doll wears a white dhoti tucked between the legs, a blue shirt, and a length of cloth like a towel thrown over the shoulder which can be twisted around the head. *Right* **Madhya Pradesh** man and woman. The female doll wears a simple blue cotton sari, with cowrie shell armlets, glass bangles and bead necklace. The male doll wears a white dhoti tied at the waist with a red sash, and a yellow scarf trimmed in red, around the shoulders. He has a red/white striped turban and a coin necklace.

Left Man and woman from **Mizoram**. The male doll wears a low white sarong-like *lungi* with an orange handwoven shawl to cover his chest. The Mizo woman wears a black jacket and a black and white handwoven shawl around her waist. *Right* Man and woman from **Rajasthan**. The male doll wears a short white shirt and a white dhoti drawn between his legs. His brown and yellow turban, many metres in length, is used in times of emergency as a rope to draw water from wells. The women of the area by contrast add splashes of colour to the vast sandy deserts with their colourful skirts or *ghagaras* and *kanchlis* or backless blouses. The female doll wears a red *odhni* or veil over her head, a yellow/red/green backless blouse, and a red skirt over a blue floral one. She wears silver jewellery on her forehead, round her neck, wrists and ankles.

'Tribes of India'. *Left* **Muria** The female doll wears a white mini-sari and a number of bead and coin necklaces. The bead head-dress is offset by a comb. The number of combs in a Muria woman's hair indicates the number of boyfriends she has had. This is the only tribe in India which permits experimental marriage: a boy and girl can live together for a short while before plunging into matrimony. *Centre* **Banjara** The Banjaras of Andhra Pradesh and the Lambadis of Rajasthan are India's native gypsies. The female doll's costume consists of the *ghagara*, a swirling skirt made of red, black and white coarse cotton, and fully embroidered blouse and drapery. The women seldom, if ever, take off the armful of metal and bone bangles and anklets. The heavy silver pendant-like earrings are held on either side by the doll's plaited hair. *Right* **Santhal** The people of the Santhal tribes are full of life and this is reflected in their style of dressing. The doll wears an orange/red striped sari reaching to her knees. The sari is worn without a blouse. Tattoo marks on the cheeks and chin, along with a bead necklace, nose pins and bangles complete her attire.

The doll wears a dark pink turban, beads around his neck, a floral yoked jacket, lightweight white dhoti, beige shoes. He is smoking a 'hubble' or water-cooled pipe.

'Tribes of India' **Naga** The Nagas were originally head-hunters, and the men are still accomplished hunters who never miss the mark with their sharp spears. The male doll wears a hand-woven shawl around his loins, and a fancy fan-like head-dress in white/black/red/yellow. The colours of the head-dress indicate his caste.

Rajasthan This 20-cm (8-inch) clay doll, with a clay pot on her head, has a caste mark in the centre of her forehead. She wears silver earrings, and necklace, a gold necklace on a black band, red head scarf, yellow blouse with blue/red trim. She has a green jacket, red dress with green border, white gathered pants.

Right A cloth doll wearing a green head scarf, silver chain, gold drop earrings, olive green floral blouse, black/yellow/orange waist-band with blue sash underneath, red skirt with white and black bands.

'Tribes of India' **Bondo** The Bondo tribes of Orissa have always been notorious as aggressive raiders and so have no intimate contact with the nearby hill people. Unmarried Bondo women wear their curly hair full, but they shave their heads after marriage. This female doll wears a small strip of multi-striped cloth around her loins like a mini-skirt and covers herself with a medley of bead necklaces and silver bangles.

established a sultanate in 1206 in Delhi, beginning 300 years of Muslim political domination. Their defeat by a Mongol chief in 1526 ushered in the beginning of the Mongol era. European influence was initiated by the Portuguese, who annexed Goa on the west coast of India in 1510.

The English East India Company, formed in 1600, received a grant of land just outside modern Calcutta from the Mongol emperor in 1701, and grew in power until the Indian Mutiny of 1857–8. The defeat of the Mongol emperor, who was implicated in the rebellion, led to the end of the dynasty, and Britain assumed direct responsibility for India in 1858.

The decision by Britain in 1905 to divide Bengal province into separate

'Indian Snake charmer'. This 13-cm (5.25-inch) doll wears a red/white floral turban, green jacket and dhoti, and yellow necklace. He has a bag over his shoulder and plays a type of bagpipe. The snake on a spring is free to sway in the breeze.

Hindu and Muslim regions was ultimately to lead to the division of India. With a major upsurge of nationalist sentiment at the end of World War II, Britain began to give India its independence, announcing it would withdraw by June 1948. Part of the arrangement was that India be divided into two new countries — India (predominantly Hindu) and Pakistan (Muslim), with the Punjab and Bengal provinces divided into predominantly Muslim and Hindu areas. India became independent in 1947 and was declared a republic in 1950. Pakistan became an Islamic republic in 1956. After wars between India and Pakistan over disputed territories in 1948 and again in 1971, East Pakistan and independent Muslim Bengal merged to become Bangladesh.
Capital Delhi.
Population (1990) 853.4 million, of which 25.5 per cent live in urban areas. 72 per cent Indo-Ayran, 25 per cent Dravidian and 3 per cent Mongoloid or other.
Religion 82.6 per cent Hindu, 11.3 per cent Muslim, 2.4 per cent Christian, 1.9 per cent Sikh, 0.7 per cent Buddhist, 0.48 per cent Jain.
Language There are two official languages — Hindi and English. Hindi is spoken by 30 per cent of the population, while another 30 per cent speak one of four languages — Bengali, Marathi, Telugu or Urdu. Other more localised languages are also spoken.

Clay and cloth dolls. *Left* **Khana** This doll has a pink turban, black beard, green gown split at sides with gold trim at front, red sleeveless jacket with gold trim, gold-edged white dhoti, and red shoes. *Centre* **Kathiawari** The male doll wears a red turban, silver chain around the neck, blue-yoked tunic, blue dhoti, and has bare feet. *Right* A male doll bought at Expo 88 wears a pink turban; white and brown tunic with collar, front opening and side splits to the waist; pink gauze dhoti; red shoes.

Indonesia (Republic of) Asia/Pacific

See also Java

The Indonesian archipelago consists of over 13 667 island with a total area of 1 904 569 square kilometres (735 164 square miles) stretching from the Malay Peninsula in the west to western New Guinea in the east. The principal islands of Indonesia are Sumatera (Sumatra), Jawa (Java), Kalimantan (60 per cent of Borneo), Sulawesi (Celebes), the Moluccas, Timor and Irian Jaya (part of New Guinea once known as Dutch New Guinea). Indonesia is divided into 27 provinces.

A selection of Indonesian dolls showing costumes of various regions. On the left is a typical Indonesian puppet.

None Jakarta A 22-cm (8.75-inch) plastic doll with 'Indonesian Dolls' on the base. She wears an orange headscarf, yellow lace jacket, brown batik sarong, gold strap sandals, and carries a silver purse. (Courtesy Vera Woodhead)

Because of their position between India and China, the islands of Indonesia have attracted considerable attention over the years. Malay peoples from western China settled in the archipelago from 3000 BC. Then from the first century AD Indonesia came into contact with the Hindu-Buddhist culture of India. Between the seventh and thirteenth centuries the Buddhist Sumatran Empire ruled the archipelago, followed from 1293 until the mid-fifteenth century by the Java-based Hindu-Buddhist Empire, which declined with the introduction of Islam by traders from the west and its subsequent growth.

In the sixteenth century Portugal gained control of the Moluccan clove trade. But by 1602 the Dutch East India Company had been formed, and from its centre in Batavia (Jakarta) it monopolised regional trade, taking control of parts of

Sinta This 21.5-cm (8.5-inch) plastic doll wears a fancy black head-dress with gold trim; black bodice with gold trim and black bead-trimmed panels at the hem edge; long yellow waist sash; brown batik sarong.

Java and other islands. Then the company went bankrupt in 1780, its charter expired in 1799, and the archipelago reverted to Dutch rule.

In the early part of the nineteenth century, while the French occupied The Netherlands, Britain temporarily took control of the East Indies. But the Dutch returned after the Napoleonic Wars and by 1910 their control had expanded to cover what is present-day Indonesia.

The archipelago was overrun by the Japanese in 1942, and during the occupation the Indonesians quietly prepared for eventual independence. Three days after the Japanese surrender in August 1945 independence was declared. Although the Dutch returned, negotiations resulted in the creation of the Republic of the United States of Indonesia on 27 December 1949.

From 1950 to 1959 six governments were formed and collapsed. Martial law was proclaimed in March 1957, but the

Straw dolls. *Left* This Tjili doll from Bali of finely woven and plaited straw (31.75 cm, 12.5 inches), is a representation of the Rice Mother sometimes used in harvest festivals, then given to children. *Right* This 25.5-cm (10-inch) doll is cleverly made from delicately coloured straw.

1945 constitution was reinstated in July 1959. West Irian (west New Guinea) was finally handed over to Indonesia by the Dutch in 1963 and renamed Irian Jaya in 1973. Although East Timor had been under Portuguese administration from 1702, moves towards self-rule began in 1974. Then Indonesia invaded the island in December 1975, and it was incorporated as Indonesia's 27th province in July 1976.

Capital Jakarta.

Population (1990) 189.4 million; with 25.3 per cent living in urban areas. 59.81 per cent live on Java (Javanese and Sundanese), 20.77 per cent on Sumatra (Minangkabaus, Acehand Batako), 6.9 per cent Sulawesi (Torajao, Minakas, Menadonese and Buginese), 4.88 per cent on Kalimantan (Dyaks), 0.88 per cent in Irian Jaya (Irianese), and 1.02 per cent on the Moluccas (Ambonese); with other ethnic groups the Madurese (Madura), Balinese (Bali), Sasako (Lombok), and Timorese (Timor).

Religion 87 per cent are Muslim, 9 per cent Christian (6 per cent Roman Catholic, 3 per cent Protestant). The 3.5 million Hindus (2 per cent) are mainly on

Bengkulu Plastic dolls (21.5 cm, 8.5 inches), 'Made in Indonesia'. The man wears a red hat with gold trim; long yellow jacket with three pockets, red buttons and gold trim on the cuffs and collar; red striped undergarment, yellow trousers. The woman has a bun at the back and flowers in her hair; gold hoop earrings and gold necklace; orange lace overdress with gold trim; gold bangles; red striped sash; wrap-around red striped skirt; yellow shoes.

Bali. There are also 1.6 million Buddhists, mostly Chinese.

Language The official language is Bahasa Indonesia, based on Malay and Bahasa Melayu, although Dutch is still spoken, and there are about 583 languages and dialects in Indonesia, including Javanese spoken by 69 million and Sundanese spoken by 26 million.

Iran (Islamic Republic of) (Persia) Middle East

With an area of 1 648 000 square kilometres (646 128 square miles) divided into 24 provinces, the southwest Asian country of Iran has borders with Iraq, Turkey,

A cloth doll with paper turban bought in Iran in the 1980s. He is reading the Koran, kneeling on a special stand. He wears a tall (6 cm, 2.25 inches) white paper turban with green top, grey beard and glasses, white background floral shirt, black waist sash, khaki trousers, long green robe with wide gold brocade trim.

Afghanistan and Pakistan. Eight per cent of the land is arable with 11 per cent forested.

Known as Persia until 1935, Iran has a history dating from the sixth century BC. The uniting of the Medes and Persians in 533 BC led to the founding of the first Persian Empire, which presided over a golden age of civilisation extending to what is now Turkey and Egypt, until conquered by Alexander the Great in 331 BC. Weakened by numerous conflicts with the Byzantine Empire, the empire of the Sassanids was defeated by Muslim Arabs in AD 637. The former empire was dismembered and ruled by various Arab and Persian governors, firstly from Damascus and later Baghdad. Persia re-emerged in the sixteenth century with borders similar to those of today. It was during this time that Shi'ite Islam became the country's official religion.

The Safavids ruled until 1750, followed by the Qajar dynasty which remained in power until 1926. Both Britain and Russia had ambitions in regard to the country because of its commercial and strategic

A pair of 35.5-cm (14-inch) dolls with head and hands of wax and inserted hair (into the wax). The female doll has a red headscarf, white bodice and blue skirt. Over this she wears a long enveloping sheer black cloak richly embroidered in gold. The male doll wears a brown headscarf/ turban, and a dark jacket with wide white hanging cuffs. His trousers are mauve and purple. (Courtesy Jenny Miller, New South Wales)

position, resulting in an agreement in 1907, with the north of the country coming under Russian influence, the south British, and in the middle a neutral buffer zone. During World War I interference from Britain, Russia and Germany left the country's internal affairs in chaos. In 1920 Colonel Reza Khan ended the short-lived autonomous Soviet Republic of Gilan that had been established in the north, became minister in 1923, and was crowned Reza Shah Pahlavi in 1926. In 1935 he changed the Hellenistic name Persia to Iran (meaning Aryan) hoping to gain favour with the Germans.

This eventually led to Britain and Russia invading Iran in 1941 and the Shah's abdication in favour of his son, Mohammed Reza. From 1950 to 1954 the Shah encountered difficulties with the West, particularly over the nationalisation of the oil industry, until a consortium of seven companies was created with Iran receiving a 50 per cent share.

Opposition to the increasing westernisation and secularisation of Iran from Islamic clergy led to demonstrations against the Shah and ultimately to his fleeing Iran in January 1979. An Islamic Cultural Revolution was launched by the new regime and stringent Islamic law came into force.

Capital Tehran (Teheran).

Population (1990) 55.6 million. 63 per cent ethnic Persian, 18 per cent Turkic, 13 per cent other Iranian, 3 per cent Kurdish, 3 per cent Arab and other Semitic.

Religion Shi'ite is the official religion (93 per cent), with Sunni Muslim (5 per cent), and 2 per cent Zoroastrian, Jewish, Christian or Baha'i.

Language Farsi (Persian) is the official language spoken by 45 per cent of the population; 23 per cent speak related languages such as Kurdish, Luri and Buluchi; 26 per cent speak Turkish languages, and 2 million speak Semitic languages.

Iraq (Republic of Iraq) Middle East

The country of Iraq in southwest Asia has borders to Saudi Arabia, Jordan, Syria, Turkey, Iran and Kuwait, and access to the Persian Gulf. It is divided into 18 governorates and covers an area of 434 924 square kilometres (167 881 square miles) of which 12 per cent is arable and 3 per cent forested.

Antique wax dolls, circa 1840, made in either England or Germany to represent ideas gleaned from the literature of the day.

The man has wax head, arms, legs; glass bead eyes; green turban; cream gown with gold braid trim; green satin cloak with gold trim and shoulder cape with gold braid trim and gold bullion edge; red shoes.

The woman has a cream head-dress with gold braid trim and gold bullion tassel, light green gown with gold braid trim; train-type cloak with gold trim; red shoes.

The doll's tag reads 'Corrines "Brides of All Nations" IRAQ'. She wears a tall multi-coloured head-dress from which falls a net veil embroidered in silver and gold; a long blouse ornamented with gold and black braid under a red bolero; trousers with tight gold-braid cuffs. (Courtesy Jenny Miller, New South Wales)

The first known inhabitants of modern Iraq were the Sumerians of the third millennium BC. When the Persians seized Babylon in the seventh century BC it became part of the Persian empire until the empire was overthrown by Alexander the Great (between 334 and 323 BC). During the centuries before and after Christ, both Rome and Parthia (Persia) fought over Iraq until it was absorbed into the Persian Sassanian empire in the second century AD.

Muslim armies from Arabia defeated the Sassanians in 637 AD and Iraq became Muslim. The Abbasids — Shi'ite Muslims — moved their capital from Damascus to Baghdad in 750, but were themselves all but destroyed when the country was overrun by Mongol hordes in the thirteenth century. Absorbed into the Ottoman empire in 1534, Iraq remained with the empire until the end of World War I.

Maintaining a consulate in Baghdad from 1802, Britain wielded considerable influence, turning Basra into a modern port during World War I when the Ottoman sultan sided with the Germans. Baghdad was taken by the British in 1917, with promises of independence, but in April 1920 Iraq was made a British mandate, with virtual colonial status.

The mandate was terminated on 3 October 1932, and Iraq became a nominally independent state.

During the years leading up to World War II relations with Britain deteriorated and German influence increased, culminating in the occupation of Basra and Baghdad by Britain in May 1941. Iraq declared war on the Axis powers in 1943, but Britain remained in occupation until the end of the war.

By 1958, due to various circumstances, Iraq was ripe for revolution and several coups followed, as well as years of bitter fighting with the Kurds of the north; but when the Shah of Iran withdrew his support for the Kurds in 1975 their resistance declined. After eight years of devastating war between Iraq and Iran, Iran with reluctance accepted a UN resolution for a ceasefire in August 1988.

Then in August 1990 Iraq invaded the southern sheikhdom of Kuwait and plunged the world into crisis. Seven months later Iraq finally agreed to comply fully with UN Security Council resolutions, and an uneasy peace ensued.

Capital Baghdad.

Population (1990) 18.8 million, with 70.6 per cent living in urban areas. 79 per cent Arabs, 16 per cent Kurds (northeast), 3 per cent Persians, 2 per cent Turks.

Religion Islam is the official religion. 60–65 per cent are Shi'ite Muslim, 32–37 per cent Sunni Muslim, 3 per cent Christian.

Language Arabic is the official language, spoken by approximately 80 per cent of the population. Kurdish predominates in Kurdish regions. About 140 000 speak Assyrian, 140 000 Persian, 60 000 Turkish, 220 000 Turkmen, and English is also widely spoken.

Ireland (Republic of) (Eire) Europe

See also Northern Ireland.

Dolls with oiled cloth faces and felt bodies by Jay Dolls, Dublin. *Far left* Dublin flower seller (12.5 cm, 5 inches), a typical colourful character supposedly with a ready wit. Black shawl, grey hair, red blouse, black skirt, white apron, pink undies, black shoes. She carries a basket of flowers. *Left* Nun. A typical Irish nun in a black habit. *Centre* Irish colleen. She wears two skirts, the outer skirt gathered up and pinned to itself. Red head scarf, black neckerchief, red/white check blouse, green shawl, green skirt, red underskirt, black waistband laced in white. She carries a basket of peat on her shoulder. *Right* Leprechaun (17.75 cm, 7 inches). Red cap, black cravat, yellow waistcoat with wide collar, green swallowtail coat, red breeches, yellow socks, black shoes with silver buckles. He holds a crock of gold under his right arm. *Far right* West Cork woman. The cloak is the traditional outer garment of West Cork and Kindale women. Married women wore a cap underneath. Black mob-cap, black cape, check blouse, black skirt, white apron, pink undies, black shoes.

Eighty kilometres (50 miles) to the west of Great Britain is the Republic of Ireland (Eire) with a land area of 70 282 square kilometres (27 129 square miles) divided into 26 counties. Eire occupies the south-central and northwest regions of Ireland, with a northern border to Northern Ireland (Ulster) — part of the United Kingdom. Although very fertile, under 15 per cent of the area is arable, and only 6 per cent forested.

Ireland was conquered by Gaelic-speaking Celts about 300 BC, and developed an artistic and literary culture with the introduction of Christianity in 432 AD. Dublin was reputedly founded by Viking raiders in 840, but their powers were effectively ended in 1014.

The Anglo-Norman adventurers extended their feudal rule to the west of Dublin, so successfully that by 1366 the Irish language was outlawed. In 1494 Poynings' Law decreed that the Irish parliament had to have the King of England's consent before legislation could be initiated, and that English law also applied to Ireland.

Efforts to impose Protestantism under Elizabeth I were firmly resisted by the Irish, who rebelled unsuccessfully, and

With the American Revolution a

Cloth dolls with resin heads by Jay, Dublin (24 cm, 9.5 inches). 'Fisherwife' wears a red headscarf, hair in a bun at the back, red/white check blouse, maroon knitted shawl, blue skirt, blue/white check apron, flannel petticoat, striped flannel knee-length bloomers, grey knitted stockings, brown shoes. 'Aran Fisherman' has grey hair and wears a white knitted beret, cable-patterned roll-neck sweater, tweed trousers, coloured cord below the waist *(crios)*, brown shoes *(pamposties)*.

gave support to England's Catholic enemies abroad, including Spain. James I's policy of granting confiscated Irish land to Protestant settlers further incensed the Irish, particularly when over 100 000 Scottish Presbyterians settled in Ulster (Northern Ireland) from 1609.

A measure of independence was granted to the Irish parliament in 1782, and Poynings' Law and various oppressive penal laws were repealed. The Dublin parliament was abolished under the Act of Union in 1800, with the Irish being given representation at Westminster.

The devastating potato famine in the late 1840s killed one million Irish and many emigrated (two million crossed the Atlantic between 1847 and 1861). Industrialisation went to the Protestant north in the mid-nineteenth century, while the agricultural south did not advance economically.

World War I deferred the pressure for home rule. The first modern Irish parliament (Dail Eireann) was convened in Dublin in 1919, and six counties of Ulster were granted home rule in December 1920. In 1921 an Anglo-Irish Treaty created the Irish Free State, a self-governing dominion within the British

Collectors' character dolls by Jay, Dublin (16.5–17.75 cm, 6.5–7 inches), with clay heads and felt over wire bodies. *Far left* '**Donegal** Man'. He usually left home for the harvesting season in England or Scotland, but wore the normal homespun coat, trousers and cap of rural Ireland. The doll wears a tweed cap, red neckerchief, grey knitted sweater, homespun coat and trousers, black shoes. He carries a *cromach* (walking stick) under the right arm. *Left* **Sligo** The doll wears a black knitted hat over red headscarf, blue jacket, blue skirt (short at the front, long at the back, and pleated), knitted shawl, floral underskirt, black shoes. 1830s style. *Middle* 'Paddy', an eighteenth century Donegal man. He has a tall black hat, red cravat, dark beige waistcoat, black swallowtail coat, black trousers and shoes. He carries a cromach over the right arm. *Right* **Connemara** Young women, noted for their hard work, usually wore a long white bainin shawl which covered the head and greater part of the body, together with a red skirt dyed with madder. The doll wears a white shawl, blue check blouse, red skirt and striped long panties, brown shoes. *Far right* 'Aran Fisherman'. Seafarers wore clothes of heavy homespun. The *crios* (plaited sash) was worn below the waist to give support when rowing. Distinctive knit patterns identified villages, useful if a fisherman was drowned and washed ashore. Their shoes *(pamposties)* were specially made to withstand rough rock. The doll wears a knitted white cap with pompon, blue neckerchief, navy knitted sweater, white jacket, tweed trousers, brown shoes, *crios*.

Commonwealth. Northern Ireland opted to stay part of the United Kingdom.

During World War II and the post-war era the Irish government remained neutral. After the 1948 election Eire became the Republic of Ireland and left the Commonwealth.

Capital Dublin.

Population 3.5 million, with 57 per cent living in urban areas. 94 per cent of the population is predominantly Celtic, with a small English minority.

Religion 94–95 per cent are Roman Catholic, with 2.8 per cent Anglican Church of Ireland, and other Protestant denominations, Baha'i and Jewish.

Language Constitutionally Irish is the first official language, with English second. Irish Gaelic, related to Scots Gaelic, is also spoken, mainly in the west.

Israel (State of) (formerly Palestine) Middle East

Located on the far eastern Mediterranean seabord (Middle East), Israel has an area of approximately 20 770 square kilometres (8017 square miles) as defined in 1949. This does not include the disputed and occupied areas of the Gaza Strip (south-east), West Bank (east) and Golan Heights (north). Seventeen per cent of the land is arable, 6 per cent forested and 11 per cent under irrigation.

Because of its situation and history, much of the land within the modern state of Israel is holy to one or all of three great religions — Judaism, Christianity and Islam — and this has led to many conflicts through the ages. Some of the earliest evidence of human life (outside Africa) can be found within the country's borders,

Moulded-plastic dolls with wire body armature (20 cm, 8 inches) by Wizo Home Industries, Israel, bought in the 1970s. *Left* 'Hasidic Rabbi' has a fur-trimmed hat with black crown *(shtreimi)*, grey beard, long ear locks, white shirt, long black jacket, prayer shawl *(tallis)*, grey trousers. He holds the Torah (Sacred Scrolls). The female doll wears a black cowl on her head trimmed with gold/red/black braid, silver decoration across her forehead, long black overdress with black and gold braid trim, long red trousers with green trim.

'Sabbath Blessing', a clay/cloth doll with wire armature (18.5 cm, 7.25 inches), handmade by Sabra-Israel. The doll wears a navy lace headscarf, blue overblouse with braid trim, black skirt, black stockings and shoes. On the table are two candles.

Clay dolls with wire armature handmade by Sabra, Israel. *Left* 'Modern Kibbutz Girl' has a green hat, fawn shirt, rucksack on her back, green trousers, and she holds the Israeli flag. *Right* This doll wears a yellow robe and purple cloak and holds an earthenware urn on her shoulder.

A cloth and wire doll marked 'Handcraft Pisanty Jerusalem Made in Israel'. The doll wears a dark brown cowl on her head, brown beads, dark tan dress with brown trousers, and holds an earthenware dish in her arms.

with the Jewish population claiming descent from the Semitic nomads (Israelites) who came to the country 4000 years ago. The history of the 12 tribes of Israel is well recorded. They were never paramount rulers because of their situation, sandwiched between Egypt and Mesopotamia.

The capital, Jerusalem, was sacked by the Assyrians in 721 BC, destroying 10 of the tribes, and the Babylonians took the rest into exile in 586 BC. The Israelites (now called Jews) rebuilt, only to be conquered by the Persians, Greeks and ultimately the Romans who set up the semi-autonomous province of Palestine in 63 BC. Christianity arose out of Judaism in the first century AD. Then in 138 a revolt against Rome cost the Jews their statehood, causing many to flee into exile with only a minority remaining in Palestine.

Palestine was ruled from Byzantium, by the Christian Eastern Roman Empire, until Jerusalem was conquered by the Arabs in 636. Most of the population became Muslim and adopted the Arabic language. In 1099 Christian rule was resumed after the Crusades, until defeat by Saladin in 1187. The Muslim Ottoman Turks conquered Arab Palestine in 1517, ruling it as a provence of Syria until 1918.

Over the centuries the descendants of the Jews that had fled dreamed of returning to Palestine, but it wasn't until 1897, when the first Zionist conference was held, that this was thought possible. Buying land from absentee Arab landlords, the Zionist immigrants began to farm Palestine and also revived the ancient Hebrew language. They founded the first modern-day all-Jewish city, Tel Aviv, in 1909. Immigration increased and by the outbreak of World War I, 60 000 Jews had settled in Palestine, compared with approximately 450 000 resident Arabs.

When Turkey sided with Germany, Britain recruited both Palestinian Arabs and Jews to help expel them from Palestine by 1917. With the collapse of the Ottoman Empire a vacuum existed in Palestine.

British promises to the Arabs and Jews were conflicting, but a statement in November 1917 'calling for a Jewish national home in Palestine as long as this did not prejudice the civil and religious rights of other communities' appeared the clearest. Jews continued to immigrate, competing for space with the indigenous Palestinian Arabs. By 1933 225 000 Jews had entered Palestine, raising their numbers to 30 per cent of the population.

Britain's plans after the war for the partition of the country were rejected by the Arabs, and Britain referred the problem in early 1947 to the United Nations, but a further plan was also rejected. Britain announced it would leave

Wood and leather dolls (16.5 cm, 6.5 inches) marked 'Handmade in Israel Frank Meisler Ltd, Old City, Jaffa, Israel'. The woman has a turned wooden pot on the head, leather head-dress over green check headband, black underbodice decorated with gold, mauve satin shirt. A black leather cloak covers all. The man wears a white head-dress with black cord, blue/white striped gown, blue belt, black cloak. He has a turned wooden hookah.

Palestine in December 1947. Civil war erupted.

The State of Israel was proclaimed in Tel Aviv in May 1948. By early 1949 Israel had survived the civil war, adding to land granted by the United Nations. Jordan had absorbed East Jerusalem on the West Bank, and Egypt had taken over the Gaza Strip in the south, causing the displacement of 780 000 Palestinian Arabs from their homes. The 760 000 Jews had become a majority.

Israel became a mixed-economy democratic state, and has the 'Law of Return' allowing any Jew to settle in Israel. At first most immigrants came from Europe, but some 640 000 Oriental Jews had entered by 1979, and their descendants are the majority in Israel today. Twenty per cent of Jews in the world are Israelis.

Capital Jerusalem.

Population 4.4 million, with 89.4 per cent living in urban areas. 83 per cent Jewish, 16.8 per cent Arab.

Religion 82 per cent Judaism, 614 000 Muslim (mostly Sunni), 76 000 Druzes, 103 000 Christian.

Language Hebrew (66 per cent) and Arabic (15 per cent) are the official languages; the remaining 19 per cent includes a diverse range of European languages and 95 000 Israelis who speak Yiddish.

Italy (Italian Republic)

Divided into 20 regions, including the islands of Sicily (Sicilia) in the southeast, Sardinia (Sardegna) in the west, Elba and approximately 70 other islands, Italy has a total area of 301 225 square kilometres (116 273 square miles). Over half the area is pasture or cultivated, and 22 per cent is forested.

Even before the Romans various civilisations, including the Estruscans in Tuscany, Latins and Sabines in central Italy, Greek colonies (south) and Gauls (north), had been established. The Latins had developed a powerful state centred on Rome by around 400 BC, and after the conquest of Taranto in 272 BC, the whole of Italy was united under Rome's rule.

During the three Punic Wars Rome won first Sicily from the Carthaginians, and then took control of Corsica (264–41 BC). After the razing of Carthage in 149 BC Rome progressively won control over most of the known world — the north coast of Africa, the Iberian Peninsula, England to Hadrian's Wall, as well as Armenia, Mesopotamia, Judea and Egypt. Christianity was officially adopted by the Roman Empire in 313 AD.

With the sacking of Rome in 410 by the barbarian Visigoths and the re-conquest of Italy by the Byzantine Empire in the sixth century, the Roman Empire was fragmented. Charlemagne, who had annexed the Lombard kingdom into his vast Frankish realms, was crowned Roman Emperor in 800, followed by Otti I of Germany in 961 who marked the beginning of the Holy Roman Empire. This led to a long struggle for supremacy between the papacy and emperors which lasted until the thirteenth century.

Several cities — Venice, Florence and Genoa — emerged as powerful city-state republics, and along with Naples were the vanguard of the Renaissance. However, due to constant wars, the Italian cities were exhausted by the end of the fifteenth century and economic conditions were changing.

Left **Milano** (Lombardio, a northern province) The 14-cm (5.5-inch) doll has a silver head-dress attached to a bun at the back of her hairdo, floral bodice, white/pink spotted shawl with pink ribbon and lace trim, white blouse, floral skirt, white apron, lace trim. *Middle* **Sorrento** (Campania) This 19-cm (7.5-inch) doll has a yellow head-dress with red trim, white blouse, black bodice with red trim, red skirt with gold braid trim, yellow apron with blue lower band and gold trim. She holds a tambourine in the right hand. *Right* **Genoa** (Ligura, a northern province bordering France) This 17.75-cm (7-inch) doll has a small circular red/orange/green head-dress, white blouse, red bodice with yellow lacing, green skirt with yellow grim, red/white striped apron, and carries a basket of flowers.

Dolls by Eros, Italy. *Left* **Napoli** (Campania, province on the western coast) The doll wears a white head-dress with mauve trim *(tovaglia)*, gold hoop earrings, white blouse with lace trim, black waistcoat with purple lining and yellow lacing, blue skirt with purple band, light blue apron with yellow trim. *Middle* **Sienna** (Toscana, a northern province on the west coast) 'Contrada Della Civetta' (ceremonial drummer). The doll wears a red hat with white trim, red collar over lace collar, long white jacket with black cuffs, black waist-coat with white trim, red cape with gold/white trim, red belt with gold trim; trousers with right leg black, left leg red and white trim. The doll holds drumsticks (the drum has been lost). *Right* **Sienna** (Toscana) The doll wears a white-brimmed hat with red band, white blouse, black corselet with red straps, and red lacing, red skirt with black trim, white apron with white braid trim.

Dolls by Eros, Italy. *Left* **Desulo** (on the island of Sardinia) The 19-cm (7.5-inch) doll wears a red head-dress with blue trim and yellow lines, white blouse, red bolero with blue edge and yellow stitching, red skirt with blue and gold trim, red apron with blue trim and yellow stitching. *Centre 'Gondolier'* (19 cm, 7.5 inches) **Venice** (Veneto province, northern Italy) wears a straw hat with red band; white shirt with blue collar and white stitching, black bow, blue/white neck insert; red cummerbund; black trousers and shoes. He holds the long oar used on a gondola in his right hand. *Right* **Florence** (Firenze, Toscana province) The doll wears a wide-brimmed straw hat with red ribbon trim, white blouse, black bodice laced in red with red straps over the shoulder, red/white spotted skirt, white apron. She holds a water ewer.

Abruzzi (on the east coast of Italy) The plastic doll wears a high red head-dress finished with gold braid. Her dress is tomato red with a lace collar and she wears a chain necklace. Her apron is orange/red floral.

Dolls with felt heads and plastic body by Eros, Italy (19 cm, 7.5 inches). All three dolls represent northern regions of Italy. *Left* **Val d'Aoasta** (northwest province bordering Switzerland) The doll wears a gold-lace head-dress with high back frill, yellow/red neckerchief, white blouse, red waistcoat with yellow piping and black insert with yellow trim, red skirt with gold band trim, black apron with black lace trim. *Middle* **Venezia** (Veneto province, a northeast province facing the Adriatic Sea) The doll has black hair with a plaited bun at the back, red dress with red/white collar, black fringed shawl with rose design. *Right* **Dolomiti** (Trentino-Alto Adige, a northern province bordering Austria) The doll has a black brimmed hat with green band and white flower, white blouse with braid collar, red waistcoat with green trim and lacing, green waistband and bow, black skirt, black floral apron.

Far left This female doll wears a white hood over blonde plaits, white blouse, wide black waistband, navy skirt with red band at the hem, pale blue apron with red/white/blue braid trim. *Left* **Milano** (Lombardia, near the Swiss border) He wears a wide-brimmed black hat trimmed with a white feather, white lace collar, green waistcoat with yellow lacing, brown jacket with brown/white sleeves and lace cuffs, green breeches finished with a black kneeband. *Centre and right* **Tirolo** (the Tyrol area near the Swiss border) The female doll wears a green hat with red band, green bodice, white blouse, red waistband, green skirt with red/yellow trim. The male doll wears a grey hat with green band and feather, white shirt, red tie, braid braces, grey *lederhosen* with a green trim, green jacket with grey lapels, white socks with braid trim. *Right* The doll has a white head-dress with yellow trim, light shawl, white blouse, blue skirt with white floral apron.

Olanda The doll wears a red hood with yellow trim, white blouse, red waistcoat with blue trim and yellow lacing, navy skirt with red trim, white apron with lace trim. *Left* **Taormina** (Sicily, an island to the south of mainland Italy) The doll has a white patterned headscarf, white blouse, maroon waistcoat with green insert and yellow lacing, green/red plaid skirt, white/blue/yellow striped apron. She carries a water ewer. *Middle* **Sassari** (a city on Sardinia, an island west of the mainland) The doll wears a bright yellow headscarf, white blouse, short waistcoat with yellow lacing, royal blue skirt with braid trim and red hem band, blue apron with pale blue trim. She carries a basket of fruit. *Right* **Calabria** (a southern province of mainland Italy) The doll wears a brown truncated-cone hat with yellow trim and fine blue/red/yellow/green ribbons, white shirt, yellow neckerchief, red waistcoat with yellow trim, chain watchband, royal blue jacket with green lapels and cuffs and gold buttons, royal blue trousers with green side stripe.

A pair of old Italian-marked celluloids, dressed in traditional costume. The male doll has a red hat trimmed with yellow. He wears a white shirt, red waistcoat and black jacket and trousers. The female doll wears a red head-dress trimmed with white. She has a white blouse and shawl, blue skirt trimmed with yellow and red bands, and a heavily embroidered apron.

Isle of Capri (off the west coast) The doll wears a blue conical hat with lace trim; a blue dress with lace collar, wide black waistband, and red braid and lace on the skirt. Her apron is decorated with yellow braid edging and a print of the Blue Grotto.

Two carved and painted dolls from the Lake Como region in northern Italy.

Messina (in Sicily) A 16.5-cm (6.5-inch) doll with a felt donkey. She has a red headdress attached to a red headband, white blouse, black corselet with red lacing over yellow insert, red skirt, white apron with red/yellow/blue stripes and lace trim. She holds a ewer in her right hand, and leads the donkey with her left. The donkey carries two woven side baskets attached to a wide red harness over his back.

Sardinia (an island off the west coast of Italy) This 26.5-cm (10.5-inch) doll has a stuffed faceless head and cotton-covered wire armature body, and stands on a 3-cm (1.25-inch) block of cork. She wears a white headscarf wound around her head, white blouse with broderie anglaise trim down the front and at the cuffs which have bands of red ribbon. Her red jacket has splits in the sleeves showing the sleeves of the blouse and is pleated at the back. A gold and orange braid waistband, long brown skirt and wide red band at the hem, and long brown apron bound with red and trimmed with a wide band of ornamental braid complete the outfit.

Ottoman conquests had cut many of the traditional trade routes; these were further affected by the new Atlantic and Cape sea routes, causing Italy to become the battleground of rising powers France and Spain. The Spanish Hapsburgs ruled Milan and Naples in the sixteenth and seventeenth centuries, and also controlled the papacy, until war ended Spain's domination in 1714. The dukes of Savoy assumed the crown of Sardinia in 1770, while the Austrian Hapsburgs gained power in northern Italy. As well as Emperor of France, Napoleon became King of Italy in 1805 after a brilliant military campaign.

After years of fighting between the various states, most of Italy was again united in March 1861 when Victor Emmanuel assumed the title of King of Italy. The province of Venetia was secured after an agreement with Prussia in 1866, and Rome was declared capital of Italy in 1870. Representative government was introduced before 1900. Eritrea and part of Somalia were acquired by 1895, and war with Ottoman Turkey resulted in Italy gaining Libya and the Dodecanese Islands.

In May 1915 Italy joined with the allies in World War I, and under the 1919 Paris peace treaty was awarded South Tyrol, Trento and Trieste.

Then in 1936 Mussolini (then leader of Italy) formed an Axis (his term) with Nazi Germany. Italy annexed Albania in April 1939 and joined the war alongside Germany in June 1940. Under the peace treaty with the Allies in February 1947, Italy was obliged to cede areas to France and Yugoslavia, the Dodecanese to Greece, and waive all rights to its former colonies. Eritrea went to Ethiopia in 1950, Libya became independent, and Italian Somalia finally became part of Somalia in

Sicily (island south of the mainland) A cloth doll with inset glass eyes. She wears a white blouse, red jacket trimmed in green with a yellow cape trimmed in green attached at the shoulder. She has a black cummerbund, red skirt with green trim and a lace-edged white lace apron, black shoes and socks.

1960. Following the promulgation of a new constitution, the Italian Republic was declared on 1 January 1948.
Capital Rome (Roma).
Population 57.7 million, with 64.7 per cent living in urban areas. 4.9 million Sicilians, 1.6 million Sardinians.
Religion 85 per cent are Roman Catholic.
Language Italian is the official language, with a German-speaking minority.

Ivory Coast See Côte d'Ivoire.

Jamaica Caribbean

Situated 144 kilometres (89 miles) south of Cuba, in the Caribbean, Jamaica has an area of 11 424 square kilometres (4411 square miles). Nineteen per cent of the land is arable with 28 per cent woodland or forest.

The Arawak Indians, probably from South America, were the first inhabitants

A 31.75-cm (12.5-inch) black cotton cloth doll jointed with wire. A woven straw hat sits on top of the doll's head over a floral cotton headscarf. She wears a simple pink floral bodice drawn in at the front, short white apron with 'Miss Jamaica B.W.I.' written on it, gathered floral skirt with the hem cut into points. *Right* The 20-cm (8-inch) jointed cloth doll has a woven straw basket with fruit on top of her head over a blue headscarf. She wears a long blouse with orange-red front and blue striped back, two-piece gathered skirt, white bib apron.

about 700 AD, and by the time the island was discovered by Columbus in 1494 an estimated 60 000 lived there. With colonisation by Spain in 1510, the Arawak Indians were gradually exterminated by war, forced labour and disease.

England seized the sparsely inhabited island in 1655. Developed into a plantation society, with imported African slaves producing sugar, the colony prospered in the eighteenth century, but the emancipation of slaves in 1838 ruined the economy.

In 1944 the first elections under universal suffrage were held, with full internal self-government introduced in 1959. Jamaica achieved independence from Britain on 6 August 1962.
Capital Kingston.
Population 2.4 million, with 49.1 per cent living in urban areas. 76.3 per cent

Clay over wire armature dolls. The 20-cm (8-inch) female doll carries a finely woven basket containing fruit on top of a white cotton turban. She wears a bead necklace, white blouse with ruffle trim at neck and elbow, bright yellow/orange floral skirt with self hem ruffle, long white apron, straw plimsolls. The 21-cm (8.25-inch) male doll wears a white straw boater with blue band trim, floral shirt (which matches the female's dress), plaited string belt, white cuffed trousers, straw plimsolls. He carries a bunch of bananas.

African, 15.1 per cent Afro-European, 3.4 per cent East Indian and Afro-East Indian, 3.2 per cent white, 1.2 per cent Chinese and Afro-Chinese.
Religion Christianity, largely Protestant (70.7 per cent), with 7–8 per cent Roman Catholic. Some spiritualist cults, such as Rastafari, continue to flourish.
Language English is the official language, but a local Jamaican patois is also spoken.

Japan (Nippon) Asia

Consisting of four principal islands — Hokkaido, Honshu, Shikoko and Kyushu — and more than 3000 islets situated off the Asian coast in the north Pacific, Japan stretches from the northern island of Hokkaido to the volcanic Ryukyo Peninsula on its southward sweep towards Taiwan. It has a land area of 377 800 square kilometres (145 869 square miles) with 11 per cent arable and 68 per cent forest or woodland. Nearly all farmland is devoted to rice, and the average farm size is only 1.4 hectares (3.5 acres).

Archaeological finds indicate civilisation in Japan dates back 30 000 years, and pottery remains dating from 10 000 BC have been found. According

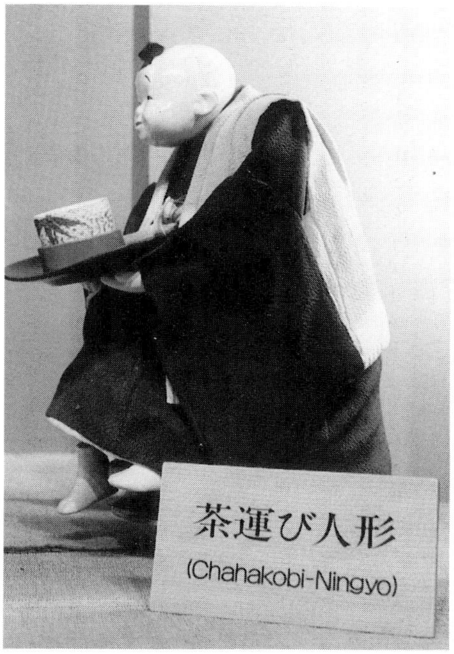

Automaton. This *karakuri chahakobi* (tea server) is a modern version of a traditional Japanese toy — a *karakuri* or moving figure first made in the seventeenth century in Japan. The top photo shows the intricate wind-up mechanism needed to power this doll. It was a toy or doll of the rich. *Above* This modern version was made by Kosei Yamazaki, one of two Japanese artists making traditional KaraKuri dolls. It was seen by the many visitors to the Japan Pavilion, Expo 88. (Courtesy Japan Pavilion, Expo 88, Brisbane)

Girls' Day Tableau. Girls' Day, 3 March, has been celebrated from around the seventeenth century, and many of the dolls are passed down through families. A few days before the festival, the dolls and their accessories are taken out of storage and arranged on a series of steps. A traditional set has 15 dolls, with the emperor and empress on the top, ladies-in-waiting, court musicians, high priests and various accessories below.

A 30.5-cm (12-inch) samurai doll representing Yoshitsune, an idealised hero, for use in the Boys' Day display of 5 May. The doll is dressed in typical samurai ceremonial costume, including a metal helmet with a woven neckguard at the back.

Small antique Hina dolls. Dolls similar to these are used in the Girls' Day display. The middle one is an empress who has lost her head-dress, the other two are ladies-in-waiting. The empress doll is clothed in an outer kimono *(karaginu)* decorated with gold and tassels. She holds a court fan *(hiogi)*.

Hina dolls—small antique dolls dressed for the Girls' Day display. The two dolls on the left are dressed as emperors, while the two on the right are musicians. The emperor doll on the left wears a brocade coat *(sokutai)* and carries a sword *(katana)*. His hat, known as a *kanmuri*, has a stiff gauze panel at the back.

Pieces similar to these are often used on the lower shelves of the Girls' and Boys' Day displays.

to Japanese tradition, still taught as historical fact as late as 1945, Jimmu was the first emperor in 660 BC.

The conquest of Korea by the Empress Jingo took place in 201 AD, and in 550 Buddhism was introduced from Korea to Japan, where it was eagerly adopted, but the Japanese saw no reason to discard their Shinto beliefs. Similarly adopted from Asia were the Chinese calendar, writing system, lacquer, silk and ceramic skills.

A strong rice-growing kingdom under the rule of the Yamato family controlled Honshu by the fifth century AD, and its people, a mixture of Micronesian, Malay and Mongol, drove the aboriginal Ainu north, ultimately to the island of Hokkaido (which did not formally become part of Japan until 1868). A fixed capital was established at Nara in 710, and moved in 794 to nearby Kyoto, which remained the capital, in theory at least, until 1868.

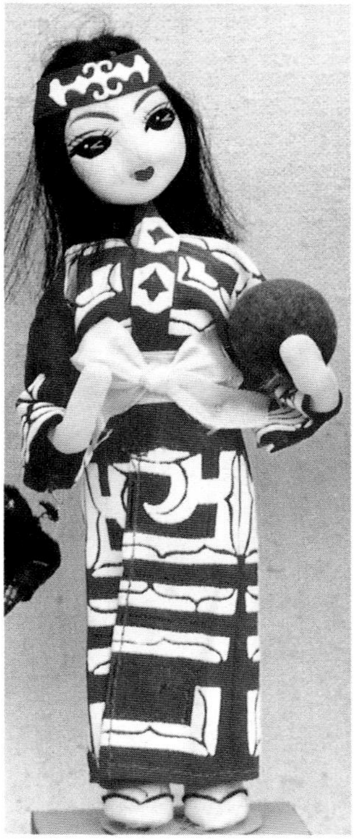

Dolls depicting Ainu, Japanese aborigines who live on the northern island of Hokkaido. The male doll wears a rope head piece tied back and front, a striking costume of black/white material, and a red overtunic. He has a *katana* (sword) slung over one shoulder and a spear in his right hand. The female doll is dressed in red and white with a yellow *obi* (sash).

The doll on the left is a geisha, the doll on the right a traditional princess (both 46 cm, 18 inches). The geisha doll wears a purple cowl over a black kimono which has the traditional short sleeves of an older woman and a floral edging. She has a striped *obi* (waist-sash). The princess doll is dressed in a beautiful orange kimono.

A small Japanese doll in her box that contains wigs showing the various hairstyles worn during a Japanese girl's life. 1930s. The doll wears a red kimono.

Baby dolls. These modern versions of very old traditional baby dolls are made in plastic and painted with a flat plastic paint so they resemble the old dolls with their *gofun* finish. They were bought in the 1970s.

Modern Yamato Ninyo and Hakata dolls.

Then in 1192 the first shogun appeared. While still maintaining the fiction of obedience to the emperor, these military-style dictators (ruling by the samurai code of conduct) wielded the real power from 1192 until 1867, when feudalism disappeared with the resignation of the last shogun.

The Portuguese discovered Japan in the mid-sixteenth century, even introducing Jesuit priests, but they were ordered out because of the Japanese fear of subversion and foreign involvement. Japanese were forbidden to travel abroad from 1639 onwards, and trading contacts were limited to a single Dutch settlement in Nagasaki harbour. In 1853 Japan's long seclusion ended when the commander of a squadron of American warships coerced the shogunal government into allowing trading rights to western powers.

A gigantic fortress had been built at Edo in the 1600s, and after a brief civil

Ichimatsu Ninyo. 1930s. The doll is wearing the *furisode* or long-sleeved kimono worn by children and unmarried girls. The textiles used for the clothing are woven, printed and tie dyed to scale. The doll has real hair and glass eyes. Under her clothing she wears a brown paper wrap with the dollmaker's name on it. The head, arms and legs are moulded from a mixture of sawdust and glue, then covered with *gofun* (made from crushed oyster shells).

Hakarta doll — a small painted ceramic doll. The wooden plaque on the left has the maker's name on it.

A 1930s Japanese baby doll, showing her composition body with a ma-ma in the front. The doll has real hair and glass eyes.

Kime Kamo Ninyo (dolls) (15 and 10 cm, 6 and 4 inches). The bodies of these dolls are made from a composition similar to compressed sawdust, with all the fold lines impressed into the bodies. The cloth fabric is then cleverly glued and pressed into the grooves to give the impression of highly padded clothing. The doll on the left is in orange brocade, the one on the right in off-white and orange. (Private collection, Rockhampton)

Daruma dolls. These four dolls, called by some 'wedding' dolls, are a fancy cloth version of the painted papier-mâché Daruma, a doll that cannot fall over. Tradition says they are based on Buddha who sat and meditated for so long he was unable to stand up. They are considered good luck dolls. These dolls have human hair, glass eyes in the larger versions (painted in the small), and are dressed in lovely brocade fabrics. Sizes range from 7.5 to 14 cm (3 to 5.5 inches).

war in 1868 Edo was taken over in the name of the emperor and renamed Tokyo. A constitution modelled on that of Bismarck's Germany was promulgated in 1889. The speed with which the Japanese adopted western ideas created in less than 50 years a state powerful enough to defeat China (1894–5) and Russia (1904–5), resulting in the annexation of Formosa (Taiwan) and Korea as a colony in 1910. With the Paris Peace Treaty of 1919 Japan also made territorial gains in the Pacific.

After seizing Manchuria in 1931 Japan launched a full-scale invasion of China in 1937. In answer to United States pressure to withdraw from China, Japan declared war in the Pacific in December 1941 with an attack on Pearl Harbor. After the Japanese surrender in August 1945 Formosa reverted to China, becoming the separate state of Taiwan, and Korea reverted to the Allied forces with the Soviet Union occupying northern Korea and a United States force occupying the south.

Far-reaching reforms implemented during the occupation of Japan by Allied forces (1945–52) resulted in a democratic constitution, increased civil liberties and land reform.

Capital Tokyo.

Population (1990) 123 million, with 76.2 per cent living in urban areas. 99.4 per cent Japanese (including the indigenous Ainu on Hokkaido); the other 0.67 per cent is mainly Korean.

Religion The majority participate in both Shinto and Buddhist rites. 115.6 million Shinto, 92 million Buddhists, with an estimated 1.7 million Christians.

Typical Japanese dolls sold as souvenirs. The colour orange is very commonly used for clothing dolls.

Kokeshi dolls. The *kokeshi* is a doll reduced to its simplest form, a simple shaped body with a round head. All these dolls are post World War II *kokeshi* as pre-war ones have straight cylindrical bodies. The pair of kokeshi on the right were sold in many Japanese souvenir shops in the early 1970s as the new world-wide mascot — Kokeshi Kissing Dolls. They had a magnet inside the head and would attract or repel, according to the different style of painted clothes.

An antique *karakuri*. This ingenious moving doll or automaton portrays an ancient magician — when the box is lifted and lowered by hand, the object on the platform appears and disappears. (Courtesy Japan Pavilion, Expo 88)

Japanese dolls depicting children, two girls and a boy (on the right) in traditional clothing.

Language Japanese is the official language. (Japanese is also spoken in Korea and Taiwan as a second language.)

Java (Jawa) (part of Indonesia) Asia/Pacific

See also Indonesia.

Because many dolls have been sold to tourists visiting this island over the years, I have included Java as a separate entity.

A beautifully carved and intricately painted wooden doll wearing a black painted hat and jacket, painted batik-look sarong.

Plastic dolls (22 cm, 8.75 inches). Labels on the base reads 'Indonesian Dolls' and 'Pengaten Jawa Jawa Tengah'. The man wears a black head-dress and jacket with silver braid trim, gold bead necklace and larger white and green bead necklace, brown batik sarong, black shoes. He carries a *kris* (sword) strung crosswise from a waistband at the back, with bead handle decoration. The woman has a fancy hairdo decorated at the back with gold hairpins, white beading and simulated white flowers; black bodice, black jacket with gold trim, white/gold brocade waistband, brown batik sarong, gold sandals.

Java was first visited by Hindus in the first century. Then about the fifteenth century the Hindu empire was overthrown by Mohammedans.

The Portuguese appeared in the islands in 1520, and later in the century Dutch traders arrived. The Dutch East India Company was formed in 1602, resulting in the gradual annexation by the Dutch of the greater part of Java. Then the island was taken by the French during the Napoleonic Wars, but after their defeat in 1811 the British occupied the island for six years, and then returned it to the Dutch. For the rest of Java's history, first under Dutch domination and then as part of Indonesia, look under the entry 'Indonesia'.

A 22-cm (8.75-inch) plastic doll. The label on the base reads 'm'bok Jamu Jawa Tengah'. She has black hair in a twirled bun, and a basket slung from her shoulder by a brown batik band. She wears a large-patterned green check sarong. She holds a bucket in her right hand.

Typical male attire of a desert Arab: long white robe and black overrobe *(aba)* with gold trim, white head-dress *(kaffiyeh)* with an *angol* of black yarn.

An early twentieth-century version of a Jordanian bride. The doll has a bisque head by Recknagel, Germany, and a jointed body. She wears a tall red head-dress ornamented with small coins, and over this a white veil trimmed with broderie anglaise; a gown of woven brown striped material with long flowing sleeves and an embroidered bodice; and a red waist-sash. Over the bodice she has a short-sleeved jacket of dark tan, embroidered at the front edges and cuffs. Around her neck she wears a chain with large pendant.

Cloth and wire dolls made at Agabat Jaber Refugee Camp, Jericho, Jordan, 1960–70s. *Left* **Biet Dajan** A 17.75-cm (7-inch) female doll, wearing a long white head-dress shawl edged with blue blanket stitch, green figured blouse, embroidered black trousers, long overdress richly hand-embroidered in red, and gold waistband. *Right* **Bethlehem** (West Bank) This 20-cm (8-inch) female doll, wears a high red conical head-dress covered with a white scarf, dark check blouse, white pants and skirt, long overdress embroidered in red down the front and sleeves, gold sash.

Jordan (Hashemite Kingdom of Jordan) Middle East

The Kingdom of Jordan is situated in southwest Asia (commonly referred to as the Middle East) and has an area of 96 188 square kilometres (37 129 square miles), part of which — the West Bank — is occupied by Israel. Jordan shares borders with Lebanon, Syria and Iraq to the north, Saudi Arabia to the east, Israel to the west, and has access to the Red Sea at Aquabah. Only a small portion of land near the Syrian border is forested.

A beautiful city was built at the oasis of Petra (in a hidden valley in the south Jordan mountains) in the second century BC. The area of modern Jordan was conquered by Muslim Arabs in the seventh century, and experienced Christian Crusader rule, based in Jerusalem, from the twelfth century, later becoming part of the Ottoman Empire in 1517.

In an effort to end Turkish domination, the country joined England in World War I, only to come under British rule after the war. Transjordan (the mandated area east of the Jordan river) was granted autonomy in 1923 and gained full independence in May 1946.

Renamed Jordan in 1949, the country annexed the West Bank, and then East Jerusalem in 1950, so that its population

Left **Jericho**, an 18.25-cm (7.25-inch) female doll, wears a red check head-dress, blue figured blouse and trousers, black overdress heavily embroidered in red down the front. She has a black roll on her back. *Right* 'Bedouin', a 19-cm (7.5-inch) doll, has a black head-dress bound with red, brown check blouse, blue trouser-like underskirt, black overskirt with blue embroidery down the front, black overblouse trimmed with blue and pink stitching.

became 60 per cent Palestinian. Efforts by the Palestine Liberation Organisation (PLO, founded in 1964) to incorporate Palestinian residents into Jordan were resisted, as they wanted separate statehood.

In the 1967 Arab-Israeli War, Jordan was ejected from the West Bank and East Jerusalem, receiving a further influx of Palestinian refugees. Martial law was imposed, and although used sparingly was in force until July 1991.

In 1986 Jordan reasserted its responsibility for the West Bank by allowing more Palestinian-held seats in an enlarged National Assembly, but later severed ties with the West Bank in July 1988, enabling the PLO to assume full responsibility for the area.

From the mid 1980s Jordan has faced increasing economic difficulties, often made worse by various trade embargos, while at the same time trying diplomatically to sponsor peace in the Middle East.

Capital Amman.

Population 2.8 million, with 66 per cent living in urban areas (plus 1.1 million on West Bank). 98 per cent Arab, 1 per cent Circassian, 1 per cent American.

Religion Over 80 per cent Sunni Muslim, 5 per cent Christian, and a small percentage of Shi'ite Muslims.

Language Arabic is the official language.

Kalimantan (Borneo) (part of Indonesia) Asia/Pacific

See also Indonesia.

The large island of Borneo, 1328 kilometres long by 960 kilometres broad (830 × 600 miles), is divided into four countries. Sabah (formerly British North Borneo) in the north and Sarawak in the west were protectorates under British rule from 1888 until after World War II and are now part of Malaysia. Brunei, also under British rule from 1888 to World War II, is now a small but very rich independent kingdom on the west coast. The largest country, occupying 512 000 square kilometres (200 000 square miles), is Kalimantan, formerly Dutch Borneo and now part of the Republic of Indonesia.

The Dutch East India Company was formed in 1602 and, operating out of Batavia (Jakarta in Jawa), established a monopoly over regional trade. When the company went broke in 1780 its charter expired and the area reverted to official Dutch rule in the early 1800s.

These three dolls are dressed to portray costumes worn by the indigenous people of Kalimantan. They are made of cloth. *Left* This doll wears a simple black wrap-around garment, and has brass earrings and a multi-circlet necklace. Her lower arms and shins are covered by wire bracelets and anklets. *Middle* The male doll wears an orange floral turban. His black jacket is trimmed with orange braid, and stitching at the cuffs. His black trousers have stitching at the side seams and cuffs. *Right* The female doll wears a black top with orange braid trim. Her black wrap-around skirt is trimmed with a rope of 'coins' wound several times around her waist and hips. (Courtesy Jenny Miller, New South Wales)

Britain took temporary control of the East Indies when France occupied The Netherlands during the Napoleonic wars, retaining the northern sections of Sarawak and Sabah; this was clarified in 1824 by the Anglo-Dutch Treaty. The Dutch retained the largest portion, known as Borneo or Dutch Borneo. When the Dutch returned to the East Indies after World War II, during which time the island had been occupied by Japan, they found that the country wanted its independence. Borneo became part of the Republic of Indonesia when it was proclaimed in August 1950.

Main city Pontianak.

Population Includes the Kalimantan Dayaks.

Kashmir (Jammu and Kashmir)

Kashmir is a divided region of 215 680 square kilometres (84 250 square miles) between India and Pakistan.

A 23-cm (9-inch) doll with cloth body and clay head. She wears a light orange gossamer headscarf trimmed with gold braid, and a long yellow jacket trimmed with gold braid, and yellow trousers. She has an elaborate jewellery adornment on her forehead, red earrings, and a green stone pendant.

Until the thirteenth century Hindu culture prevailed in the area, although Buddhism was also present. Mohammedan dynasties destroyed the Hindu civilisation, and in 1581 Kashmir became part of the Mogul empire. Then in 1756 it was incorporated into the Durani (Afghan) empire. The Sikh conquest began in 1819, and by 1820 Kashmir had become a feudal dependency of the Punjab.

In 1948 war broke out between India and Pakistan over the Muslim majority state of Kashmir, whose Hindu leader wanted union with India. The conflict was unresolved by 1949, and after a negotiated ceasefire by the UN Kashmir was divided between the two countries. In August 1965 India and Pakistan again fought over Kashmir, with peace negotiated in January 1966. A secessionist rebellion erupted in 1990–91, and a determined India asserted its authority by imposing direct rule on the area. An uneasy peace prevails.

Kazakhstan The doll wears a green pillbox hat with gold painted decoration, cream dress with green sleeveless jacket edged with gold. She has a yellow belt with red stone buckle. (Courtesy Jenny Miller, New South Wales)

Kazakhstan Central Asia

Kazakhstan is a land-locked country in southern Eurasia with an area of 2 717 000 square kilometres (1 048 762 square miles); it has borders with the Russian Federation, China, Kyrgyzstan and Uzbekistan, and a coastline to the Caspian Sea.

Around 1812 Russian incursions began against the Muslim khanates of Central Asia and five Islamic nations were annexed by the Russian empire during the nineteenth century, including Kazakhstan. These colonies were quickly seized by the Communists after the Revolution and in 1922 they became part of the Russian Federated Soviet Socialist Republic. In 1936 Kazakhstan became the Kazakh SSR.

When Kazakhstan became independent in 1991 it was one of only two nations that retained the hammer and sickle as part of their flag.

Capital Alma Ata.

Population 16.2 million, with 40.8 per cent of the population Russian, 36 per cent Kazakh, 6.1 per cent Ukrainian, 2.1 per cent Tartar.

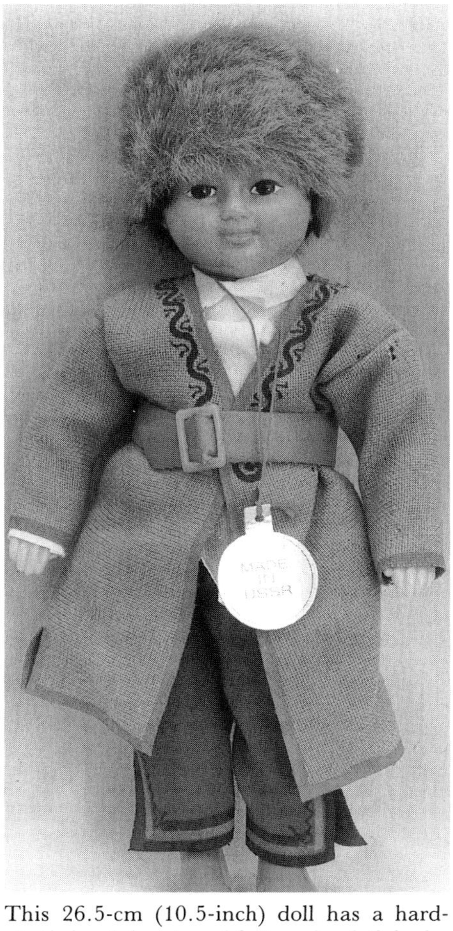

This 26.5-cm (10.5-inch) doll has a hard-plastic head, hands and feet, and a cloth body. He wears a brown fur hat with green satin flat top, white overshirt with collar, dark red trousers split to the knee with decoration around the hem and split. His long fawn knee-length jacket is edged in red with green decoration down the front to the waist, and is held by a wide leather belt around his waist.

Kenya (Republic of)

Kenya sits astride the Equator on the east coast of Africa. Divided into 8 provinces, it covers an area of 582 640 square kilometres (150 943 square miles) of which over 13 400 square kilometres (5000 square miles) is water in the form of lakes. Only 3 per cent of the land is arable and 4 per cent is forested. Kenya shares borders with Tanzania, Uganda, Sudan, Ethiopia and Somalia, and faces the Indian Ocean in the east.

The remains of Stone Age and Iron Age cultures indicate that the earliest

Samburu tribe A one-piece, all-clay, hand-modelled doll (14 cm, 5.5 inches) with pierced eyes and mouths. The female figure has breasts and earrings; both figures are decorated with charcoal and ochre (earth pigment) colours. Beads are used for forehead and earring decoration. A cloth skirt is wound around the dolls. (Courtesy Sherry Morgan, Clearwater, Florida, USA. Photograph: J. Maxson)

A tribal man of carved wood (30.5 cm, 12 inches). He has silver coil earrings and a wide silver coil necklace, and carries a spear in his right hand and a shield made of fur-covered hide in his left.

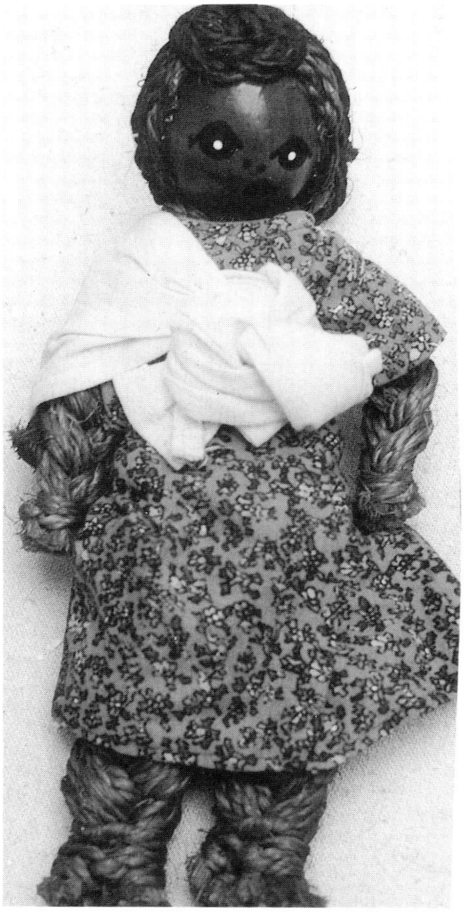

A plaited jute doll with wooden bead head and baby. The woman (25.5 cm, 10 inches) has black string hair wound around her head and a red floral dress. A yellow shawl, tied at the front, holds the baby in a back fold. The baby (14 cm, 5.5 inches) is made of string. She has black hair and a green check skirt with wide white bands over the shoulders.

This 12.75-cm (5-inch) hard-plastic doll carries a bundle of timber on top of her black turban. She wears a coloured bead necklace, blue floral top and skirt, with a wide red/white cummerbund and a white apron.

known ancestors of modern man lived in what is now Kenya. From the tenth century Arabs settled along the coast, and through intermingling with the local people the Swahili language and culture were formed. In the sixteenth century Portugal established forts and trading posts, but the Arabs had regained control by the seventeenth century and took over the slave trade in the nineteenth century. By late in the century epidemics and civil war had taken a great deal of power away from the Masai highland pastoralists.

Missionaries and explorers from Europe aroused interest in the region in both Britain and Germany. The British East Africa Company traded until 1895 when the British East African protectorate was established. Large areas of African land began to be taken over by Europeans, South Africans and other white immigrants, and by the end of the 1800s the seeds of resentment had been sewn. Indian labourers were brought in when Africans refused to build the Ugandan railway, staying on as traders.

During World War I, white settlers strengthened their hold on the government, and in 1920 the country became Kenya, a British colony. African rebellion reached its peak in 1952, when the Mau-Mau led a campaign to restore the land to Africans, and a state of emergency was declared that lasted nearly eight years. On 12 December 1963 Kenya became independent and was declared a republic a year later.

Capital Nairobi.

Population (1990) 24.6 million, with 19

A 17.75-cm (7-inch) carved wooden *m'zee* (old man) sitting on a stool. The doll is painted black and has a wool cape. In his right hand he holds a fly whisk, and in his left a cane. (Courtesy Sherry Morgan, Clearwater, Florida, USA. Photograph: J. Maxson)

A 17.75-cm (7-inch) doll made from dried banana leaves, decorated with seed beads and cowrie shells. She wears a blue leather dress and has wire arm bands. Bought in Nairobi, Kenya. (Courtesy Sherry Morgan, Clearwater, Florida, USA. Photograph: J. Maxson)

per cent living in urban areas. 21 per cent Kikuyu, 14 per cent Luhya, 13 per cent

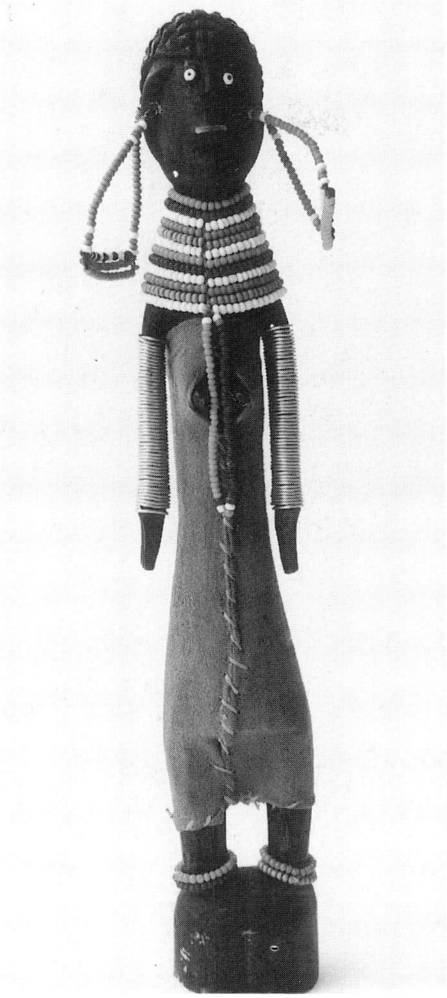

Masai tribe Carved wooden doll — 28.5 cm (11.25 inches) including 4-cm (1.5-inch) base. The doll has bead eyes, slit mouth, carved hair, pierced ears, carved, pointed breasts. She wears a brown cloth gown, long silver wire bracelets on both arms and bead anklets. Bought in the Amboseli Game Park, Kenya. (Courtesy Sherry Morgan, Clearwater, Florida, USA. Photograph: J. Maxson)

Luo, 11 per cent Kalenjin, 11 per cent Kamba, 6 per cent Kisii, 6 per cent Meru — some of the 70 ethnic groups — plus 1 per cent Asian, European and Arab. *Religion* 38 per cent Protestant, 28 per cent Roman Catholic, 6 per cent Muslim; the remaining 26 per cent follow traditional animist/indigenous beliefs. *Language* English and Swahili are the official languages, with three other principal ethnic language groups.

Korea (South) (Republic of Korea) Asia

With an area of 98 484 square kilometres (38 015 square miles) divided into nine provinces, South Korea occupies the southern half of the Korean Peninsula. Twenty-one per cent of the land is arable, with over 66 per cent forested.

Evidence of human habitation dates back to 3000 BC with the arrival of nomads migrating south from the Asian mainland down the Korean Peninsula. Because of frequent intervention from the Chinese, as well as the establishment of competing kingdoms, a long period of instability occurred in the area. In 668 AD

Left This doll dressed in pink and white ornamented with gold represents a dancer with two fans in her hands. The middle pair represent an historical king and queen. The male doll wears a tall crown, a long blue gown with green/red sleeves, tall boots. The female doll has elaborate hair ornaments, a pink blouse, and red skirt decorated in gold. *Right* This doll is dressed in a traditional high-waisted Korean dress in green and red.

Three dolls dressed in traditional costume. *Left* This female doll's dress has a white bodice trimmed with green and green skirt with long streamers from a bow down the front. *Middle* The male doll wears a white shirt and trousers, sleeveless purple jacket, and has a cane basket on his back. *Right* The female doll wears a bodice with multi-coloured bands, red skirt, and blue/red drape over her left arm.

A 1980s version of traditional Korean costume. These dolls have padded wire armature bodies and painted cloth faces. Their clothes are decorated with gold paint. The male doll, who represents a nobleman, wears a tall black pointed head-dress tied at the back and with two streamers down the back; a long pale blue gown, mauve trousers, and blue overcape. The female doll has a long plait tied with red ribbon. Her dress has a yellow bodice and long red skirt, and is trimmed with a long red ribbon. She holds a gold mirror in one hand and a white fan in the other.

the kingdom of Shilla was finally established, succeeded by the kingdom of Koryo (from which the name Korea was derived) in 935. Founded in 1392, the Yi dynasty ruled from Seoul for the next 518 years. Then in 1644, weakened by wars with the Chinese, Japanese and invading Mongols, the territory became a vassal state of China.

After Japan's war with Russia in 1904–05 Japan formally annexed Korea as a colony in 1910, and by 1919 it was treated as an integral part of Japan. Then at the end of World War II Korea was divided into two, as agreed by the Allies, with the territory in the north occupied by Soviet troops and the south by United States forces. In 1948 this division was formalised with the proclamation of the Republic of Korea (south) and the Democratic Peoples Republic of Korea (north). After the withdrawal of both United States and Soviet troops in 1948–49 hostilities between the two countries escalated into full-scale war (1950). An armistice was signed in July 1953 when the 38th parallel became the established border between the two countries.

Despite considerable political problems, Korea has, with United States help, achieved economic prosperity. In the last few years contacts between the two Koreas have become more frequent.

Capital Seoul (Soul).

Population 43.2 million, with 65.4 per cent living in urban areas. 99.9 per cent Korean, 0.1 per cent Chinese.

Religion Confucianism, Mahayana Buddhism and ancestor worship are practiced by 66 per cent; Christianity by 28 per cent.

Laos (Lao People's Democratic Republic) Asia

Laos is a landlocked country situated in the middle of the Indochinese Peninsula. With an area of 236 800 square kilometres (91 405 square miles), Laos has borders to Vietnam, Cambodia, Thailand, Burma and China. Four per cent of the land is arable, with 58 per cent either forest or woodland.

The Lao can trace their heritage to the migration of the Tai people from southern China between the sixth and eighth centuries to lands on the edge of the great Khmer Empire of Angkor. A number of scattered principalities were brought together in 1352 to form the powerful kingdom of Lan Xang. Both Vietnam and Siam (Thailand) were able to take large areas of land from the principalities in the seventeenth and eighteenth centuries as they were weakened by rivalry between the princes.

Hill tribes dolls made of cloth. *Left* This doll has a woven straw hat with a tall inner crown and decorated with fine beading. She wears red flowers in her hair. Her jacket and long wrap-around skirt are of the same material: red background with black/white stripes. She has a small basket between her hands. *Middle* The doll wears a black turban with black/white edging and red flower trim. She has silver earrings and a three-coil silver necklace. Her bodice is black with red borders, and she has a green waist-sash. Her skirt is black with a red/white front panel, and over this a black embroidered tabard with red and green trim. *Right* The kneeling doll wears a striped headscarf that goes around body and crosses over at the front. She wears large silver earrings, and gold beads and a silver necklace. Her jacket and long skirt are black, and she carries a woven cane basket. (Courtesy Jenny Miller, New South Wales)

France had colonised all of Vietnam by 1885, including some Lao territory, and by 1893 all the Lao territory to the east of the Mekong River had been given to France by Siam. France wasn't interested in Laos except as a buffer zone between Siam and the French colony of Indo-China (Vietnam).

Japan occupied Laos during World War II, and in 1945 after the defeat of the Japanese the Lao seized power and proclaimed their independence, only to have France regain control and designate Laos as a free state within the French Union.

In 1954 Laos was granted full independence. After years of trying to form a successful government the third coalition government was established in 1973. The Lao People's Democratic Republic was declared in December 1975.

Capital Vientiane.

Population 3.9 million, with 17 per cent living in rural areas. The population consists of Lao 67 per cent, Palaung-Wa 12 per cent, Thai 8 per cent, Man 5 per cent.

Religion Buddhist 58 per cent, tribal religions 34 per cent, Christian 2 per cent, Muslim 1 per cent.

Language Laotian is the official language and French is also spoken.

Lapland (Lappland) Europe

This is not a country, but a well-known region covering the north of Finland, Sweden and Norway and bordering the Arctic Ocean, with almost the whole region within the Arctic Circle. It covers an area of approximately 394 240 square kilometres (154 000 square miles). Most of the Finnish and Swedish area of Lapland is situated on low plains merging into tundra, whereas Norwegian Lapland is a wild country of mountainous terrain, glaciers and fiords.

The Lapps are a nomadic race of Asiatic origin.

Cellulon Schildkrot dolls (24 cm, 9.5 inches) made in Germany in the 1960s. The male doll wears a navy peaked hat with large red pompon and red and yellow bands, red scarf, navy jacket with yellow/red trim, black leather belt, navy trousers, fur shoes with red/yellow pompons. The female doll wears a red helmet hat with green braid and white trim, red scarf, navy jacket with yellow/red trim, yarn brocade belt, navy trousers, fur shoes with red/yellow pompons.

Finland region Plastic dolls (16.5 cm, 6.5 inches) with a tag reading 'Made in Finland'. The male doll wears a royal blue cap with red/yellow trim and fur edging; royal blue jacket with red/yellow trim on the front edge, cuffs and hem; royal blue trousers; simulated white fur boots. The female doll wears a red felt cap with yellow trim and lace edging, long red jacket with blue/yellow edging, white shawl with neck clasp, red trousers, white 'fur' boots. (Private collection)

Plastic dolls (17.75 cm, 7 inches). *Left* The male doll wears a black 'hat of the four winds' with yellow headband and red/white/green trim; black jacket with red/yellow trim, red braid sash, and red/yellow/green pompon at the waist; black trousers with green trim; grey shoes. *Middle* The female doll wears a red cap with lace trim, red jacket with yellow/green trim, white shawl with red/yellow/green pompons, red trousers with green/yellow trim, grey shoes. *Right* The female doll wears a red cap with yellow/white trim, check undershirt, blue dress with red/white trim, long black pants, and painted black boots.

Latvia Europe

Situated between Estonia and Lithuania facing the Baltic Sea, Latvia has an area of 64 000 square kilometres (24 704 square miles).

Latvia was formerly part of the Russian Empire, from 1795 until it was proclaimed a republic on 18 November 1918. The Soviet Union occupied Latvia along with Lithuania and Estonia in 1940, and the country remained a Soviet 'republic' until the dissolution of the USSR in 1991.

Capital Riga.

Population 2.6 million. Latvian 53.7 per cent, Russian 32.8 per cent, Byelorussian 4.5 per cent, Ukrainian 2.7 per cent and Polish 2.5 per cent.

Religion Mostly Lutheran.

Language Latvian, a member of the Indo-European family of languages, closer to Sanskrit than any other living language.

Latvia This doll has a wooden head with painted features; the body and formed skirt are made from flax. She holds a bouquet of flowers in her left hand. The bottom of the skirt is trimmed with handwoven braid.

Two modern dolls dressed in traditional costume by a lady from Latvia in the early 1980s. *Woman* A 30.5-cm (12-inch) plastic doll. She wears a tall 'crown' head-dress richly ornamented with beads and braid; off-white woollen blouse with stitched collar and silver braid decoration at the neck; white sleeveless jacket with embroidered black-trim; red woollen skirt with embroidery trim. *Man* 'Ken' by Mattel. He wears a white shirt with stitched collar and plaited tie; handwoven sash in red/white; fawn trousers; hand knitted and embroidered socks; brown shoes.

Lebanon (Republic of) Middle East

The Republic of Lebanon is located on the east coast of the Mediterranean, and is divided into five regional governments or moafazats, with a total area of 10 400 square kilometres (4014 square miles). The country has borders with Syria and Israel. Twenty-one per cent of the land is arable, with 8 per cent forested.

From around 300 BC Lebanon was part of the Phoenician Empire and the Hellenic world before coming under Roman rule in the first century AD. The country was Christianised by the fourth century and Islam was introduced by conquering Arabs in 635. During two centuries (the eleventh to thirteenth) of Christian-Muslim confrontation Lebanon was crisscrossed by the Crusades,

Dolls with clay heads and clay-covered wire frame bodies, bought in the early 1970s. The male doll's head is shaped in clay then painted to represent a turban and wound round with cream ribbon. He wears a purple shirt, gold lamé sash, black pants and shoes. He holds a cream handkerchief. The female doll wears an orange head scarf, yellow blouse, gold sash, gold lamé skirt trimmed with gold ric-rac, black painted boots. She holds a red handkerchief. ('Made in Lebanon' on the underside of the base.)

This doll of clay and wire wears a high cream turban with black band, black/gold shirt and baggy trousers, wide blue sash, red shoes. He holds a long sword in his right hand.

providing opportunities for merchants who remained after the Crusaders had left.

Conquest by the Ottoman Turks in 1516 brought more religious tolerance, but with the decline of the Ottoman Empire, the great powers of the time grew interested. In 1832 they intervened to prevent Lebanon being taken over by the Egyptian Maronites, and it was established as a French protectorate in 1860.

The British and French conquest of the Ottoman Empire during World War I led to Lebanon being mandated to Britain and France in 1920. It was included in the French mandate for Syria, but separated from Syria in 1926 and established a semi-autonomous republic.

Lebanon's leaders, both Christian and Muslim, declared the country's independence in November 1941, effective from 1 January 1944. Lebanon received its first wave of Palestinian refugees after the 1948–49 Arab League's war against Israel. After various skirmishes between the PLO-backed Lebanese Muslims and the Maronites (Christian) armed militia — the Phalange — full-scale civil war broke out in August 1975.

In May 1991 Parliament voted to give Muslims an equal number of seats, ending almost 50 years of Christian domination. By July 1991, in a bid to reassert national sovereignty, the Lebanese army took

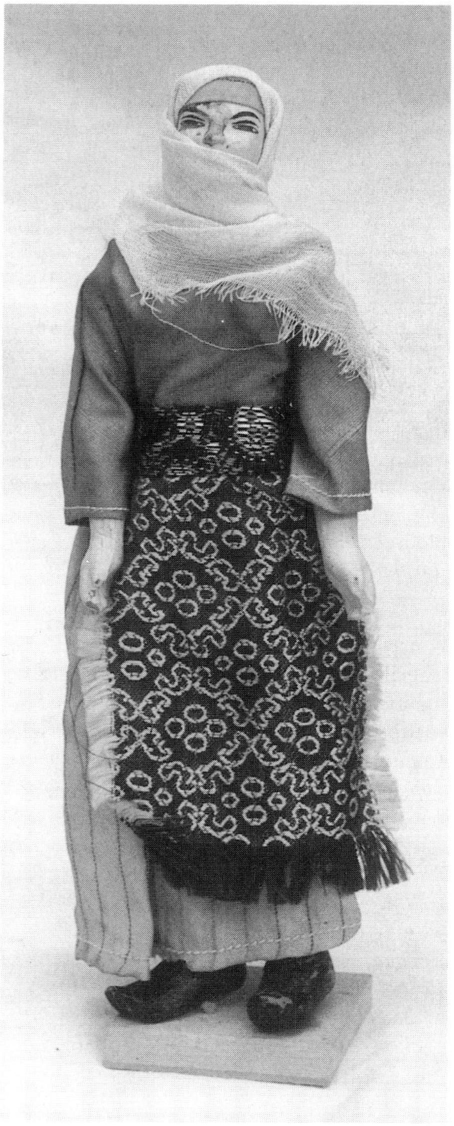

A 21.5-cm (8.5-inch) doll of clay over wire, circa 1965. The doll wears a cream headscarf over a light orange cap, olive green blouse, black braid waistband, orange skirt, black apron with gold embroidery and fringe, black shoes with turned-up toes. Russet (dark orange) trousers are seen underneath.

The doll has a large pot balanced on her head. She wears a white scarf, that also acts as a face veil, with a black headpiece. She has a red blouse, beige bolero trimmed in red, floral purple sash, blue floral skirt and red shoes.

A 17.75-cm (7-inch) cloth doll made by members of the Lesotho Co-op Handcrafts. The doll wears a woven straw hat — these top-knotted hats are still worn by both men and women; blanket held by a colourful bead-trimmed pin (the people like to wear different distinctive patterns); simple blue figured wrap-around dress.

These 14-cm (5.5-inch) hard-plastic dolls with 'Made in England' on the back were sold in the 1960s as being from Basutoland. *Left* The male doll wears a tall cone-shaped straw hat with top loop, blue shawl held with a pin, black trousers, gold earrings. *Right* The female doll wears a tall conical straw hat looped at the top, white blouse, yellow skirt covered by a long multicoloured cloak with serrated edge and pinned at the shoulder, gold earrings and anklets, bead necklace. She holds a red bundle in her left hand.

control of the last of the Palestinian guerilla outposts used as staging bases against Israel, and two Palestinian refugee camps also came under Lebanese control.
Capital Beirut.
Population Estimated 3.5 million, with 83 per cent living in urban areas. 93 per cent Arab; 7 per cent Armenian, Kurdish, Assyrian, Turkish and Greek.
Religion Estimated 75 per cent Muslim, 25 per cent Christian.
Language Arabic (93 per cent) and French are both official languages. English and Armenian (6 per cent) are also spoken, with English widely used for trade and commerce.

Lesotho (Kingdom of) (previously Basutoland) Africa

Covering an area of 30 350 square kilometres (11 715 square miles), and divided into 10 districts, Lesotho is a landlocked country within the Republic of South Africa. Ten per cent of the land is arable, with very little forestation.

The Zulu-speaking Nguniin had largely displaced the earlier inhabitants, the San people (Bushman hunter-gatherers) by the eighteenth century. Sotho-speaking tribes settled in the region until attacked by the Zulu early in the nineteenth century. After having repulsed the Zulu, the king negotiated with Britain for protection in 1843. The country — then known as Basutoland — became a British territory in 1868. Without the consent of the Basotho the country was annexed to Cape Colony in 1871, to finally become a British crown colony in 1884.

From 1906 Basutoland, Bechuanaland and Swaziland were all administered as one. Steadfastly opposed to being incorporated into South Africa, Basutoland was given a new constitution by Britain in 1960, and became the independent Kingdom of Lesotho within the Commonwealth in October 1966.
Capital Maseru.
Population (1990) 1.8 million, with 19 per cent living in urban areas. 99.7 are Sotho (including various subgroups), with Zulu, Tembu and Fingo tribes, 1600 Europeans and 800 Asians making up the remainder.
Religion 80 per cent Christian, mainly Roman Catholic, with 20 per cent observing traditional indigenous beliefs.
Language Bantu (Lesotho or Southern Sotho) and English are the official languages. Zulu, Afrikaans, French and Xhosa are also spoken.

Liberia (Republic of) Africa

Divided into 13 counties with a total area of 111 369 square kilometres (42 988 square miles), Liberia is situated on the West African coast with borders to Sierra

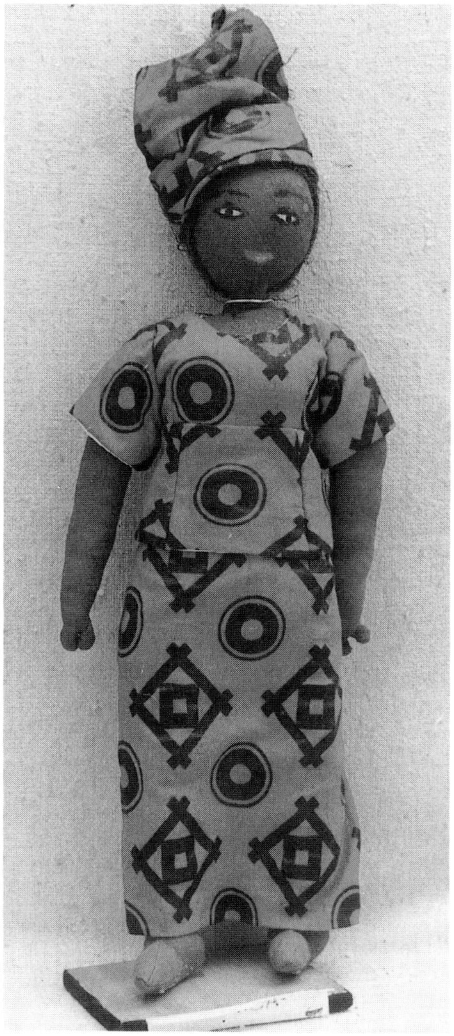

This 25.5-cm (10-inch) brown cloth doll with painted features represents a woman of Monrovia. She has a tall red/black print turban, black hair, gold necklet, and red/black print blouse over matching skirt.

Leone, Guinea and Côte d'Ivoire. Only 1 per cent of the land is arable; 39 per cent is either forest or woodland.

The American Colonisation Society, with the help of a United States Congressional Grant, began in 1816 to transport freed slaves who wished to return to their homeland back to Africa. Some 22 000 former slaves (75 per cent from America) were settled along the west coast.

The Republic of Liberia was declared on 26 July 1847, but until the 1890s the government based in Monrovia controlled only the isolated coastal settlements. The people of the interior staunchly resisted the influx of settlers and it wasn't until the 1930s that this resistance was subdued.

From 1870 the Liberian government was dominated by the '300 families' who, with their Christian faith and American colonial style, formed the settler social elite. Unrest continued, until in 1984 a new constitution approved by referendum introduced for the first time universal adult suffrage without property qualifications. However, animosity and political coups remain destabilising influences.

Capital Monrovia.

Population (1990) 2.6 million, with 38 per cent living in urban areas. 95 per cent are indigenous African tribes, 5 per cent Americo-Liberian (descendants of freed slaves).

Religion 70–75 per cent follow traditional animist beliefs, 20 per cent Muslim, 10 per cent Christian.

Language English is the official language, but 20 languages/dialects are also spoken.

Liechtenstein (Principality of) Europe

A landlocked alpine principality surrounded by Austria and Switzerland, Liechtenstein, the fourth smallest country in the world, occupies an area of only 160 square kilometres (61.8 square miles). Twenty-five per cent of the country is arable with 18 per cent forested.

The fiefs of Vaduz and Schellenberg, created in the fourteenth century, were acquired in 1699 and 1713 (respectively) by the Austrian Liechtenstein family. Bearing the family name, it became an independent principality within the Holy Roman Empire in 1719. During the Napoleonic era the country came under French control, but regained independence within the new German Federation in 1815.

The principality declared its permanent neutrality in 1868, which was respected in both World Wars I and II. In 1919 Liechtenstein's external affairs, previously handled by Austria, were entrusted to neutral Switzerland. Since World War II Liechtenstein has achieved one of the world's highest per-capita incomes.

Capital Vaduz.

Population 28 074. 95 per cent are Liechtensteiners of Alemanis origin. The remainder (5 per cent) are Italian, with other minorities of European origin.

Religion 87 per cent Roman Catholic, 8.6 per cent Protestant.

Language German is the official language.

Hard-plastic dolls (14 cm, 5.5 inches). The woman wears a black bonnet with stand-up back and with gold braid trim over her blond plaited hair. She is dressed in a white blouse with lace trim, red waistcoat with white lacing, black skirt with braid trim, blue brocade apron with black brocade bow, white stockings, black shoes. The man has moulded hair under a stiffened, shaped black hat trimmed with flowers and feathers. He wears a white shirt, black tie, red vest, grey jacket with black trim, multicoloured brocade sash, black breeches, white stockings, black shoes.

Lithuania Europe

Bounded by Latvia, Belarus, Poland and the Baltic Sea, Lithuania has an area of 65 000 square kilometres (25 090 square miles).

Lithuania was constituted in 1918 from the former Russian territories of Kovno, Suvalki and Vilna (Wilno), and was a republic until invaded, along with Latvia and Estonia, in 1940. It remained a Soviet 'republic' until the declaration of independence from the USSR in 1990.

Capital Vilnius.

Population 3.6 million. Lithuanian 80.1 per cent, Russian 8.6 per cent, Polish 7.7 per cent, Byelorussian 1.5 per cent.

Luxembourg (Grand Duchy of) Europe

With an area of 2586 square kilometres (998 square miles), the landlocked country of Luxembourg is situated in the middle of Europe, surrounded by France, Belgium and Germany. It is divided into three districts and 12 cantons, with 24 per

Lithuania The doll has a wooden bead head and wire armature body. She wears a pillbox hat with red/yellow woven band, white blouse with red/white trim and lace collar, black waistcoat with green trim, yellow bead necklace, multi-coloured check skirt under a long white woven apron with red/green woven trim. (Courtesy Jean Krukelis, Queensland)

The doll wears a lace-edged mob-cap, white blouse with lace and gold trim, red waistband, blue skirt with lace and red/white braid trim, white apron with gold and lace trim and decorated with the Luxembourg coat of arms.

An 11.5-cm (4.5-inch) plastic doll wearing a white lace bonnet with lace edging at the back, pink dress with lace at the front and around the hem. Her white lace apron has Luxembourg worked on the lace.

cent of the country arable and 21 per cent forested.

Luxembourg was settled by the Franks in the fifth century AD, and became an autonomous county within the Holy Roman Empire in 963. Created a duchy in 1354, it was under French Burgundian jurisdiction from 1443, before becoming part of the Hapsburg Empire in 1482. From 1555 the country became part of the Spanish-ruled Low Countries (except for a period of French rule, 1684–97), then in 1714 it came under the Austrian Hapsburgs.

Revolutionary France annexed Luxembourg in 1795, only for it to become a grand duchy within the United Kingdom of The Netherlands (including Belgium) in 1815. When Belgium seceded from The Netherlands in 1830, the greater part of Luxembourg went with it. (Today this section of Belgium is Luxembourg province.) The remainder of the area won autonomy in 1848, and by 1867 Prussian troops had been withdrawn. The link with The Netherlands was finally severed in 1890.

After being occupied by Germany in World War I, under the Versailles Treaty in 1919 Luxembourg was declared perpetually free from all German ties. But it was again overrun by the Germans in World War II and annexed to the Third Reich in 1942, to be liberated in 1944.

Capital Luxembourg-Ville.

Population (1990) 378 400, with 77 per cent living in urban areas. Most of the population are of French and German extraction, with a foreign population of 99 400 — mostly Italians.

Religion 95–97 per cent Roman Catholic.

Language Letzeburgish (Moselle-Frankish in origin) is the official spoken language, with English widely understood.

Macedonia Europe

Lying east of Albania and west and northwest of the Aegean Sea, Macedonia is a region in the Balkan Peninsula, partly

These 15-cm (6-inch) dolls depict the costumes worn in the northern part of Greece. The doll on the left wears a basket on top of a pink headscarf trimmed with gold. Her long green jacket is trimmed on the bodice with gold braid and the large reverse of the jacket/skirt are trimmed with red and white bead decoration and gold braid. Under these revers can be seen her red apron worn on top of a pink skirt with lace ruffles at the hemline. The doll on the right wears a blue helmet-like head-dress trimmed in gold. Her white blouse has a high white collar. She wears a long blue coat or jacket with gold bodice and gold and lace trim on the turn back; and a red apron with lace and blue stitching over her white skirt.

in Greece and partly in the former Yugoslavia.

Macedonia was incorporated in the Ottoman Empire at the end of the fourteenth century, and the Berlin Treaty of 1878 left the district still under Turkish rule. The Balkan Wars of 1912–13 led to the partition of the area between Greece, Serbia and Bulgaria.

It was invaded by the Allied forces in 1918, and after World War I the district was divided between Greece and the new Yugoslavia. In 1923–24 the League of Nations undertook the settlement of Grecian Macedonia, introducing large numbers of Greek exiles from Asia Minor and Thrace and arranging for the transfer of minority elements in the population to other Balkan states.

So today we have the emerging state of Macedonia (from the former Yugoslavia) and the Macedonian part of Greece.

Malaysia (Federation of) Asia

Malaysia is divided into two by the South China Sea: to the west is mainland Malaysia on the southern portion of the Malay or Kra Peninsula (area 131 598 square kilometres, 50 797 square miles), and to the east the states of Sarawak (124 449 square kilometres, 48 037 square miles) and Sabah (78 710 square kilometres, 28 452 square miles), on the northern section of the island of Borneo (the southern section is part of Indonesia). The 63 per cent of the territory covered by tropical rainforest is home to one of the world's most diverse bird populations.

Evidence points to what is modern Malaysia having been inhabited as long ago as 50 000 BC. The peninsula was subject to various external cultures, chiefly Indian and Hindu, from the third to fourteenth centuries AD. The Javanese Majapahit empire had extended as far south as Singapore by 1300. Then a base was established in Malacca by the Thai Ayuthia empire in 1400, leading to the founding of the Malacca sultanate. Arab merchants, trading from East Bengal, brought Islam to Malacca, converting the sultan.

Malacca had extended its control to the area of Pahang, Terengganu, Kedah and Johore before it fell to Portuguese invasion in 1500. Because of the isolation from their other trading outposts in Goa and the Moluccas, Portugal eventually succumbed to the Dutch, when they joined with the sultanates to gain control of Malacca in 1644. Despite Dutch efforts to revive the port, it was to be exploited by the Buginese from the Celebes, who after penetrating the peninsula installed one of their own as sultan of Selangor in 1745.

British interest grew in the eighteenth century with the decline of Dutch and Buginese influence, particularly the interest of London merchant houses which wished to trade with China. The East India Company set up a trading post in Penang in 1786, in Malacca in 1795 and in Singapore in 1819. Singapore, Malacca and Penang were incorporated into the Straits Settlements in 1826, coming under direct control of the British Colonial Office in 1867. Lack of administrative control in areas other than the Settlements led to European and Chinese merchants petitioning Britain to restore order.

Britain accepted responsibility for Perak in 1874, Selangor, Negri Sembilan and Pahang by 1888, bringing the four states together in 1896 as the Federated Malay States with Kuala Lumpur as capital. British authority encompassed the whole peninsula when the five remaining states — Kedah, Perlis, Terengganu, Kelantan and Johore — were united in 1914.

Left A 19-cm (7.5-inch) hard-plastic doll with a scarf over her head, sheer long jacket (over shapeless bodice), batik sarong, black sandals. *Middle* A 27-cm (10.75-inch) cloth doll with painted features. She wears a bead necklace, dark pink/yellow jacket with folded-back lapels, sheer fabric scarf over the right shoulder, batik sarong and gold scuffs. *Right* This 23-cm (9-inch) felt and wire armature doll wears a sheer green scarf over her head, bead necklace, apricot brocade satin top, batik sarong and red sandals.

With the invasion of the Malay Peninsula and the fall of Singapore to the Japanese in 1942, Britain's power in the area was greatly undermined. Returning to Malaya in 1946, Britain proposed that the sovereignty of the Malay states be transferred to the British Crown, and that all states (except Singapore) be unified into a Malayan Union. After negotiations, it was agreed to form the Federation of Malaya, inaugurated in February 1948, with the sultans retaining sovereign control of their respective states.

Malaysia was established in September 1963, uniting the Independent Federation of Malaya, the self-governing state of Singapore and the British colonies of Sarawak and North Borneo (Sabah), with Brunei declining at the last moment. The number of Malaysian states was reduced to 13 when Singapore was removed from the Federation in August 1965.

Capital Kuala Lumpur.
Population (1990) 17.77 million, with 40 per cent living in urban areas. 59 per cent Malay and indigenous people of both west and east Malaysia; 32 per cent Chinese; 9 per cent Indian, Pakistani and Sri Lankan.
Religion Muslim 53 per cent, Buddhist 17.3 per cent, Confucian Taoist 11.6 per cent, Christian 8.6 per cent, Hindu 7 per cent, folk/tribal 2 per cent.

Malta (Republic of) Europe Mediterranean

Situated in the central Mediterranean, the Maltese archipelago consists of the islands of Malta, Gozo and Comino, together with the uninhabited islets of Cominotto, Filfla and St Paul, with a total area of 316 square kilometres (122 square miles). Thirty-eight per cent of the land is arable, but there is no proper woodland.

Under Phoenician, Carthaginian, Greek and Roman rule before falling to the Arabs in 870 AD, Malta was conquered by first the Count of Sicily in 1090, and then Spain (1282), before being granted by the Hapsburgs to the Knights Hospitallers in 1530. Under the Knights of Malta the country resisted a Turkish siege in 1565, Valletta was established, and churches, palaces, hospitals and fortifications built.

Napoleon invaded Malta and expelled the Knights in 1798, only to be expelled

The tag reads 'A Souvenir of Malta LADY IN FALDETTA'. A 23-cm (9-inch) plastic doll wearing a black enveloping cape (the *faldetta*) gathered at the right side (near the ears) and with a stiffened straight edge on the left-hand side; brown blouse with lace collar and trim; black skirt. The *faldetta* is traditional apparel.

by British forces a year later. Britain took over the island in 1800 at the conclusion of the Napoleonic wars, and it became a major British base.

Malta was given its first constitution in 1887 and a representative assembly in 1921. Because the island withstood heavy bombing by the Axis powers during World War II it was awarded the George Cross in 1942. Malta was granted self-government in 1947, with full independence achieved in 1964, and it became a republic within the Commonwealth in 1974. In 1979 Malta declared its neutrality and non-alignment.

Capital Valetta.

Population (1990) 400 000 with 84 per cent living in urban areas. 94 per cent native islanders of mixed Arabic, Sicilian, Norman, Spanish, English and Italian origin.

Religion 98 per cent Roman Catholic.

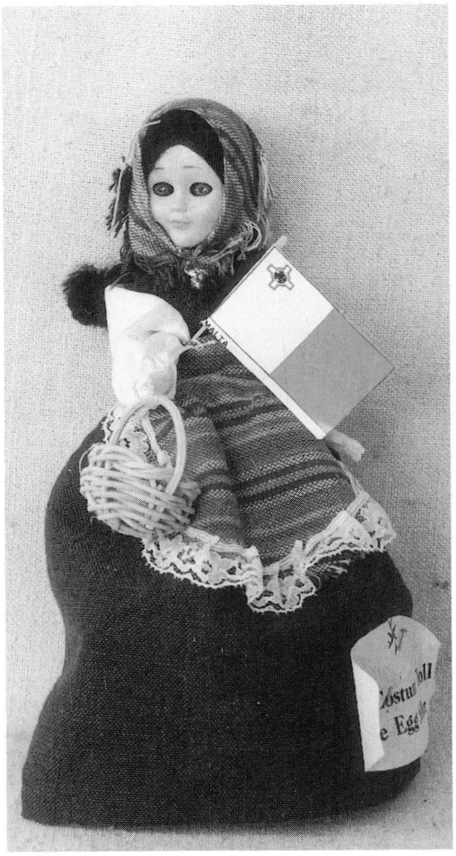

The tag reads 'Malta costume doll VILLAGE EGG SELLER'. The 19.5-cm (7.75-inch) plastic doll has black plaits under a striped headscarf, a lace-trimmed matching apron, small royal-blue fringed shawl over a white blouse, royal blue skirt. She carries eggs in a case basket. (Courtesy Vera Woodhead)

Language English and Maltese are the official languages. Maltese is related to Arabic dialects spoken in Algeria and Tunisia, and is the only Arabic idiom using the Latin alphabet.

Martinique Caribbean

Situated in the Caribbean, the island of Martinique has an area of 1100 square kilometres (425 square miles).

As with many other islands of the Caribbean, the earliest inhabitants of Martinique were Arawak Indians succeeded by the Caribs of South America. Although the island was discovered during Columbus's voyages, no attempt was made to settle it before a French colony of 1635. African slaves were imported to work on the large sugar and coffee plantations.

The British occupied Martinique from 1762 to 1763, and again during the

Malta 'Maltese Bride', a 19-cm (7.5-inch) hard-plastic doll with dress trimmed with the famous handmade Maltese lace. She wears a fine Maltese lace veil over a white taffeta wedding gown which features a collar and bodice insert and an overskirt, all of Maltese lace.

Revolutionary and Napoleonic Wars. It was confirmed as a French territory in 1816, and slavery was abolished in 1848. The island's old capital, St Pierre, was completely destroyed during a volcanic eruption in 1902.

Martinique became a department of France in 1947, and in 1974 a region of France, and was later granted a measure of autonomy in 1982.

Capital Forte-de-France.

Population (1989) 331 511.

Religion Mainly Roman Catholic, with a small Hindu minority.

Language French, with a creole patois.

Mexico (United Mexican States) Central America

Mexico, the largest country in Central America, has an area of 1 958 201 square kilometres (761 404 square miles) and is divided into 31 states and the federal district of Mexico City. It is situated south

Martinique An early 1900s SFBJ (France) bisque (china) head painted brown on a composition body. The doll wears a dark pink headscarf, silvery beads, pale green blouse with darker green lapels and lace trim, pale green skirt with lace trim, pink striped overskirt tucked up at the waist.

Mexico Two dolls completely made from woven straw. The 20-cm (8-inch) male doll wears a plaited red sombero with yellow trim, green woven jacket with flower trim, red trousers and yellow/purple woven cane serape. The 21-cm (8.25-inch) female doll wears a green woven straw sombrero with yellow trim, red blouse with flower trim, natural colour woven jacket, multi-striped woven skirt. (Courtesy Vera Woodhead)

Plastic and cloth dolls (23 cm, 9 inches). The male doll wears a large straw sombrero with orange trim, navy jacket and trousers trimmed in white, striped serape, brown shoes. He holds a wooden guitar. The female doll has black braids with green bows, a white blouse with braid trim, dark pink skirt with green/white trim, green scarf, straw sandals. She holds a basket of fruit.

Oiled cloth and cloth dolls, made in Toluca, Mexico, and bought in the 1970s (25 cm, 9.75 inches). *Left* 'Bandido' wears a wide straw sombrero, pink/white check shirt, white trousers, fine leather thonged sandals, bandoliers over the shoulders. He holds a gun in his left hand. *Centre* The female doll has long black plaits, a white blouse with lace trim, red/white spotted skirt with flounce at the hem, leather sandals. She holds two woven cane baskets. *Right* The male doll wears a wide straw sombrero, red/white check shirt with white collar, green serape over the shoulder, white trousers, leather thong sandals. He has flowers in a sheath on his back.

of the United States and is bordered by Guatemala and Belize to the south, the Gulf of Mexico to the east, and the Pacific Ocean to the west. Although nearly 25 per cent of the country is tropical rainforest, 50 per cent experiences arid to semi-arid conditions and only 12 per cent of the land is arable.

Mexico's past includes the most highly developed pre-Columbian civilisation in Latin America from the tenth century, followed by the Aztecs from the middle of the twelfth century. It is estimated that the Aztecs may have numbered nearly 15 million when Cortez and 600 conquistadors landed in 1519, but within two years the Spanish had defeated their leader Montezuma II and captured the city of Tenochtitlan.

Because of rich silver strikes between 1546 and 1558, Mexico (or New Spain) became an important centre in the Spanish empire. The Indians were reduced to a form of semi-slavery until this was finally abolished in 1829.

From 1810 events on the Iberian Peninsula triggered moves for independence from Spain, and in 1821 the Spanish viceroy was forced to leave Mexico. A federal republic was established in 1824. In an attempt to regain control, a Spanish expedition was sent to Mexico in 1829, but by 1836 Spain had formally recognised Mexico's independence.

From 1823 Texas (then part of Mexico) was opened to United States colonisation, with Texas declaring its independence from Mexico in 1836. This caused war to break out between the United States and Mexico in 1846. In 1848 modern California, New Mexico, Arizona, Nevada, Utah and part of Colorado were ceded by Mexico to the United States on the payment of a considerable sum, and the cancellation of debts owing to the United States.

Political turbulence and war took a heavy toll of Mexico's economy, and in 1861 the suspension of payments on foreign debts provoked a swift reaction from France, Spain and Britain. In 1863 Napoleon III took Mexico City and installed an Austrian Hapsburg as archduke-emperor; he was later killed

Left This 10-cm (4-inch) plastic female doll wears a white headscarf with coloured stitching trim, white blouse with white/red/blue braid trim, green sash, multi-striped blue woven skirt. She carries a cane basket of flowers held by a cord around her head. *Right* A 10-cm (4-inch) clay female doll wearing a red/yellow shawl, white blouse with red/blue cross stitch trim, black peplum with white braid trim over a black skirt with red trim. Her white apron is trimmed with a blue/white band. She carries a net in her right hand, a fish in the left.

Left A 17.75-cm (7-inch) vinyl doll wearing a red sombrero, white blouse, red skirt with gold decoration. *Middle* 'Rosita', a 26.5-cm (10.5-inch) cloth doll with painted features, black yarn plaits under a red/green headband with bow, gold earrings, white blouse with red trim, bead necklace, red/green skirt with green straps and trim, and leather sandals. *Right* This 17.75-cm (7-inch) cloth doll wears a straw sombrero, maroon jacket, fawn trousers, yellow serape. He holds a wooden flute in the left hand.

after French troops were withdrawn in 1867.

An era of considerable stability ensued until the country became embroiled in a guerilla war in the north and a peasant revolt in the south from 1911. A new constitution was promulgated in 1917, but reforms were only gradually introduced, leading to another revolt between 1926 and 1929.

Mexico's collaboration with the United States war effort during World War II resulted in a better economy, and political stability which has fortunately continued even through several serious economic crises.

Capital Mexico City.
Population (1990) 88.6 million, with 69.7 per cent living in urban areas. 60 per cent mestizo (Indian-Spanish), 30 per cent Amerindian, 9 per cent white.
Religion 93 per cent Roman Catholic, 3.3 per cent Protestant, and some Baha'i.
Language Spanish is the official language (92 per cent), and there are some 59 distinct native dialects.

Moldova This plastic doll has black hair covered by a red babushka, with a spray of leaves on the left side. She wears a three-strand bead necklace, pale ivory blouse with simulated embroidery, black bolero with gold trim, red sash, black skirt with a wide painted design, yellow apron with red edging and simulated embroidery, knee length red boots.

Moldova (Moldavia) Europe

Moldova is a landlocked country surrounded to the north, east and south by the Ukraine, and with Romania to the west, it has an area of 34 000 square kilometres (13 124 square miles).

Moldova was part of a region known as Bessarabia that over the years had historically been part of Romania, Turkey and the Russian empire. The Russians seized the area from Turkey in 1812. Romania was granted part of it in 1918 after World War I, and in 1924 the remainder was merged with the Ukraine, becoming an autonomous republic within the Ukraine in 1925. The Moldavian Soviet Socialist Republic was established on 2 August 1940, and the country became independent 51 years later as Moldova.

Capital Kishinev.
Population 4.2 million. Moldovian 63.9 per cent, Ukrainian 14.2 per cent, Russian 12.8 per cent, Gagayz 3.5 per cent, Jewish 2.0 per cent, Bulgarian 2.0 per cent.

Monaco (Principality of) Europe

Situated on the Mediterranean coast, an enclave in southeastern France, is the tiny

Left This 14-cm (5.5-inch) plastic female doll wears a straw hat, light red blouse with lace trim, red/white diamond-check skirt with black band, red apron with black Monaco print and lace edge. *Right* 'Monaco Policeman', a 13-cm (5.25-inch) plastic doll, wears a white helmet with red feather trim, white shirt, black tie, white jacket with red/white cord and epaulettes, white belt, white trousers, black shoes.

A 19-cm (7.5-inch) celluloid doll by Poupées Magali. She wears a finely woven wide-brimmed straw hat slung at the back of the neck, white blouse, black sleeveless bodice, red sash, red/white diamond-check skirt with black trim, red floral apron with black trim. She carries a woven straw basket of flowers.

principality of Monaco with an area of only 1.9 square kilometres (0.75 square miles).

Featured in turn in the early history of Monaco are the Phoenicians, Greeks, Romans, Visigoths and Saracens. The principality's name stems from a sixth-century Ligurian tribe, the Monoikos.

Following the construction of a fortress in 1215 AD by the Genoese, the house of Grimaldi imposed lordship in 1297. Then as a reward for service by the Grimaldis, France recognised Monaco's independence in 1489. Monaco accepted protection from Spain in 1542, but had reverted to French protection by 1641. Uniting with France in 1793, Monaco regained its independence in 1815 under Sardinian protection, to again come under French protection in 1861 after the Franco-Austrian War.

Princely absolutism gave way to constitutional rule in 1911, and Monaco's sovereignty was accepted by France in 1918. Then the country was occupied by the Italians in 1940, followed by the Germans in 1943.

Post-war Monaco became a major tourist centre. In 1959 Prince Rainier asserted his sovereign powers, but a revised constitution promulgated in 1962 guaranteed representative government and renounced royal divine right.

Capital Monaco-ville.
Population 28 200. 47 per cent French, 16 per cent Monegasque, 16 per cent Italian, 21 per cent other.
Religion 95 per cent Roman Catholic.
Language The official language is French; but Italian, English and Monegasque are also widely spoken.

Mongolia (Mongolian People's Republic) Asia

Situated in northern Central Asia, landlocked Mongolia is divided into 18 counties *(aimag)* and has an area of 1 565 000 square kilometres (604 090 square miles). One per cent of the land is arable, 10 per cent forested, and the pasture land of the steppes occupies 79 per cent of the total area.

Home to pastoral nomads since the

A 25.5-cm (10-inch) plastic doll wearing a white fake-fur straight-sided hat, red robe trimmed with golden-yellow braid and with slits at the side, black boots with red trim.

second millennium BC, the Central Asiatic Plateau produced a succession of tribal empires from the third century BC. In 1206 Genghis Khan consolidated the Mongol tribes into the first Mongol state, and over the next 60 years Mongol armies conquered territories from eastern Europe to the Pacific Ocean.

The Mongol empire began disintegrating in the fourteenth century, to collapse in the seventeenth when it was overwhelmed during the expansion of Manchuria. The Mongol princes finally accepted Manchu Chinese overlordship in 1691. However, upon the collapse of China's imperial regime in 1911, the province of Outer Mongolia declared itself an independent monarchy, and the Living Buddha of Urga (the head of the Lamaist Church) became head of state.

In 1915, after war with China, Mongolia (which was actually a de facto Russian protectorate at the time) became autonomous under Chinese suzerainty. China abrogated Mongolia's autonomy in 1919–20 and occupied the country, but was expelled in 1921. Independence was proclaimed, but in fact the country was firmly under Soviet direction, and in 1924 a Soviet-style constitution established the People's Republic.

In 1946 China formally recognised Mongolia's independence and industrialisation began in 1948. From 1984, slowly at first, Mongolia began to emulate Soviet reform policies, finally rushing to embrace the change sweeping the Soviet bloc in 1990.

Capital Ulan Bator.
Population (1990) 2.2 million, with 51.8 per cent living in urban areas. 90 per cent Mongol, 4 per cent Kazakh, 2 per cent Russian, 2 per cent other.
Religion Tibetan Buddhist Lamaism (repressed in the 1930s and restored in 1990), 4 per cent Muslim.
Language 90 per cent speak Khalka Mongol; Russian and Chinese also spoken by minorities.

Montenegro Europe

Situated in the Balkans, with an area of 13 182 square kilometres (5331 square miles), Montenegro, part of the former Yugoslavia from the 1920s, is one of the smallest provinces to have become independent with the disintegration of that state in the 1990s.

Montenegro separated from the Serb states in the fourteenth century. It acted

This male doll is dressed in a black pillbox hat with red crown. He wears a white shirt, red wrap-around vest with gold braid trim, red jacket with floating sleeve panels and trimmed with gold braid and yellow embroidery. He has a yellow waistband, black trousers, white socks and white shoes.

This female doll wears a black pillbox hat with red crown. She has a white blouse, red short-sleeved vest with gold edging, long green jacket with red lining and gold braid trim.

The doll wears a black pillbox hat with red crown, white blouse, red jacket with gold braid trim, long white jacket with braid trim. She has gold chains draped over her white skirt.

as a buffer state between the growing commercial expansion of Venice and the conquests of Turkey, but in 1484 the Montenegrins were forced to withdraw to the mountains and change their original capital for Cetinje. A printing press was set up and some of the earliest Slav books were printed, but culture was soon sacrificed to the necessity of self-preservation.

From 1516 until 1696 Montenegro was continually at war with the Turks, who twice captured the city. A dynasty founded in 1697 stamped out Islam and entered into friendly relations with Peter the Great of Russia. A senate was founded and education encouraged from 1830 to 1851. In the 1850s the Turks were finally beaten, ensuring independence, and a constitution was granted.

Rather unwillingly the country joined the Balkan League, and the attack on Turkey in 1912 resulted in Montenegro increasing its territory; negotiations went ahead for union with Serbia. Both countries found themselves in opposition to Austria-Hungary in World War I. Montenegro joined with Serbia when the Serbian monarchy united the former Austrian-Hungarian territories of Slovenia, Dalmatia, Croatia, Bosnia, Hercegovina and Vojvodina into the new Kingdom of Serbs, Croats and Slovenes in December 1918. The country's name was changed to Yugoslavia in 1929.
Capital Titograd.
Population 584 310.
Religion Predominantly Eastern Orthodox.

Moravia Europe

A region rather than a country, Moravia was once a province of Czechoslovakia, but is now situated between Silesia and Bohemia in the Czech Republic and the new country of Slovakia and Austria. It has an area of 22 067 square kilometres (8620 square miles).

Many of the dolls sold as souvenirs of the former Czechoslovakia were actually dressed in the colourful and distinctive costumes of this region.

Cellulon dolls with moulded hair (28 cm, 11 inches). *Left* The male doll wears a black hat with red/green/yellow/white braid around the brim, white shirt with black braid collar under a black waistcoat with red/blue embroidery at the front and back. He has a blue waistband, and navy trousers embellished with lace and blue embroidery at the front and side seams. He wears black boots. *Middle* A female doll dressed in a red headscarf trimmed with red braid; white blouse with puffed sleeves and lace cuffs and collar, black embroidery down the front and on the shoulder. She has a blue brocade waistcoat with green lapels and red embroidery on both back and front. Her dark red brocade skirt with blue band has floating lace and braid panels at the front and a pleated black insert at the back. She wears black boots with embroidery trim at the top. *Right* This male doll wears a black hat, white shirt with a brocade collar, brown belt, and white trousers trimmed with red at the side. His heavy white coat is held across the shoulders with braid.

The main city is Brno (Brunn).

Religion The majority are Roman Catholic.

Morocco (Kingdom of) Africa

Covering an area of 446 550 square kilometres (172 368 square miles) and divided into seven provinces, Morocco is situated on the northwest coast of Africa. Its coastline stretches from the Mediterranean to the Atlantic, with Tangier just across the Straits of Gibraltar from Spain. It has borders with Algeria to the east, and Western Sahara to the south. Eighteen per cent of the land is arable, 12 per cent forested.

Berbers, Masmoudas and Sanhajas were the first inhabitants of Morocco, and for many centuries the country was divided by clan loyalties. Morocco, Tunisia and Algeria form a natural unit embracing the Atlas regions. The Carthaginians established colonies west

Vinyl dolls (17.75 cm, 7 inches). *Left* This female doll has black hair piled up over a headdress, with a white braid headband. The veil over her head is held at the ears with fancy bead pins. She wears a long red gown with gold emrboidery trim and white/gold braid down the front and around the hem and cuffs; yellow harem pants. *Right* The doll wears a coloured floral veil held on the head with an ornamental green band, and also pinned at the waist. She has long black plaits and large medallion (coin) earrings. She wears a long-sleeved floral blouse, yellow brocade overdress with wide gold braid sash, red harem pants, green pointed shoes. She carries a distaff in her hand.

A pre-World War II doll made of leather. He wears a cowled jacket of brown flecked fabric, white shirt and trousers. He has a leather pouch slung over his shoulder and a leather belt. (Private collection, Townsville)

A mother carrying a baby — cloth dolls with painted faces, circa 1930s. The doll wears a large plaited straw hat over a long white head shawl that envelopes the baby as well; pink/red check headscarf (the baby wears a red one); beige floral top, red/white striped trouser-like skirt, and red lace-up boots.

along the coast from Tunis. This region was extended by Rome, which established the province of Mauretania. In the fifth century AD the Roman province was replaced by the Vandal kingdom of Africa.

Late in the seventh century the Saracens crossed the Libyan deserts and established an empire in Barbary, converting the Berbers to Islam. A revolt in 739 overthrew Saracen power in Spain and Africa, and by 1200 a Berber empire was established by the Amoravides who dominated North Africa through to Egypt. During the thirteenth century, in a rapid decline, the empire was reduced to the size of modern Morocco. For a time, a revival under the Saadian dynasty (1550–1668) succeeded in arresting further disintegration. Today's ruling dynasty captured Morocco from the Saadians in the middle of the seventeenth century.

Berber pirates (corsairs) harried European shipping until France secured victories in the seventeenth and eighteenth centuries, paving the way for later dominance. Algeria was conquered in 1830, but as various other European powers had economic interests in Morocco, French influence there was not effective until after agreements with Britain and Spain in 1904. In 1909 there was a serious outbreak by the Moorish tribes, which was suppressed by large French and Spanish armies.

A French protectorate was set up in 1912, and the Spanish zone of influence defined by agreement, limiting it to the northern area of the country. In March 1956 the French protectorate became the independent Sultanate of Morocco, and a month later the Spanish protectorate was joined to the sultanate. The sultan changed his title to king in 1957, and a constitution was adopted in 1962.

Since the mid 1970s Morocco has been embroiled in conflicts over its attempts to annex the Western (formerly Spanish) Saraha, from which the Spanish withdrew in 1975.

Capital Rabat.

Population (1990) 25.6 million. 55 per cent Arab, 44 per cent Berber, 0.7 per cent non-Moroccan, 0.2 per cent Jewish. 23 per cent live in urban areas.

Religion The state religion is Islam, 98.7 per cent Sunni Muslim. 1.1 per cent Christian.

Language Arabic is the official language, with a number of Berber dialects spoken. French is widely used for commerce.

Musicians

Throughout history music has played an important part in human life, whether by bringing pleasure to one person or thousands, or leading armies into war. A musical instrument, either simple or ornate, can capture and enhance mood by means of scale and tempo.

India Dolls with wooden head and wire-covered armature (12,75 cm, 5 inches). 'Mrudanga [drum] girl'. The female doll wears a blue veil brought to the front waist, silver earrings, two gold neckbands and a gold necklace, long red jacket, metal belt, yellow skirt with a check hem. A long drum hangs from her neck by a long cord. The male doll is dressed in a striped turban, long white jacket, blue waistcoat with silver decoration, white trousers. He holds a red tambourine in his left hand.

China This cloth and plastic doll wears a fancy straw hat on her head, pink *cheongsam* with gold neck circlet, and has a musical sitar-like instrument on her lap. (Courtesy Hilary Dunford)

Japan *Left* Typical musicians used on either the Girls' Day or Boys' Day tableau. The doll on the left is dressed in dark blue-green with orange, the doll on the right in bright orange with black. Both outfits are richly embossed with gold. The dolls have drums under their left arms.

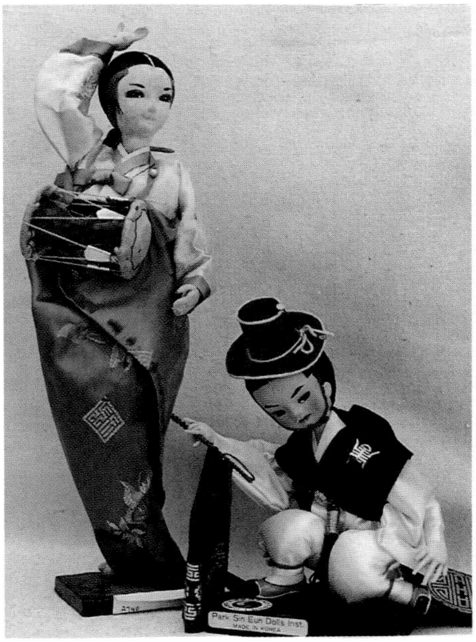

Korea 'Dancing to the Changku' (the *changku* is Korea's traditional drum for dancing), made at the AC Kwang Orphanage Kojo-Do, Korea, in the 1970s. *Left* This 29-cm (11.5-inch) cloth doll has black hair with a rod through the back bun. She wears a white top, green bow and green skirt, and a red drum hangs from a cord around her neck. *Right* The 12.75-cm (5-inch) sitting doll with cloth head and hands and plastic feet was bought at Expo 88. He wears a tall red hat with yellow cord trim, white neck scarf, lemon shirt, blue jacket, red waistcord with tassel, lemon trousers with blue trim at the ankles, blue shoes. He holds a red and blue banner in one hand. This outfit is worn in a Korean dance.

Italy *Left* 'Siena Trombetto di Palazzo' — a 17.75-cm (7-inch) doll by Eros. The doll wears a blue cap with green brim, red long-sleeved jacket split at the sides (showing white shirt), green and blue tabbard with white edging; understockings with right leg white, left leg black; peaked overstockings with black right leg, white left leg; and black shoes. He holds a trumpet with attached pennant featuring a black and white square under a red oblong with a white lion. *Middle* 'Naples', a 17.75-cm (7-inch) doll wearing a long red cap ending in a red tassel, white shirt with purple ties, red bolero, multi-coloured waist-sash, blue knee breeches trimmed at the sides with yellow dots, long white stockings, black shoes. He carries a mandolin on a cord around his neck. *Right* 'Contrada della Civetta' 'Flag Bearer', a 17.75-cm (7-inch) doll by Eros. The doll wears a red truncated hat with white top and white braid trim, black bodice, full long white sleeves with large red side capes trimmed in gold, short white skirt edged in gold, red belt with gold trim. His leggings are right leg black, left leg red, with white trim; black shoes. He carries a red flag edged in white with a black and white emblem. In real life the flag bearers perform marvellous feats with their flags.

Madeira, Portugal Besides portraying musicians, this pre-World War II ensemble is also an action piece probably used at a festival. The five dolls have heads made of a cork-like compound with celluloid mask faces; their bodies are cloth and wire. Each wears a black cap with long black tassel. The male dolls are dressed in white with red waistbands. The female dolls have white blouses, red skirts with embroidered trim, red scarves. They all have full-size wooden castanets tied to their backs. The dolls are on a wire circle attached to a rod and when the rod is pushed up and down the castanets make a noise and the middle doll hits his silver bell. (Author's collection)

A 25.5-cm (10-inch) doll made of brown felt and marked 'Wenco Design HERERO NAMIBIA'. She has black yarn hair and wears a green turban, bead necklace, green crochet shawl over a brown/white dress, and long green slip.

Namibia (Southwest Africa) Africa

Bisected by the Tropic of Capricorn, and with an area of 824 290 square kilometres (318 176 square miles), Namibia is situated on the southwest coast of Africa. Included in the area is the South-African-claimed enclave of Walvis Bay. Only 1 per cent of the land is arable, with 22 per cent woodland or scrub.

Originally occupied by the Khockhoi, the San (Bushmen) and the Bantu-speaking Herero, the country's first contact with Europeans was in the 1840s when Portuguese navigators explored the coastal regions at Cape Cross, Walvis Bay and Dias Point. Dutch and British explorers followed from the seventeenth to early nineteenth century, with the German connection beginning in the 1840s.

In 1878 Britain annexed Walvis Bay, and an Anglo-German agreement acknowledged German control of Southwest Africa. Walvis Bay was retained by Britain and administered as part of Cape Colony (South Africa).

South African troops defeated the Germans during World War I, occupying the territory which in 1920 was mandated by the League of Nations to South Africa. They were to administer the territory on behalf of Britain. In 1946 the United Nations rejected the request by South Africa to incorporate Southwest Africa, and in 1950 it was ruled that the territory remain under international mandate. In 1966 the United Nations revoked the South African mandate and from 1968 the territory was referred to as Namibia. After a great deal of discussion between the indigenous people of Namibia, the United Nations and South Africa, an internationally recognised settlement provided for the United Nations to supervise elections prior to independence in 1988.

The constitution was formally adopted in February 1990, with independence on 21 March 1990. South Africa and Namibia are negotiating over Walvis Bay, the principal harbour serving Namibia.

Capital Winhoek.

Population 1.7 million. 86 per cent black, 6.5 per cent white, 7.5 per cent mixed. 45 per cent of the population belong to the Ovambo ethnic group.

Religion Approximately 90 per cent Christian, 10 per cent traditional animist beliefs.

Language Afrikaans and English are the official languages. 60 per cent speak Afrikaans, the rest English or German. There are also a number of indigenous languages.

Nepal Carved wooden dolls (16 cm, 6.25 inches) on a 4-cm (1.5-inch) wooden plinth. The man wears a blue turban, green jacket and trousers, white waistband. He carries a pole on his shoulder, with wooden baskets. The woman wears a green blouse, orange shoulder sash and wide waistband, blue skirt pleated at the front. She has a carved wooden basket on her back.

Cloth dolls (25.5 cm, 10 inches). The woman has plaits wound in buns over her ears. She wears a homespun blouse, cord necklace, wide lemon sash, black pleated skirt with red trim. The man wears a red/blue print turban, red/black striped jacket and trousers, lemon shoulder scarf/strap and waistband. (Courtesy Nepal Pavilion, Expo 88)

Nepal (Kingdom of) Asia

Situated along the southern slopes of the Himalaya, in southern Asia, with an area of 140 800 square kilometres (54 349 square miles), Nepal is surrounded by India and Tibet (China). Seventeen per cent of the land is arable with 33 per cent forested.

In 568 BC the Buddha was born in southern Nepal and the Buddhist culture has flourished from the fourth century BC. From 500 to 700 AD strong trading and cultural ties linked Nepal with Tibet.

A number of hill principalities had been created by Rajput nobles fleeing the Muslim invasion of India in the sixteenth century. When the King of Gurka conquered the valley he moved his capital to Kathmandu in 1769, laying the foundations of modern-day Nepal. Nepal's boundaries were set by a series of wars with her neighbours.

The border war with the East India Company in 1814–16 led to the beginning of Britain's influence over Nepal. Power in Nepal passed from the king to a succession of influential families — the Thapas (1806–37) and the Ranas (1846–1951) who became hereditary prime ministers.

In 1959 Nepal's first constitution was promulgated and the first elections were held in February 1959. However, the constitution was suspended by the king in December 1960, and it wasn't until the 1990s that the king became a constitutional monarch. Nepal's first multi-party election for three decades was held in May 1991.

Capital Kathmandu.
Population (1990) 19.1 million, with 8 per cent living in urban areas. 58.4 per cent Nepalese (native Mongolian), 18.7 per cent Bihari (including Maithiri and Bhojpuri), 3.3 per cent Tamang, 3 per cent Newar.
Religion Nepal is the only official Hindu state in the world. 88–90 per cent Hindu, 5 per cent Buddhist, 3 per cent Muslim, and approximately 35 000 Christians.
Language Nepali is the official language, spoken by approximately 58 per cent. There are 20 other local languages.

Netherlands (Kingdom of The Netherlands) (Holland) Europe

Situated on the western coast of Europe, the Kingdom of The Netherlands covers an area of 41 863 square kilometres (16 159 square miles) of which 33 940 square kilometres (13 101 square miles) is dry land. Twenty-five per cent of the land area is arable, 34 per cent pastures or meadows and 9 per cent forested.

The southern part of the country was

A pair of unusual dolls, 'Alkmar', made with wooden bead heads and wire armature bodies wrapped with white plastic coils. Cheese carriers, the dolls wear flat-topped yellow plastic hats and their clothing is depicted by the coiled plastic. A sled laden with plastic cheeses is strung between the two.

These 30.5-cm (12-inch) vinyl dolls bought in the early 1970s both have tags reading 'Genuine Rozetta Dolls, Amsterdam'. The female doll wears a winged lace cap, black blouse with floral insert and trimmed with dark braid, long multicoloured skirt under a black apron with floral top section and braid waistband, wooden clogs. The male doll wears a black hat with red crown, red crossover jacket over a black/white striped shirt with gold buttons at the neck, black trousers with gold buttons, and wooden clogs.

colonised by the Romans, and later in the fifth century was fully Christianised as part of the Frankish Empire (seventh to eighth centuries AD).

Between the ninth and tenth centuries, Viking invasions fragmented the area into feudal fiefdoms, with a loose allegiance to the Holy Roman Empire. These 'Low Countries' were first dominated by the Dukes of Burgundy, but passed, through marriage, in the late 1400s to the Hapsburg dynasty. With the joining of the Spanish and Austrian successions Hapsburg rule extended over half the known world by the beginning of the 1500s.

When the Austrian and Spanish Hapsburg lines separated in 1555, the Low Countries became a province of Spain. During the merciless Eighty Years War (1568–1648) the northern provinces declared their independence from Spain, and in 1581 became the United Provinces of The Netherlands, conceded by Spain in 1609.

It was a golden age for the new republic. The powerful United East India and West India companies built Dutch

Vinyl dolls (28 cm, 11 inches) from the fishing village of **Urk** (1976). The female doll wears a close-fitting white lace bonnet edged with yellow lace, padded floral bodice with black sleeves, multi-striped skirt apron with finer stripes on a white ground, black stockings and shoes. The male doll wears a flat-crown black hat with turned-back brim laced at the side, double-breasted red/white/black shirt with red collar, black tie, full black trousers with two silver buttons, black stockings and shoes.

This 28.5-cm (11.25-inch) vinyl **Zeeland** doll wears a lace cap with square brass decorations to each side and a fillet for support *(ooryzer)*, coral beads, black dress with floral yoke. A shawl (or *doek*) of the same floral fabric with yellow piping trim is tucked into the black/white apron; black socks, wooden clogs.

A 46-cm (18-inch) German celluloid doll with glass eyes, circa 1930s. She wears a white head-dress, traditional red coral beads, black top, fringed shawl, black skirt, gold brocade apron.

These 16.5-cm (6.5-inch) plastic dolls represent 'Marken'. The female doll wears a white cap under a blue cap with red front trim, red bodice, red braid belt, black skirt, black apron with blue bib, and wooden clogs. The male doll wears a tall black hat, black/white check shirt with red collar, black jacket and baggy trousers, wooden clogs.

Arnhem 12.75-cm (5-inch) plastic dolls. The male doll wears a black cap, check shirt, red jacket, black trousers, clogs. The female doll wears a white lace cap, black bodices and apron with floral trim, red/white striped shirt. Both dolls wear a brooch with the name 'Arnhem' and dangling clogs pinned to their waistline.

A 21.5-cm (8.5-inch) plastic doll. She wears a white cap with metal hat pins, red coral necklace, red cape, black dress, blue check apron, wooden clogs.

A pair of pre-World War II celluloid dolls, 15 cm (6 inches) tall. The female doll wears a white cotton cap, black dress, mushroom apron, black stockings, clogs. The male doll wears a black peaked cap, red/white striped shirt, blue jacket, black trousers with silver buttons, clogs.

A cloth doll made in England by Farnell's Alpha Toys. She has a mask face, velvet skirt and hat, blue check blouse. (Courtesy S. McKay, New South Wales)

empires in Asia, Africa and the Americas. After a series of Anglo-Dutch naval wars, the Dutch surrendered their North American colony of New Amsterdam (later to become New York) to England in 1666. Instead of competing in the European power struggle, the Dutch retreated and made Amsterdam a major financial centre.

A French Revolutionary army overran the whole of the Low Countries in

A pair of composition dolls in traditional Dutch costume. (Private collection, Kempsey, New South Wales)

1794–95 causing the Dutch provinces to become the Batavian Republic (1795–1806), then a kingdom ruled by Napoleon's brother, and lastly a province of the French Empire.

In 1813 the Dutch reasserted their independence. Between 1815 and 1840 Ceylon, Cape Colony (South Africa) and half of Dutch Guiana were ceded to Britain, but the rest of the colonial empire in the Americas and East Indies was restored to The Netherlands.

The southern provinces (including the greater part of Luxembourg) declared their independence as Belgium in 1830 which was recognised by The Netherlands in 1839.

The Netherlands stayed neutral in World War I, but the country was overrun by the Germans in World War II, and the Dutch East Indies colonies were occupied by the Japanese.

After the war, the Dutch failed to re-establish colonial authority in the East Indies. In 1949 much of the area gained virtual independence as Indonesia, with the final links severed in 1956. Western New Guinea, which had remained under Dutch rule until placed under UN administration in 1962, was ceded to Indonesia to become Irian Jaya in 1963.

In 1954 Dutch Guiana (Surinam) and The Netherlands Antilles were granted internal autonomy leading to Surinam becoming a fully independent republic in 1975.

Capital Amsterdam.

Population (1990) 14.9 million, with 88.4 per cent living in urban areas. 99 per cent Dutch (German/Gallo/Celtic), 1 per cent Indonesian/Surinamese.

Religion Christianity. 40 per cent Roman Catholic, 30 per cent Protestant, 5 per cent atheist/agnostic.

Language Dutch is the official language. It is also the parent tongue of Afrikaans (South Africa).

New Caledonia (New Caledonia and Dependencies) Pacific Ocean

With a total area of some 19 000 square kilometres (7334 square miles), New Caledonia and Dependencies is a territory administered by France in the South Pacific Ocean 1750 kilometres (1087 miles) east of Australia.

Settled by the indigenous Kanak people as far back as 4000 BC, New Caledonia was first visited by European navigators, particularly the Spanish, in the sixteenth and seventeenth centuries; the islands were named by Captain Cook in 1774.

France annexed the territory in 1853, and by the end of the nineteenth century settlers owned 90 per cent of the land, to the extreme detriment of the diminishing Kanak population.

A black French celluloid doll wearing a red and white floral dress with white lace cuffs and blue ribbon trim on the bodice and hem.

The islands played a vital role as a headquarters for United States forces in the Pacific during World War II. By 1946 they had become a French Overseas Territory.

After years of dissension between the settlers and the Kanaks an accord was signed in 1988, dividing the territory into three administrative regions with elected regional assemblies (two under Kanak rule).

Capital Noumea.
Population 163 000 of which 43 per cent are Melanesian Kanaks, 37 per cent settlers of European descent, 10 per cent Polynesian.
Religion 70 per cent Roman Catholic, 16 per cent Protestant, 4 per cent Muslim.
Language French is the official language; there are also Melanesian-Polynesian dialects.

New Guinea See Papua New Guinea.

New Hebrides See Vanuatu.

New Zealand Pacific Ocean

Located in the South Pacific Ocean, New Zealand consists of two main islands (North and South) divided by Cook Strait, Stewart Island and a number of smaller islands. With a combined area of 269 057 square kilometres (103 856 square miles), New Zealand is divided into 13 statistical divisions, with meadow and pasture covering 63.9 per cent of the land area and 5.1 per cent forested. Associated territories of New Zealand are the Cook Islands, an autonomous South Pacific island group; also Niue, autonomous; the Ross Dependency in Antarctica; and Tokelu, an island dependency between Kiribati and Western Samoa.

Hard plastic dolls of the 1950s and 1960s dressed as Maoris.

A 1930s celluloid Maori doll wearing a coloured woven headband, hemp cloak (formerly feather cloak), green *tiki* (good luck amulet), skirt of painted string to represent the flax skirt, over a red underskirt. (Courtesy B. Cooper, New South Wales)

The early colonists of New Zealand came from eastern Polynesia (the vicinity of the Cook, Society and Marquesas Islands) around 800 AD.

A Dutch East India Company expedition led by Abel Tasman probably brought the first Europeans to New Zealand, reaching the South Island which Tasman named Staaten Island; later it was named Nieew Zeeland.

James Cook, in 1769, was the first European to land on the islands, and from the 1790s European sealers, whalers and traders made landfall. In 1814 missionaries (mainly from New South Wales) arrived, followed by the first permanent settlers in the 1830s.

Because of trouble between the settlers and the native Maoris, in 1828 New Zealand was named in a British Act 'as a place not under British Sovereignty'. Instead the state of New South Wales (Australia) was given the power to maintain order, extended in 1828 to cover British subjects in New Zealand.

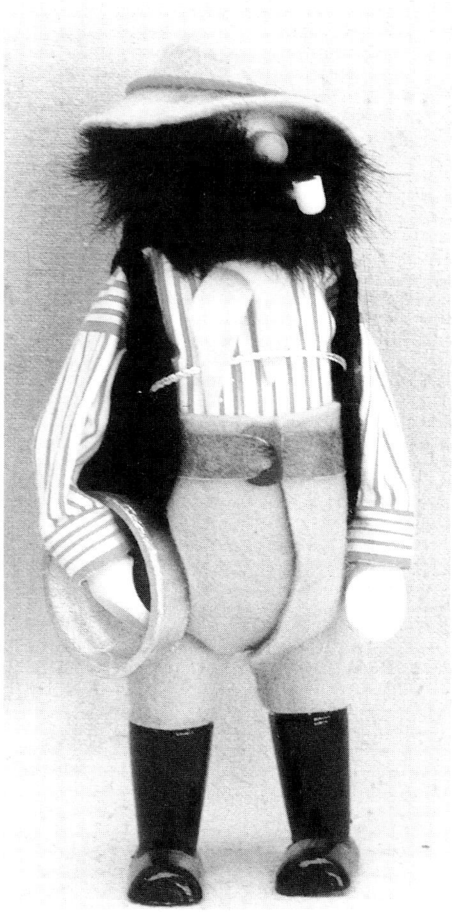

A 20-cm (8-inch) wooden doll representing a gold miner from South Island. He has a fawn hat with red band, bushy beard, pipe, yellow scarf, red/white shirt, black waistcoat, gold watch chain, brown leather belt, fawn trousers, black boots. He holds a gold panning dish in his hand.

Under the Treaty of Waitangi all rights and powers of sovereignty were ceded to Queen Victoria on 6 February 1840. For a number of compelling reasons, New Zealand became a British territory in May 1840, and was made a separate colony with Auckland as capital in 1841. Large tracts of land were bought from the Maoris by the increasing number of new settlers and by the end of the nineteenth century less than 20 per cent of the land was under Maori ownership.

Wellington was made the capital in 1865, and large groups of Scandinavian, English and Irish migrants arrived under special settlement schemes in the 1870s. New Zealand was the first country in the world to give women the vote in 1893. New Zealand became a Dominion under the British Crown in 1907; and in November 1926, along with Australia, Canada, South Africa and Newfound-

Beautifully modelled dolls made by a modern New Zealand doll artist. They wear the special Maori cloaks — these are waiting for their feathers, which will come, with special permission, from kiwis that have been killed on the roads by cars. (Courtesy Emily R. Schuster, New Zealand Maori Arts and Crafts Institute, Rotorua)

land, became a self-governing Dominion (with status equal to that of Britain) as a member of the British Commonwealth.

Full independence was achieved by the Statute of Westminster, adopted by the British parliament in 1931 and accepted by New Zealand in 1947.

Capital Wellington.

Population 3.3 million, with 83.7 per cent living in urban areas. 84.5 per cent are native-born New Zealanders, and of the foreign born 196 872 are British, 46 839 Australian, 24 159 Dutch, 33 864 Samoan, 15 540 Cook Islanders. In 1986 Maoris made up 9 per cent of the total population.

Religion 81 per cent Christian.

Language English is the official language; the indigenous Maori language is also spoken.

Nigeria (Federal Republic of) Africa

Situated on the Gulf of Guinea on the south coast of West Africa, Nigeria is divided into 19 states and a federal capital territory, with a total area of 923 770

Three wooden dolls carved in a light-weight wood, with painted features and decorations. They were made in eastern Nigeria by the Ibibio tribe. (Courtesy V. Bowen, Cairns)

square kilometres (365 575 square miles). Thirty-one per cent of the land is arable with 15 per cent forested.

Evidence of various stone-age cultures has been found throughout Nigeria. A civilisation known as Nok, which covered a large area of central Nigeria, flourished from 500 BC to 200 AD.

The history of the various regions of Nigeria differs greatly from one to another. The Hausa people in the north evolved a series of city states with fortified walls, which became important centres of Islam as well as commercial centres in the trans-Saharan trade in gold, slaves and cotton. During the seventeenth century the Oya kingdom in the northern part of the southwest started to expand, conquering other Yoruba states, and by the end of the eighteenth century was the dominant power in Yorubaland. On the Niger Delta the states were mainly fishing communities, who with the development of Atlantic trade controlled trading networks extending far into the interior.

Nigeria's first contact with Europeans was with Portuguese traders in the fifteenth century, with the Gulf of Guinea becoming a major centre for the slave trade. After the abolition of this trade, British merchants established a firm presence around Lagos in Southern Yorubaland and along the Niger Delta, with formal colonisation beginning with

Hard-plastic dolls. The female doll wears a tan turban with black braid trim, long tan jacket trimmed in black and a tan skirt with black band. She wears a gold bead necklace around her neck and carries a black bag. The male doll wears a tan turban-like head-dress with black trim, tan gown with very long wide sleeves trimmed with black bands. (Courtesy J. Miller, New South Wales)

the annexation of Lagos in 1861. The Royal Niger Company, who feared French domination, were the main impetus for colonisation and in 1885 the company was given responsibility for government along the Niger and Benue Rivers. Their charter to govern was later revoked and in 1900 the British protectorate of Northern Nigeria was established. The colony of Lagos was incorporated into the newly formed protectorate of Southern Nigeria, with the two protectorates joined together in 1914 to form the colony of Nigeria.

In 1954 the constitution established a loose federal system of government and a timetable for independence, which came into force on 1 October 1960. The British-administered UN trust territory of the Cameroons was incorporated into Nigeria in June 1961.

Capital Lagos.

Population (1990) 118.8 million, with 16.1 per cent living in urban areas. Of the 250 or so ethnic groups, the Hausa and Fulani (north), Yoruba (southwest) and Ibo (southeast) constitute 65 per cent of the total population.

Religion 50 per cent Muslim, 40 per cent Christian; 10 per cent practise indigenous animist faiths.

Language English is the official language, although the African language Hausa is the most widely spoken.

Northern Ireland (Ulster) Europe

Part of the United Kingdom, Northern Ireland occupies the northeastern section of Ireland, an area of 13 404 square kilometres (5236 square miles). The rest of the island constitutes the Republic of Ireland (Eire).

For the early history of this area, look under 'Ireland'.

When Ireland separated into two regions in 1925, with the southern part becoming the Irish Free State (now the Republic of Ireland), the northern counties of Antrim, Armagh, Down, Fermanagh, Londonderry and Tyrone voted to stay part of the United Kingdom and became known as Northern Ireland or Ulster.

Over the years, Northern Ireland has been continually beset with internal problems, mainly resulting from Irish Republican Army (IRA) incursions into Northern Ireland, although some parts of Northern Ireland are also in favour of the unification of Ireland.

Capital Belfast.
Population 1.5 million.

'Irish Country Dancers', resin (plastic) dolls by Peggy Nisbet, England. The male doll has a white lace jabot, green jacket, mustard yellow plaid and kilt, painted stockings and shoes. The female doll wears a green dress with braid decoration, green cape with mustard yellow lining.

An antique, bisque-headed doll by Simon & Halbig, made in Germany. She is wearing her original clothes, depicting the Hardanger area of Norway: red hat with green ribbon and white bead trim, white blouse with broderie anglaise cuffs, red vest with green trim and embroidered infill, black skirt, white apron with broderie anglaise trim — a lovely old original outfit. (Courtesy Joyce Ross, Queensland)

A 20-cm (8-inch) cloth doll with wrist tag reading 'Made in Norway by Ronnaig Petersen', circa the late 1930s. The doll has a red scarf over blonde hair, white blouse, red embroidered vest, red mittens, navy trousers, red socks, black shoes. She holds a pair of ski poles.

Norway (Kingdom of) Europe

With an area of 324 220 square kilometres (125 149 square miles), divided into 19 counties *(fylker)*, Norway occupies the western portion of the Scandinavian Peninsula. Only a small proportion of the land is arable, mainly in the lakeside/fiord valleys, and 27 per cent is forested.

Settlement of present-day Norway dates back over 10 000 years. Germanic tribes first settled in the early centuries BC, establishing numerous small kingdoms that were unified around 900 AD. Christianity was introduced in the ninth century.

Between 800 and 1100 Norwegians participated in the Viking expansion and

Yarn dolls (4 cm, 1.5 inches) bought from the Norwegian Folk Museum, Oslo, in 1976. *Left couple* 'Telemark'. The woman has blonde hair, white blouse, red jacket (laced), coloured waist sash, black skirt with embroidered design, red stockings, black shoes. The man has a black hat, white shirt, black vest, black breeches with tassels at the knees, white socks, black shoes. *Right couple* 'Ramsdal'. The woman has blonde hair, white blouse, red vest with embroidery trim, blue skirt with embroidered band, white apron, red purse, red stockings, black shoes. The man has a black hat, white shirt, red waistcoat, black breeches, white socks, black shoes.

A late nineteenth-century antique doll dressed to represent a Hardanger bride.

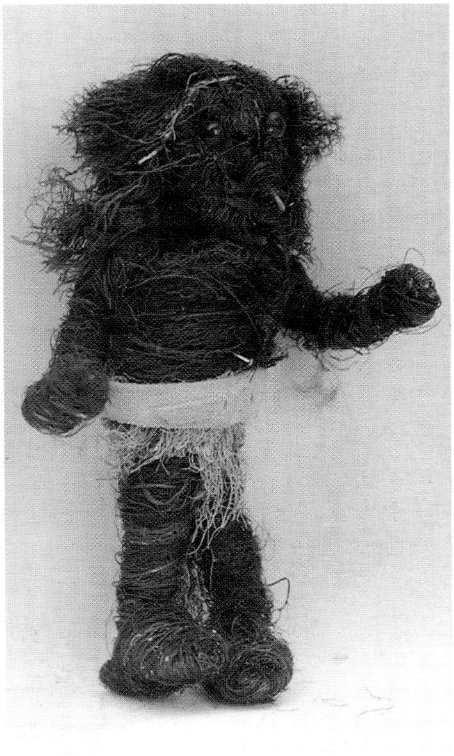

'Hulder', 11.5 cm (4.5 inches), a mythical figure. 'Hulders were daughters of mountain trolls who could change themselves into beautiful maidens but could never hide or disguise their ugly tails.' Made of sisal over a wire armature, the doll has sisal hair, glass eyes, a long sisal nose, red embroidered mouth, sash with short skirt, long plaited tail at the back.

'Setesdal', yarn dolls (4 cm, 1.75 inches) bought in Oslo in 1976. The woman wears a black hat, white blouse, black tunic with green/red/white trim, black stockings and shoes. The man wears a black hat, white shirt, black waistcoat with green/red trim, black breeches with green trim, white stockings, black shoes.

conquest of Normandy, Ireland, Greenland and parts of Britain, even reaching as far west as North America.

The Norwegian and Swedish crowns were united in 1343, and in 1380 both Norway and Sweden came under the Danish crown. Although Sweden became independent in 1523, Norway remained a Danish province for four centuries. Denmark's influence was strengthened with the adoption of absolute monarchy in 1660.

In 1624 when medieval Oslo was destroyed by fire, the new city of Christiania was made the capital.

Sweden had ambitions concerning Norway, but these were not achieved until Norway was transferred to the Swedish crown in 1814 after the defeat of Napoleon. The Norwegians rebelled, resulting in a Swedish invasion, but a compromise was achieved, allowing Norway to retain its own parliament and some autonomy under Swedish sovereignty. Nationalism became a dominant force in the nineteenth century, and in 1905 Sweden formally agreed to the separation of Norway.

Remaining neutral during World War I, Norway enjoyed an economic boom. In 1925 the capital Christiania reverted to its old name Oslo. With other Scandinavian countries, Norway declared itself neutral at the beginning of World War II, but was overrun by Germany in 1940.

After the war, as a result of territorial changes, Norway acquired a northern border with Russia, so it abandoned neutrality, joining NATO in 1949. The country's economy was strengthened from the 1970s with the discovery of off-shore gas and oil.

Capital Oslo.

Population (1990) 4.2 million, with 74 per cent living in urban areas. 97 per cent of Germanic (Nordic, Alpine, Baltic) origin, with 20 000 Sami/Lapps living in the extreme north.

Religion Christianity, 94 per cent belonging to the Evangelical Lutheran Norwegian State Church.

Language Norwegian. Two forms are officially recognised: Bokmal, the more urban Dano-Norwegian language, and Nynorski (New Norwegian) taught in 16–20 per cent of schools. There are also small Lappish and Finnish-speaking minorities in the far north.

Pakistan (Islamic Republic of) Asia

Situated in the northwest of the Indian subcontinent, Pakistan is divided into four provinces and a federal capital territory, with a total area of 803 940 square kilometres (310 321 square miles). Twenty-six per cent of the land is arable, with the help of the largest irrigation system in the world (13 million hectares, 32 million acres); 4 per cent is forest or woodland.

What is now Pakistan has been inhabited for centuries, with an expansion of agricultural settlements around 3500 BC, culminating in the Indus civilisation around 2500 BC.

The Indo-Ayrans (semi-nomadic pastoral tribes) who arrived from the west were in sharp contrast to the urban culture of the Indus (Harrapans). Tribal identities made way for territorial ones, and independent kingdoms of various sizes. By 710–16 AD Sind and southern Punjab had been conquered and Islamic law introduced; by 1026 Muslim power had spread to all parts of northwest India, Bihar and to Bengal in the east.

A 25.5-cm (10-inch) cloth doll wearing a red head-scarf trimmed with gold fringe, long blue bodice with gold braid trim, red skirt with blue hem ruffle trimmed gold. (Courtesy Vera Woodhead, Queensland)

This 25.5-cm (10-inch) cloth doll wears a sheer mauve veil over black hair tied at the nape, divided and tied again; silver earrings, necklace, bangles and ring; a long mauve top with side splits and gold braid trim; full mauve trousers with wide frills and gold trim.

A 19-cm (7.5-inch) cloth doll with 'GAKARA' on the base. She has black hair in a single plait, a blue headscarf with gold edge, gold neck circlet, long blue jacket with gold trim at the front, blue/gold gathered trousers, gold shoes.

A 23-cm (9-inch) clay and cloth doll with 'Pakistan' and 'SWATI' on the base. She wears a silver pillbox hat over a black figured shawl with orange edging, long matching top, with orange lace yoke, black trousers with orange trim, red shoes. She also wears a chunky necklace and earrings.

A 26.5-cm (10.5-inch) cloth doll wearing a red headscarf with gold border, gold filigree necklace, gold loop earrings, long red blouse with gold trim, pleated red skirt with gold trim. The skirt is lined with Pakistani newspaper to give it body and thickness.

Sind was annexed in 1842, followed by the Punjab in 1849, as Britain expanded via the East India Company. After the mutiny of 1857, the Company ceded governmental power to the British crown.

Then during the 1930s and early 1940s demands increased for the establishment of a separate Muslim state where Muslims were a numerical majority. Partition of India and Pakistan took place on 14 August 1947, and the Indian Empire ceased to exist when power was trans-

Hunza A northern area of Pakistan. The doll wears a sheer veil over her head, yellow blouse with blue braid trim at the neck, front, cuffs and hem. Around her neck she wears a large brass medallion. She has baggy black pants and black shoes.

ferred to the two new dominions by Britain.

Pakistan was declared an Islamic republic in 1956. In 1971 the reluctance of West Pakistan to accept an East Pakistan-dominated government ended in civil war and war with India. This resulted in the separation of East Pakistan from the western part of the country and eventually the emergence of a new state — Bangladesh.

A new constitution in 1973 set up a parliamentary system with power divided between central government and the provinces. Pakistan left the Commonwealth in 1972 over Bangladesh's membership, but was readmitted in October 1989.

Capital Karachi.

Population (1990) 114.6 million, with 29.8 per cent living in urban areas. 66 per cent Punjabi, plus Sindhi, Pasthan (Pathan), Baluch and Muhajir, and over 3 million Afghan refugees.

Religion 97 per cent Muslim (77 per cent Sunni and 20 per cent Shi'ite), with the remaining 3 per cent Christian, Hindu, Parsee and Buddhist minorities.

Language Urdu and English are the official languages, but 64 per cent speak Punjabi, 12 per cent Sindhi, 8 per cent Pashto, 7 per cent Urdu, 1 per cent Baluchi and Brahvi.

Palestine Middle East

Originally the name of Palestine referred to the biblical land of that name and the Roman state that followed. The Arabs that lived there were called Palestinians. The descendants of these people who were dispossessed by the creation of Israel in 1948 still refer to themselves as Palestinians, a word which is now as much a political definition as a cultural or ethnic one.

Today there is no Palestinian state although approximately 4 million people who call themselves Palestinians live either within the borders of historical Palestine or throughout the Middle East and in other countries. Approximately 50 per cent of the population of Jordan is Palestinian; there are 700 000 Israeli Arabs within Israel itself and some 1.6 million Palestinians live under Israeli rule in occupied territories.

Carrying the ethnic past of both Philistine and Jew, as well as the invaders of the land (Persian, Crusader and Turk), today's Palestinians are mostly Arabs, whose ancestors gave them not only their language (Arabic) but also their religion (Islam). About 10 per cent are Christian.

The land of Palestine was ruled for over four centuries (1517–1918) by the Ottoman Turks who allowed the Palestinians only a very limited autonomy. Palestine became a British mandate after the Ottoman defeat in World War I and remained as such until after World War II and the creation of Israel. About 780 000 Palestinians left Israel during the Israeli War of Independence (1948–49). Hundreds of thousands of Palestinians have lived, been born and raised in refugee camps over the last 40 years. In 1994 parts of the Occupied Territories were returned to Palestinian control.

Both dolls are tagged: 'Hand made product of THE HOLY LAND BETHLEHEM'. These 16.5-cm (6.5-inch) dolls have wooden bodies and clay heads and are dressed in the traditional costume of what was Palestine. The woman wears a tall red conical hat *(tarboose)* with gold decoration, covered by a white veil head-dress (denoting a married woman); black embroidered blouse, teal blue velvet waistcoat with gold/black trim, coiled and padded red/white waistband, red skirt with wide black inserts back and front and embroidery trim. The man wears a white head-dress *(kaffiyah)* with *angal* of black yarn, long brown/black striped gown with wide waistband and black overrobe *(aba)*.

Panama (Republic of) Central America

With an area of 78 200 square kilometres (30 185 square miles), Panama occupies the southern end of the isthmus linking North and South America. The country is bisected by the 67.5 kilometre (42 mile) long man-made Panama Canal that connects the Atlantic Ocean to the Pacific. Six per cent of the land is arable and 54 per cent covered with rainforest.

The early Indian tribes of the area, the Guaymis and Cunas, never reached the sophistication of the Mayans, Aztecs or Incas. Panama was the seat of government for the Spanish colonial system, which stretched as far south as Peru. When Panama gained independence from Spain in 1821, it was incorporated into Gran Colombia between 1821 and 1830.

The building of a canal was first suggested in the sixteenth century to enable Peruvian mineral wealth to be shipped to Spain, but it wasn't until the Americans raised the idea in the late 1800s that the Panama Canal was built and eventually completed in 1914. The Canal Treaty of 1903 gave the United States sovereign rights in the Canal Zone for $10 million, an arrangement revised in 1936 and 1955.

An 18.5-cm (7.25-inch) plastic doll with black hair in two richly ornamented plaits. She wears an off-the-shoulder blouse with full lilac cape collar edged in braid and lace and a blue pompon at the neckline; full lilac skirt with blue waist sash and bow, and braid and lace trim; gold necklace and earrings.

All elections in Panama between 1908 and 1928 were supervised by the United States.

Two new canal treaties were negotiated with the United States between 1968 and 1981, abolishing the Canal Zone and preparing for the transfer of the Canal to Panamanian jurisdiction by the year 2000.
Capital Panama City.
Population (1990) 2.4 million, with 52.2 per cent living in urban areas. 70 per cent of the population are mestizo (Indian/European ancestry), 14 per cent West Indian, 10 per cent white, 6 per cent Indian.
Religion Christianity: over 93 per cent Roman Catholic, 6 per cent Protestant.
Language Spanish is the official language, but 14 per cent speak English.

Papua New Guinea South Pacific

Situated off the northeastern tip of Australia, Papua New Guinea occupies half of a large island, the other half of which is Irian Jaya, part of Indonesia. Papua New Guinea also encompasses the Solomon Islands (Bougainville and Buka), the Bismarck Archipelago (New Britain, New Ireland and Manus) and approximately 600 smaller islands, with a total area of 461 691 square kilometres (178 212 square miles).

A 30.5-cm (12-inch) doll of carved wood, circa 1920. She wears a grass skirt. (Courtesy Jan Jones, Tasmania)

First inhabited by settlers from Asia approximately 50 000 years ago, the island's first European contact with the arrival of Spanish and Portuguese sailors and explorers in the 1500s. Between 1526 and 1527 the island was given the name Ilhas dos Papuas (from a Malay word meaning 'frizzy hair'), and New Guinea by a Spaniard who thought the people were similar to those of Guinea on the African coast.

A pair of dolls especially made by Metti/Netta Australia to be dressed in Papua New Guinea representing one of many tribal costumes. The man wears a multicoloured head-dress with shell front band, shell decoration over the torso, woven wrist and knee bands, fibre front piece. The woman has a shell headband, and long woven bag *(billum)* that drapes down her back. She wears shell decoration, and woven bands on the arms and legs, similar to those of the man.

Two Australian-made dolls 'by Moldex (Melbourne) Pedigree, a division of Lines Bros' (1960s). They were sold in Papua New Guinea and dressed in national costume.

Dutch, English and French explorers quickly followed. Seeking to protect their East Indies empire, in 1828 the Dutch formalised their long standing claim over the western portion of the island. Germany formally took possession of the northern part of the territory in November

Vinyl dolls specially manufactured in Australia by Metti/Netta for sale to Papua New Guinea where they were dressed to represent the various highland tribes, often to raise money for charities like the Red Cross or Scouts.

1884, followed three days later by Britain (pressured into the move by the Australian colonies) which declared a protectorate over the southern portion of the island. This southern section was annexed outright by Britain in 1888.

British New Guinea became the Territory of Papua in 1906 and was formally transferred to the new Commonwealth of Australia. Australia also took over control of German New Guinea at the outbreak of World War I, and the country became a mandated trustee territory in 1920. The whole of the mandated Territory of New Guinea and the Territory of Papua were embroiled when Japan invaded the island in 1942.

After the war the eastern half of New Guinea reverted to a single colony under Australian control, and was known as the Territory of Papua and New Guinea. The first Legislative Council for the combined territories was inaugurated in 1951.

Indonesia took control of Dutch New Guinea in 1963, and this territory became part of Indonesia as Irian Jaya.

Selfgovernment for Papua New Guinea was achieved in December 1973 and the country achieved full independence on 16 September 1975.

Capital Port Moresby.

Population (1990) 4 million with 14.3 per cent living in urban areas. The country is peopled by two principal groups: Papuans (over 80 per cent) who dominate the mainland interior and south coast, and Melanesians (less than 15 per cent) who populate the northern and eastern regions and many of the islands. 33 000 non-indigenous inhabitants include 17 000 Australians.

Religion (1980) 64 per cent Protestant, 33 per cent Roman Catholic, with widespread traditional rituals.

Language Motu is the official parliamentary language. English is spoken by 2 per cent of the population. There are approximately 750 indigenous languages, including 'Pidgin' which is spoken by over 1 million.

Persia See Iran.

Peru (Republic of) South America

With an area of 1 285 220 square kilometres (496 095 square miles) divided into 24 departments, Peru is situated on the northwest coast of South America. Lake

A 6-cm (2.5-inch) sitting doll of clay and thread-covered wire representing a weaver. The doll wears two long plaits, a red hat with black top, handwoven orange shawl, woven purple skirt with woven braid trim. She is weaving on a simple handloom.

Dolls of clay and cloth (25.5 cm, 10 inches). The woman wears a wide-brimmed flat hat, floral on top, red underneath, long red cloak with green trim falling from her head to the hem of her skirt. She has two plaits worn to the front, a white blouse, brown jacket with green/white trim, green handwoven skirt with braid and embroidery trim. She carries a small cloth bundle. The man wears a black hat with red underside over a red-painted helmet-shaped cap, white shirt, fawn waistcoat, grey jacket, red handwoven *serape*, black trousers and sandals.

Paper dolls (4.5 cm, 1.75 inches) from the 1970s. Both dolls are made from paper wound around wire, and then fully dressed in paper clothing. They came in their little perspex boxes. The man has a yellow hat, red hair, white shirt, black belt, red trousers. He is holding a twisted paper rope. The woman has an orange hat with turned-back brim edged with paper cord, black hair, white blouse, short black cape, green waistband, orange skirt with black/white trim. She holds a paper lei.

Dolls with clay heads and wire armatures covered with wool (12 cm, 4.75 inches). The woman wears a red hat with turned-up brim, black on top, blue trim. She has two black plaits; a woven shawl over a white blouse; dark purple woven skirt with red/yellow braces, wool trim and woven brocade border. She holds a spinning distaff. The man wears a red hat with orange trim, black on top. He has painted red helmet cap, white shirt, wide straight-sided woven cloak caught at the underarm, dark grey trousers with red decoration. He carries a load of fine sticks on his back and a wooden flute in his hand.

Titicaca, the world's highest navigable body of water (3812 metres, 12 507 ft) above sea level, is situated in the south of Peru near the Bolivian border. Three per cent of the land is arable and 55 per cent forested.

Humans are known to have lived in Peru from about 8000 BC, with advanced cultures starting up around 1250 BC. The Incas were much later with their 13 emperors dating from around 1200 AD until 1533, when the emperor of the time was captured and executed by the Spanish. A dynasty which had once ruled from present-day Colombia to central Chile came to an end when the last Inca leader was beheaded in 1572.

After more than two years of civil war between the Spanish authorities and the conquistadors, Spanish rule was fully restored in 1569. Because of the massive mineral wealth gained from the silver mines, Peru emerged as the most powerful of the Spanish viceroyalties and Lima was established as a cultural and commercial centre.

With colonial reform in the eighteenth century, Peru lost Ecuador, Venezuela and Colombia to the Viceroyalty of New Granada, and between 1779 and 1810 Peru also lost the territory of Upper Peru with all its mineral wealth to the viceroyalty of Rio de Plata.

While its neighbours proclaimed their independence from Spain, Peru remained loyal until 1824, when it became independent. A liberal constitution was passed in 1828, but sporadic fighting over territorial rights between Peru and both Bolivia and Ecuador in the 1840s took their toll. However, guano (a first-class fertiliser) found in abundance in the coastal region boosted the country's economy, Peru trading first with France and later with Britain. The country has been in a state of political turmoil for most of the twentieth century.

Capital Lima.

Population 22 million, with 70.2 per cent living in urban areas. 45 per cent of the population are South American Indians, 37 per cent mestizo, 15 per cent white, 3 per cent Chinese, black or Japanese.

Religion 90 per cent Roman Catholic.

Language Spanish (spoken by 65 per cent) and Quechua (27 per cent) are both official languages, while 3 per cent speak Aymara.

Philippines (Republic of the) Asia

Situated 800 kilometres (497 miles) off the coast of mainland Asia, in the west Pacific Ocean, the Philippines archipelago consists of 7107 separate islands with a total area of approximately 300 000 square kilometres (115 800 square miles). The two largest islands are Luzon to the north (which includes the capital Manila) and Mindanao in the south. Twenty per cent of the land is arable and 40 per cent is forested.

Prior to Ferdinand Magellan's voyage to the archipelago in 1521, each island had a separate identity, but in the century afterwards Spain increased its control on the islands. This was due mainly to their important position on the trade route between Latin America and the Far East. Islam had been adopted in the southern islands a century or so before the arrival of the Spanish who introduced Christianity to the northern islands.

Plantations were established during the

Clay and wire dolls (23 cm, 9 inches) representing farmers. The woman has black hair rolled into a bun at the back, black/red/white dress, yellow sash, apron with black trim. She carries a woven basket. The man wears a red hat, floral shirt, black trousers and sandals. He once had a hoe in his right hand.

Cloth dolls with painted faces from the 1930s and 40s (28 cm, 11 inches). *Left* An authentic replica of the costume of a **Moro** man — an upper-class Muslim living in the southern islands of the Philippines. He wears a purple check scarf, mauve shirt, black trousers open at the ankles, medallion trimmed and laced. The Moro are reputed to be fierce fighters. *Middle and right* **Tagalog** people wearing authentic replica costume called *Balintawak*. The Tagalog are found mostly in Central Luzon and around Manila. The woman wears a large woven cane hat, bead necklace, sheer red blouse, scarf over her shoulder, two-tiered red/white skirt, wrap-around brown/white short skirt, white undies, maroon sandals with wooden soles and heels and red trim. The man wears a straw hat with turned-up brim, cotton singlet, sheer striped long shirt of pineapple cloth, striped trousers, mustard sandals.

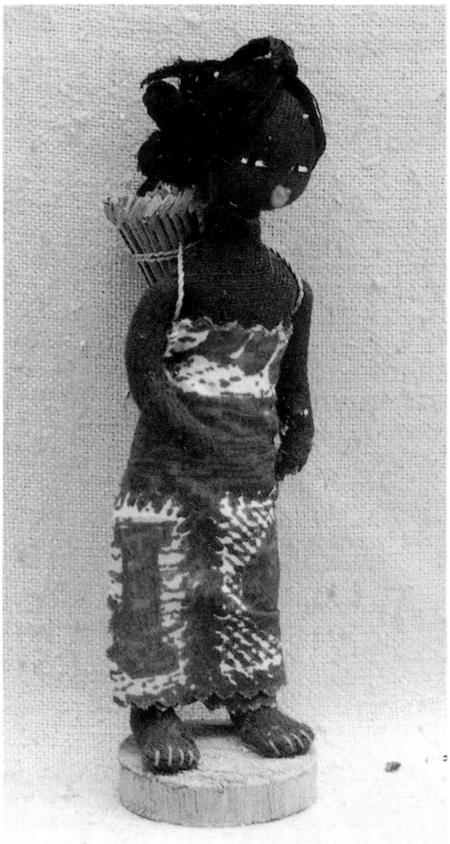

A brown cloth doll representing a woman of the Philippines **Benquet**, a mountain tribe near Baguio. She wears a multicoloured sarong-like dress and carries a bundle of sticks on her back.

Cloth dolls (19 cm, 7.5 inches) depicting the **Igorots**. The man wears a red band, red loin cloth with a short sword in the waistband. He has yarn hair and painted features. The woman wears a red headband, yellow blouse, woven skirt and carries a woven cane basket. She has yarn hair, painted features.

From left to right A female cloth and plastic doll (16.5 cm, 6.5 inches) wearing a white dress, white shawl with red trim, silver necklace, lace-trimmed tiered skirt. A 15-cm (6-inch) male doll of cloth and wire wearing a coloured overshirt, red bow, blue trousers, red sandals. 'Assandas Makati'. A 28-cm (11-inch) female doll wearing pearl jewellery, a white blouse, pink shawl, pink skirt. A 22-cm (8.75-inch) female doll wearing a straw hat over a red headscarf, necklace, green floral bodice, green/yellow scarf over her shoulder and around her waist, floral skirt. She carries a flat basket. A 20-cm (8-inch) female cloth doll wearing gold jewellery, a white blouse and shawl, pink tiered skirt with white lace trim.

eighteenth century and with the introduction of steam power in the nineteenth century the Philippines became a large sugar producer. As the colonial influence of Spain declined, better economic development eventually led to an independence movement by the end of the nineteenth century. During the Spanish-American War of 1898 United States forces occupied the Spanish colony, with the colony being formally ceded to the United States by the Treaty of Paris. Although significant concessions were given towards selfgovernment, the pressure for full independence continued and in November 1935 the Commonwealth of the Philippines was established.

Japan captured the Philippine Islands in 1941, and under Japanese urging, the territory was declared independent in October 1943. The Philippines were liberated in 1945 and the Republic of the Philippines was proclaimed as an independent sovereign state in April 1946.

A 1930s clay doll wearing a green dress with cape collar, sheer dark green apron with flower trim. (Courtesy Mary Judge, Townsville)

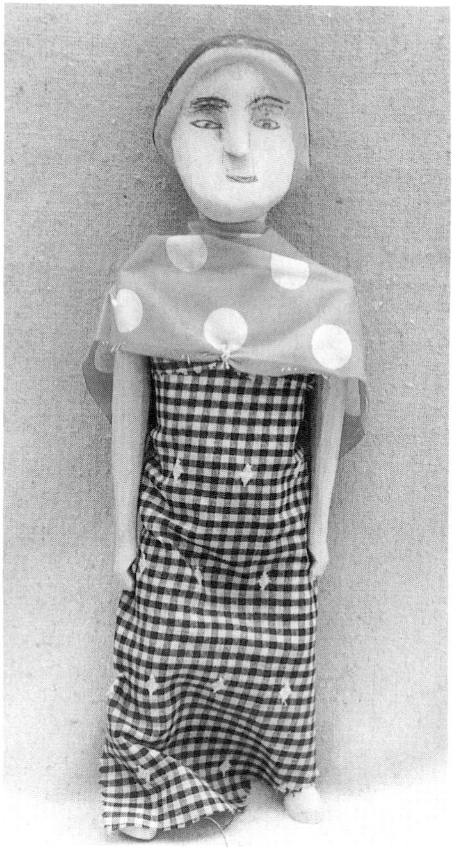

This simple 30.5-cm (12-inch) wooden doll carved from very light wood, has its head and body carved as one piece; the arms and legs were made separately and joined on. The hair and features are painted/drawn in black. The doll wears a simple pink/white polkadot shawl over a navy/white check dress.

Typical wooden Polish play dolls in simple costume. The woman has a pleated cap with red band and red streamers, white blouse, white skirt with pink trim, pink apron, dark blue waistcoat. The man has a black brimmed hat with striped headband and feather trim, white shirt with red stitching, tan waistcoat, red trousers, brown shoes. He has 'WARSAW' on a ticket at the back.

Capital Manila.
Population (1990) 66.1 million, with 41 per cent living in urban areas. The Filipinos, because of the country's history, are of Malay origin, with Chinese, United States and Spanish influences.
Religion 83 per cent Roman Catholic, 9 per cent Protestant, 5 per cent Muslim, 3 per cent Buddhist.
Language The national language is Filipino (from the Malay dialect Tagalog), with English the other official language. Over 87 languages are indigenous to the Philippines.

Pitcairn Island Pacific Ocean

Situated in the South Pacific, the British Crown Colony of the Pitcairn Islands has an area of 27 square kilometres (10 square miles).

Originally settled by Polynesians, the small, rather isolated island gained notoriety in 1790 with the mutiny against Captain Bligh of the HMS *Bounty*. Some of the mutineers stayed on the island and it is their descendants who now people the island. Pitcairn Island is one of the last British colonies left.
Capital Adamstown.
Population 60.

Poland (Polish Republic) Europe

Situated in northern Central Europe, Poland has borders with Germany, the Czech Republic, Slovakia, Ukraine, Belarus and Lithuania. It has an area of 312 680 square kilometres (120 694 square miles) of which 50 per cent is arable land and 29 per cent forested.

Around 400 BC Celtic tribes arrived in what is present-day Poland, in the footsteps of a Neolithic culture which began around the fourth millennium BC.

Wooden nesting dolls. The largest doll is 9 cm (3.5 inches) tall. Each doll is hollow, cut in half to enable another doll to nest inside. Each has black painted hair, red babushka, black/red trim, over varnish.

In the first century AD Germanic tribes moved into the area, to be followed by the Huns and Avars who overran the country in the fifth and sixth centuries. Slavs settled there in the seventh and eighth centuries and by 966 Christianity had been introduced; the first king was crowned in 992. Poland fragmented as rival branches of the dynasty fought for supremacy from 1138.

Through marriage, a dual Polish-Lithuanian realm was created in 1386. Then a commonwealth (or 'republic') was

Left The male doll wears a red hat with red/black brim and red ribbons at the side; white shirt; long black waistcoat with red edging, small green tassels and gold buttons; brown belt; red/white trousers; black boots. *Centre* The doll wears a brown hat with russet trim, russet-brown cape, fawn jacket, brown belt with gold trim, white trousers with red/green embroidery, brown shoes. *Right* The male doll has a blue cap, white shirt, long grey coat with black trim, grey trousers, black boots.

Clay and wire dolls (17.75 cm, 7 inches). *Man* 'KRAKOW Doll in Polish Regional Dress' (under base). He wears a blue four-cornered hat with grey brim, white shirt, red tie, black waistcoat, black breeches, black boots; dark brown coat with blue lapels and cuffs, red trim and sash. *Woman* She wears a cap with silver crown and white finely pleated brim, white bow at the back and under the chin; maroon jacket with blue trim on the bodice and at the cuffs; gathered maroon skirt with finely pleated band at the hem and blue decoration; black boots. Marked 'WARMIA Doll in Polish Regional Dress' (under base).

The 23-cm (9-inch) man/horse represents the Polish king and his entourage who disguised themselves as horsemen to outwit Mongol invaders, an exploit commemorated in the annual Pageant of Lajkonik. The doll has a green conical hat, black beard, yellow jacket, green sleeves, stylised horse. The two small dolls are labelled 'SPOLDZ ZRZESZENIE CHAULUPIN — WARSZAWE'. The 12.75-cm (5-inch) man is painted with a brown hat, white shirt, brown cummerbund, white trousers, and decorated. The woman is painted with a green scarf, lace cap, white blouse, fancy black waistcoat, green floral skirt, white apron, red leggings.

A wooden doll wearing a black hat, white shirt, red tie, black waistcoat with red belt, multi-striped trousers, black boots.

A cloth doll with mask face, marked 'LOWICZ'. She wears a floral headpiece over two plaits, white blouse with lace trim, bead necklace, green waistcoat, grey skirt with red trim, red apron with green/pink/gold edging.

Two traditional men's costumes. *Left* The doll wears a black hat, long black jacket with red/brown cord edging, blue blouse, white trousers, black boots. *Right* The doll wears a black hat, long cream coat with red cape collar, blue jacket with bead trim and corded edge, white trousers, black boots.

A wooden doll wearing a red hat with black band and feather, white shirt, red tie, blue waistcoat, black belt, red/white trousers, red boots.

The man has a black hat with red/white band and feather, white shirt, wide black waistband with silver decoration, cream trousers with black embroidery; heavy cream jacket with green trim, red/yellow embroidery trim and red bow. The woman on the right has a blond plait coiled around her head, red bead necklace, white blouse with lace cuffs and collar, embroidered waistcoat, lemon floral shawl with fringed border, maroon skirt with purple bow, white knee-length knit stockings, beige shoes. The small cloth doll has blond plaits, a white blouse, black vest, embroidered red bow, green skirt, brown shoes.

A celluloid doll wearing a red scarf, white blouse, black waistcoat, with red trim, multi-coloured skirt and apron with green/white black trim.

effected in 1569 and at its zenith was the largest nation in Europe, stretching to the Black Sea. Gradually declining from 1572, Poland-Lithuania became a Russian protectorate in 1717, but was split amongst Russia, Prussia and Austria between 1772 and 1795, literally wiping the country off the political map.

Reincarnated as the Duchy of Warsaw during the Napoleonic Wars (1807–13), Poland was annexed by Russia after the French defeat. The Congress Kingdom of Poland was established as an autonomous government within the Russian Empire in 1815, only to be dissolved in 1864 as Russia adopted policies to suppress Polish culture. Similar suppression was also instituted in the Prussian (German) section in the 1870s.

Poland re-emerged at the end of 1918 as an independent country, with the Treaty of Versailles (1919) fixing the frontiers with Germany, but this was not done with Russia. A parliamentary democracy was established in March 1921.

However, the country was invaded by Germany in September 1939, and the leaders of Britain and the United States, without consulting the Poles, agreed to Russia's territorial claims to eastern Poland. At the end of the war Poland was compensated with former German territory to the west. This was recognised by the German Democratic Republic in 1950 and the Federal Republic of Germany in 1970. Even then Poland was only approximately half the size it was before World War II.

From 1947 Poland was under Soviet rule, until in August 1989 the first non-communist prime minister in the Eastern bloc was elected. The country's name was changed to the Polish Republic at the end of 1989.

Capital Warszawa (Warsaw).
Population (1990) 37.8 million, with 60.2 per cent living in urban areas. 98.7 per cent of the population is Polish, 0.6 per cent Ukrainian, 0.5 per cent Belarus, and less than 0.5 per cent Jewish.
Religion 95 per cent are Roman Catholic.
Language Polish.

Portugal (Portuguese Republic) Europe

With an area of 88 880 square kilometres (34 308 square miles), Portugal occupies the western half of the Iberian Peninsula. The Azores and Madeira Islands, two semi-autonomous archipelagos in the Atlantic, belong to Portugal, as does the territory of Macao, a Portuguese enclave on the coast of China (which is to be returned to China in 1999). Thirty-two per cent of the land surface is arable and 40 per cent is forested.

When the ancient Lusitanians came under Roman rule in the second century BC, they had already absorbed invasions of Celts and Phoenicians. Germanic tribes moved into the area in 410 AD, and these in turn were conquered and Christianised by the Visigoths in 585. Then followed a period of Muslim Moorish rule by caliphs in the 700s, eventually disrupted by Viking raids which weakened Moorish authority. Portugal became Christian once again.

Portugal became independent in 1128 after defeating the Moors. During the 1300s it entered an age of discovery and expansion, and from the middle of the 1400s had a vast empire reaching from Africa and India to the Far East and the Americas. Brazil was claimed by Portugal in 1500, and the Moluccas (now part of Indonesia) in 1529.

Portugal was seized by Spain in 1580

Hard plastic dolls (16 cm, 6.25 inches). The man is labelled 'HOMEM DA MADEIRA PORTUGAL'. He wears a blue cap with red triangles at the sides and long blue tassel, white shirt, white waist sash and breeches. A red sash over his shoulder holds a gourd. The woman is labelled 'MULHER DA MADEIRA PORTUGAL'. She wears a blue hat with red triangles at the sides and blue tassel, small lace cap on top of black hair in a bun, white blouse with collar and front trim, red waistcoat with yellow lacing, red shawl with yellow trim, red skirt with yellow/green/white/ blue stripes and yellow hem trim, leather boots. She carries a bouquet of flowers.

Both dolls are 16 cm (6.25 inches), hard plastic. The man is labelled on the base 'ESTUDANTE DE COIMBRA PORTUGAL'. He wears a black hat drooped to the left, white shirt, black tie, black jacket with long black cape attached, black trousers and shoes. He carries a black leather satchel with red ribbons at each end. The woman is labelled 'TRICANA DE COIMBRA PORTUGAL'. She wears a white headscarf tied and gathered at the nape, white blouse with lace trim, black fringed shawl slung over her right shoulder, black skirt, white apron with lace trim, white painted stockings, black shoes. She carries a terracotta jar.

Cloth dolls by Maria Helene (37 cm, 14.5 inches). The woman is labelled 'ALENTEJO' on the tag. She wears a black hat with red/blue flowers, red/white headscarf/neckerchief tied at the back, green floral overblouse with lace trim, green draped pants (skirt pulled up at the front to form pants), red floral apron with yellow trim, red /white striped stockings, beige shoes. The man is labelled 'BEIRA ALTA'. He wears a black hat, double-breasted brown shirt or jacket, dark fawn chaps over brown trousers. A wide tapestry shawl with pocket each end and decorated with tassels is draped over his left shoulder.

From left to right This 14.5-cm (5.75-inch) female yarn/wool doll wears a straw hat, but the rest of her costume is mainly woollen threads: red headscarf, braid bolero, red skirt with black/red stripes and black hem band, red apron with embroidered band. A female cloth doll of late 1960s tagged VENDEDEIRA DE LISBOA (vendor of Lisbon). She has a basket of vegetables on her head, red scarf, green check blouse, green skirt, red apron, fawn shoes. A male cloth doll of the 1960s tagged 'Maria Helena Doll VILAO DA MADEIRA' (banana vendor). He wears a black cap with red band, white shirt, white sash, white trousers, fawn boots with red trim. He holds a bunch of bananas. A 15-cm (6-inch) female plastic doll tagged 'NAZARE' (Fisherwoman). She has a cane basket on her head, black hat with pompon at the front, black veil/shawl, navy/white blouse with lace trim. A blue/grey check skirt is worn over a traditional seven petticoats — all lace-trimmed; red embroidered apron with lace trim.

resulting in economic decline and the loss through war of many of its Far Eastern possessions to either England or The Netherlands. But it reasserted its independence in 1640. An ally of Britain during the Napoleonic wars, Portugal was invaded by France in 1807; these forces were eventually expelled in 1811.

A liberal constitution was first accepted and then altered between 1822 and 1823, initiating a century of political struggle. Slavery was abolished in the Portuguese colonies in 1869, increasing the already acute poverty in Portugal.

Portugal was declared a republic in October 1910. The country supported Britain in World War I, but remained neutral in World War II.

Portuguese Goa, on the western coast of India, was seized by Indian troops in 1961. From 1974–75 Portugal recognised the independence of the former Portuguese colonies of Guinea-Bissau, Mozambique, Cape Verde, Sao Tome and Principe, and was powerless to stop the seizure of East Timor by Indonesia.
Capital Lisbon.
Population (1990) 10.4 million, with 29.6 per cent living in urban areas. 99 per cent of the population are Portuguese with small minorities of Cape Verdean, Brazilian, Spanish and British.
Religion 97 per cent Roman Catholic, 7 per cent Protestant, with approximately 15 000 Muslims.
Language Portuguese.

Puerto Rico (Commonwealth of) Caribbean

Situated in the Caribbean Sea, the island of the Commonwealth of Puerto Rico has an area of 9104 square kilometres (3514 square miles).

The Arawah Indians who reached the island about 800 AD are the earliest known inhabitants. Columbus discovered Puerto Rico during his 1493 expedition and by 1508 the Spanish had settled on the island, but because of Carib raids and the arrival of pirates and European adventurers, the colony grew slowly. Slave labour for the sugar and coffee plantations and cattle ranches was imported from Africa. Slavery was abolished in 1872. During the eighteenth century refugees arrived from neighbouring territories.

Demands for either greater integration with Spain or for independence grew and by the end of the nineteenth century greater autonomy was preferred by most Puerto Ricans. This was eventually granted in 1897, but not implemented due to the outbreak of the Spanish American War.

This highly varnished and painted doll wears a lace mantilla over her head, earrings, a red bodice with white trim, red skirt with lace tiers to the hem. She holds a blue fan.

Invaded by American troops in May 1898, the island was ceded to the United States in December 1898. United States citizenship was granted to Puerto Ricans in 1917 after the island became an unincorporated territory of the United States. Puerto Rico was granted a new constitution in 1952, and the island became a 'commonwealth' in association with the United States.

Capital San Juan.
Population (1990) 3.3 million.
Religion Christianity, mainly Roman Catholic.
Language Spanish is the official language, but English is widely spoken.

Religion

Some of the diversified clothing worn by the various branches of different religions throughout the world is shown in this section.

India *Guru* or holy man. This clay and cloth doll has grey hair, a grey beard and painted markings on his nose and forehead. He is dressed in an orange gown and wrap-around skirt, and wears wooden beads around his neck. He has a roll of cloth over his left shoulder and a musical instrument in his right hand.

Far left A Jewish Rabbi from **Israel**. He is dressed in black with his white and black prayer shawl around his shoulders and holds the Torah. *Left* A Jewess from **Israel** giving the sabbath blessing. She has a blue blouse, black head shawl and skirt. *Centre* A **Greek** orthodox priest, fully dressed in black. *Right* One of the famous **Swiss** Guards from the Vatican. The doll wears a black beret and medieval-type costume in red with blue/yellow stripes. *Front* A **Munich** monk — the symbol of Munich from which the city's German name was derived. The doll wears a very dark brown cowl and habit trimmed with bright yellow.

From **Asia**. *Left* A Lama from **Tibet**. The doll wears a tall semi-conical red hat trimmed with fur. He has a blue scarf at his neck and a red draped robe. He carries a Tibetan prayer wheel in his left hand. *Centre* This Tjili doll from **Bali** represents the Rice Mother and was originally a votive idol used in the harvest ritual. *Right* **India** A *guru* (teacher) dressed in simple orange robes and carrying his very few possessions or food in his shoulder sling.

An **American Indian** kachina doll of carved and painted wood. These dolls were once used in many American Indian rituals.

Plastic dolls portraying a Roman Catholic monk and nun.

Amish, USA *Left* An 18.5-cm (7.25-inch) male doll dressed in a flat black hat, black jacket and trousers, blue shirt. *Middle* An 18.5-cm (7.25-inch) plastic doll dressed as a woman in a black hood over a white cap, black shawl, red dress, black apron, stockings and shoes. *Right* An 18.5-cm (7.25-inch) plastic doll dressed as a boy in a black hat, black/white check shirt, black trousers with braces. *Front* An 8.25-cm (3.25-inch) china doll (1930s–50) with black hood, shawl and apron over a dusky pink dress.

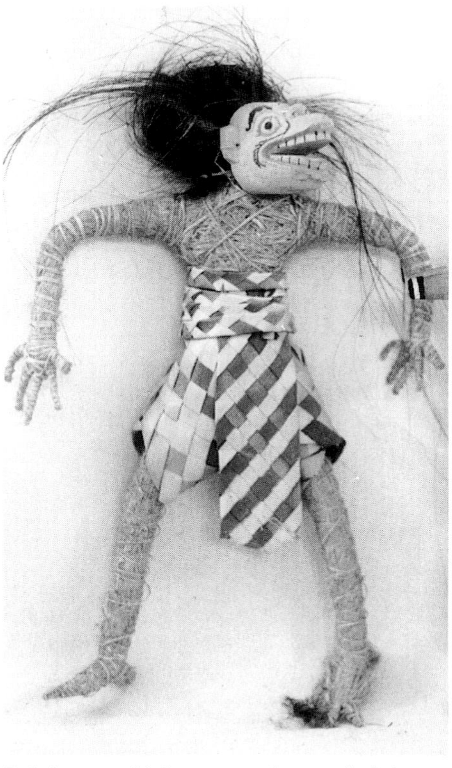

Left A straw idol representing a witchdoctor from **Bali**, Indonesia. It has a carved mask and straw body.

Sri Lanka 'Devil Dancer', a 23.5-cm (9.25-inch) cloth doll with wooden painted mask, wears a red jacket with white/black trim, white waist sash, two-tiered black skirt with various coloured bands.

'Reverend Mayfield' by Rosa Blackman, USA. A 1940–50s hand-sculpted American-made doll depicting a black southern Baptist pastor standing at the bible lectern. (Author's collection)

A ceremonial temple dancer from **Japan**. This 14-cm (5.5-inch) cloth doll wears a golden face mask over a gold brocade hood. He has an orange/gold brocade robe under an orange tabard with red waist cord and tassels at the front. A short apron is also worn at the front under the tabard, with a longer one at the back. He has green/gold trousers. The maker's name is on the board to the left.

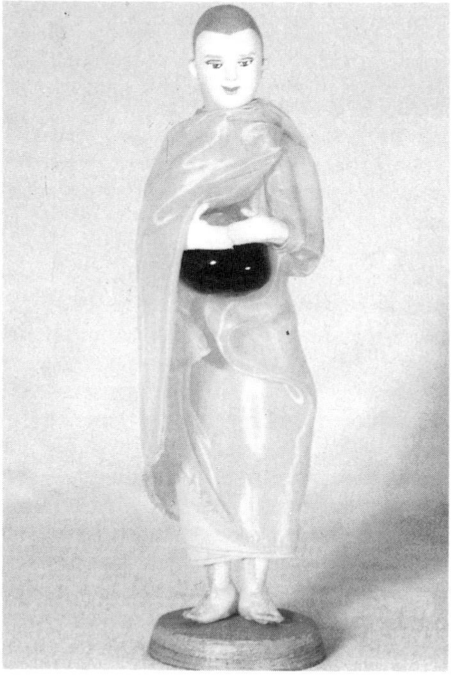

This doll from **Thailand** depicts a Buddhist monk in his saffron robes with his begging bowl.

India A lovely bisque-headed 'SFBJ 60 Paris' doll dressed in Salvation Army missionary costume of the 1920s. The 37.5-cm (14.75-inch) doll wears a white hat with maroon band, maroon blouse, pink sari with maroon stitching, maroon sandals. She still has her original box with the label 'Eden Bébé'. (Private collection, New South Wales)

A series of dolls made from various substances including resin, vinyl, hard plastic and a 1940s cloth doll (second from left). The dolls portray different Roman Catholic orders.

Nepal 'Spirit Dancer', a 16.5-cm (6.5-inch) carved wooden doll with painted tin mask. The doll wears gold coil earrings and also has gold coil ornaments on the bodice; red shawl and skirt with gold trim, short green wrap-around skirt with gold trim. Large bells hang from a wide gold waistband.

Romania Europe

Romania is divided into 41 counties, with a total area of 237 500 square kilometres (91 675 square miles). Situated in the southeastern section of Europe bordering the Black Sea, Romania shares borders with Bulgaria, Serbia, Hungary, Ukraine and Moldavia. Forty-three per cent of the land is arable with 28 per cent forested.

Part of the Roman Empire from 106 to approximately 273 AD, Romania was invaded by the Slavic peoples in the seventh and eighth centuries and the Magyars between the ninth and eleventh. During the ninth century most of the population was converted to Orthodox Christianity.

Hungary conquered Transylvania in the eleventh century; it later came under Ottoman domination in 1526, with the Hapsburgs (Hungary) regaining the region in 1699.

A 26.5-cm (10.5-inch) all-cloth doll (1960–70s) labelled 'Product of the Handcraft Co-operatives of Romania Folk art object 'Zona Radauti'. The doll has embroidered features. He wears a black crocheted hat, white shirt, cream overshirt/jacket with embroidered trim, braid waistband, cream sleeveless jacket with black braid and embroidery trim, white trousers, white knitted socks, leather moccasins with black lacing. He holds a wooden walking stick/crook.

Hard plastic dolls. The female doll (19 cm, 7.5 inches) wears a long gauze scarf-like headdress with black/white braid trim, gold medallion necklace, white blouse with black/silver embroidery, wide black/silver waist sash. She has a white skirt trimmed with black embroidery, over which is worn a gold/black wrap-around skirt. The male doll (21.5 cm, 8.5 inches) wears a tall black *curicurl* hat, white shirt with lace trim on collar and cuffs, red woven waistband with black/white decoration, white sleeveless jerkin with black embroidery trim, white trousers with black embroidery trim, white stockings, laced pointed-toe shoes. He holds a wooden instrument known as a 'nosepipe'.

Dolls with plastic heads and hands, over wire armature bodies. The man (21.5 cm, 8.5 inches) wears a straw hat with red bobbles and red band, white shirt, short overjacket with wide sleeves and embroidery trim, white gathered trousers with embroidery trim, black boots, white bag over his shoulder. He carries a small axe in his right hand. The woman (19.5 cm, 7.75 inches) has blond hair with a plait wound around her head and two plaits at the back, a white blouse trimmed with purple/gold braid, purple wrap-around skirt with white underskirt, red waistband, white socks with blue embroidery, brown laced shoes. (Courtesy Vera Woodhead, Queensland)

'Carding and Spinning', plastic resin dolls. *Left* The 19.5-cm (7.75-inch) doll wears a black headscarf, white blouse with red/black embroidery trim, black bolero ornamented front and back, white pleated skirt with lace insert and lace hem trim, black apron embroidered and ornamented with black lace edging, black boots. She is using a simple teasing/carding piece of wooden equipment. *Right* The 18.5-cm (7.25-inch) doll wears a black headscarf, white blouse with black embroidery trim, ornamented black bolero, white skirt with black embroidery trim, black pleated apron with green/pink embroidery and black lace edging, white stockings, black shoes and ankle straps. She holds a ball of spun wool or 'top'.

The separate principalities of Walachia and Moldavia merged under Romanian rule in the thirteenth and fourteenth centuries, with the Ottoman Empire establishing suzerainty over Walachia in the late 1500s and over Moldavia a century later.

Ideas of Romanian national unity and liberation spread in the nineteenth century. In 1856 Walachia and Moldavia became independent within the Ottoman Empire and the two principalities were united in 1861.

Taking advantage of the Russo-Turkish War, Romania declared the country's full independence in 1877; this was internationally recognised in 1878. Neutral at the beginning of World War I, Romania joined the Allies in 1916. A post-war settlement in 1920 gave Romania Transylvania, taken back from Hungary, as well as Bessarabia (Russia) and southern Dodrudja (Bulgaria), thus doubling the country's size. Although neutral at the beginning of World War II, Romania was obliged to restore the territories acquired in the 1920 settlement to their previous owners. In late 1940 Romania became an ally of Germany but renounced this alliance in 1944 by declaring war on Germany when Soviet troops were at the frontier.

A peace treaty in 1947 confirmed Romania's loss of Bessarabia and southern Dodrudja, although all of Transylvania was restored to Romania. A

Plastic, cloth and wire dolls. The 19-cm (7.5-inch) female doll wears a white babushka tied at the back over a single plait, red/blue bead necklace, white blouse with red embroidery trim, black/silver wrap-around skirt over a white underskirt, yarn brocade waistband, grey leather jacket with painted decoration and fur trim. She carries a black/white check bag, and has white stockings and black shoes. The 23-cm (9-inch) male doll wears a black flat-topped hat with turned-up brim, white cotton shirt tucked at the front, long full white trousers tucked at the hem, long white apron with tuck trim, leather jacket with painted ornamentation on the back and fronts and fur trim. He has a red water/wine bottle slung over his shoulder, and wears long black boots.

Plastic dolls. The 23-cm (9-inch) male doll wears a black hat decorated with beads on the crown and brim, blue/yellow/red hat band and streamers, long white jacket with multi-coloured braid trim and waistband, white trousers with red/yellow/blue tassel decoration, brown laced shoes. He holds a wooden rod in his hands. The 20-cm (8-inch) female doll wears a sheer white headscarf with painted design, heavy white jacket with black/red trim, white blouse with red embroidery and mirror trim, red woven wrap-around skirt over a white underskirt trimmed in red, white stockings, and black laced shoes.

This 25.5-cm (10-inch) doll from Shankars Doll Museum, Delhi, India, represents a woman from the **Banjara** tribe, one of the ethnic groups of northern India, and a possible origin of the Romany. The doll has an abundance of silver jewellery; a headpiece ornaments down the sides of her shawl, necklace, bracelets and anklets. She wears a red head-shawl edged in yellow, and a richly ornamented red bodice with white trim. Her skirt is red and black, with a wide decorative border of green, white and red, and small mirror ornaments. Her hands are richly decorated with fine henna drawings. She has a woven cane basket holding simple farm tools under her left arm, a hoe in her right.

People's Republic was declared in December 1947.

Withdrawal of Soviet troops was negotiated in 1958 and from 1961 Romania increasingly asserted its independence from the Soviet Union. Continually promoting this line, Romania was the only Warsaw Pact country to compete in the Olympic Games in 1984.

By November 1989 one of the most dramatic of the upheavals to sweep Eastern Europe had started in Transylvania (home of 2 million ethnic Hungarians), leading to the overthrow of the Soviet-supported government by the end of December 1989. An interim administration took over until a largely free and fair election was held in May 1990.

Capital Bucharest.

Population (1990) 23.3 million, with 50.8 per cent living in urban areas. 89.1 per cent of the population are Romanian, 7.8 per cent Hungarian, 1.5 per cent German, 1.6 per cent Ukrainian, Serb, Croat, Russian and Turk, with approximately 1 million Romany (Gypsies) (the largest Gypsy population in Europe).

Religion 80 per cent Romanian Orthodox Christian, 6 per cent Roman Catholic, 4 per cent other Protestant denominations, and approximately 30 000 Jewish and 40 000 Muslim.

Language Romanian is the official language, with four major dialects. Hungarian and German are also spoken.

Romany (Gypsies)

The Romany do not have a country but are a distinctive ethnic group of often-transient people who are thought to have originated in India, and have spread throughout Europe and the rest of the world. One of the tribes of India, the Banjara, still traders and makers of simple farm tools, is probably the origin of today's Romany. Their love of colour has probably influenced many costumes during their hundreds of years of nomadic travelling.

Byzantine writings refer to Gypsies, and they are known to have been in Europe in the early part of the fourteenth century and by 1417 were in Germany and in England by 1500. Over the centuries the Gypsies' fierce dusky appearance and strange language often frightened European peasants. Their language has now been recognised as closely related to that of some of the northern Indian dialects. However, due to the evolution of both the Romany and Indian languages over the years no close comparisons can be made.

Because of what people thought were strange habits, Gypsies have long been persecuted and even killed. Many fled to Britain after being harassed in Germany early this century, and many more were murdered under the Nazi regime.

Romania has the largest population of Romany (approximately 1 million) to be found in Europe, with another fairly large population in Spain.

Russia (Russian Federated Republics) Europe/Asia

See also Armenia, Azerbaijan, Belarus, Estonia, Georgia, Kazakhstan, Latvia, Lithuania, Moldova, Tajikstan, Turkmenia, Ukraine, Uzbekistan.

Stretching across the north of both Europe and Asia, from almost the Baltic Sea in the west, north to the Arctic Ocean and east to the North Pacific, Russia is the largest country in the world, with an area of 17 075 000 square kilometres (6 590 950 square miles).

All these dolls were made before World War II and depict various old peasant costumes. They wear specially woven shoes that represent the shoes made out of tree bark for use in wet marshy areas. These shoes would dry quickly. *From left* The boy doll (10 cm, 4 inches) has a mask face, cloth/wire body. He wears a black cap, white shirt/jacket with fine red stripes and a cord tied at the waist, navy breeches, white strapped leggings, fawn shoes. The male cloth doll (20 cm, 8 inches) wears a black cap with visor (turned back), red/white shirt, brown/white knee breeches, navy coat, white wound stockings (after the Revolution legs were often wound in coarse cotton instead of stockings), woven shoes. The cloth woman doll (15 cm, 6 inches) wears a red headscarf over two headbands (underneath one white, top red/white), blue dress, brown overcoat, white leggings, woven shoes. She has a staff in her hand. A tag sewn on the dress reads 'PEASANT GIRL ON THE ROAD Made in Soviet Union'.

A lovely teapot cover made to represent a doll dressed in Russian costume. She has moulded cloth features, a white blouse with embroidered trim, white shawl, red skirt, white apron with embroidered trim.

The vast plains of northern Eurasia were settled by nomads from around the second millennium BC. Apart from the Scythians of Greece who settled on the northern coast of the Black Sea from the second century BC, and the ancient civilisations found in Transcaucasia, the nomads were the only inhabitants until the sixth century AD.

When the Slavs migrated eastward from Europe, settling between the Carpathian Mountains and the Upper Volta River, they were followed by Norse warriors and merchants who followed the river trade routes from the Baltic to the Black and Caspian Seas. In the ninth century Slav principalities along the trade routes were gathered together into what was the first unified Russian state, known as Kievan Rus, with Kiev as the centre. In 988 Byzantine influence led to the conversion of Kievan Rus to Orthodox Christianity.

Internal power struggles led to the decline of Kievan Rus in the twelfth century. Overrun by the Tartars from Mongolia (1237–40), the Russian principalities became part of the Mongol-Tartar Empire that stretched from Europe to the Pacific Ocean. The Russian princes took up arms against the Tartars in 1380 and within a century had totally thrown off their overlordship.

During this time Muscovy had emerged as the paramount principality and between 1462 and 1505 had annexed the other principalities and republics as well as beginning the territorial expansion that led to modern Russia. Muscovy expanded eastward across the Volga into the Urals and Siberia, reaching the Pacific in 1639.

After an uprising in 1612 that ousted the Polish forces who had occupied Moscow in 1609, the Romanov tsars oversaw Muscovy's recovery and began to expand westward and absorb western ideas. Between 1696 and 1725 Moscovy was formally renamed Russia; Estonia and Latvia were annexed from Sweden; and a new capital city, St Petersburg, was founded at the head of the Gulf of Finland.

By 1796, due to the partition of Poland

This 1930s cloth doll depicts a typical costume once worn by the Russian peasants. She wears a simple floral pinafore with dark straps over a blouse with sleeve trim to match the main part of the bodice. The woven shoes represent the shoes made out of woven tree bark worn in marshy areas or during wet weather.

Matrouska dolls. These turned wooden dolls come in several forms. All are cut around the middle and are hollow, so that one can fit inside the other.

Traditional Russian costume. The doll wears a tall decorative coronet on her fair hair that is gathered into one long plait at the back. She has pearl earrings and necklace. The long frock is orange, ornamented down the front, and has white sleeves. There should be a thin veil falling from the back of the coronet. When it is cold a sleeveless jacket is worn. This dress is only worn by maidens and is often worn for traditional dances.

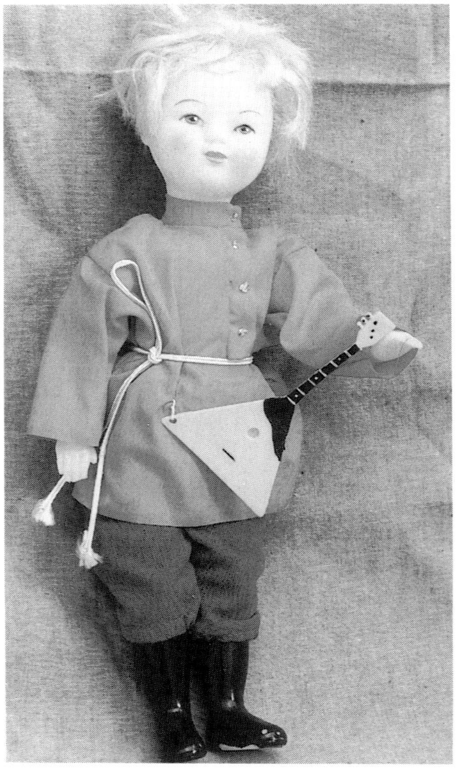

This doll wears a traditional red side-buttoning jacket with cord tie around the waist. He has blue trousers and black boots, and holds a balalaika in his left hand.

A 28-cm (11-inch) plastic doll. She wears her hair in a single plait, and has a red headband with red/white braid and a white pompon on each side of her head. She wears a white blouse with red trim on the sleeves, long blue pinafore with red straps and red hem trim, yellow apron with a wide decorated band, black shoes.

and war with Turkey, Russia had added the territories of Lithuania, Byelorussia (Belarus), Ukraine, Crimea and North Caucasus. Georgia was annexed in 1801, Finland seized from Sweden in 1809, Bessarabia (Moldavia) from Turkey in 1812, and incursions were begun against the Mulsim khanates of central Asia.

After Napoleon's abortive invasion of Russia in 1812, a Russian-led army of Russian, Austrian and Prussian forces pursued Napoleon's armies, entering Paris in 1814. This triumph led to Russia further extending its territory with the acquisitions of the Duchy of Warsaw, to frontiers in Europe that remained virtually unchanged for the next 100 years.

The country's humiliating defeat in the Crimean War (1853–6) led to revolutionary movements being formed amongst the people, further enhanced by Russia's retreat in World War I and culminating in the Russian Revolution of 1917. Spontaneous demonstrations and strikes broke out in the capital, St Petersburg, in March 1917 causing the tsar to abdicate, and a provisional government forfeited popular support by continuing with the war against Germany. A bloodless coup overthrew the provisional government in 1917, establishing a Council of People's Commissars.

The war against Germany ended in March 1918, and under the Treaty of Brest-Litovsk, Russia was forced to surrender Estonia, Latvia, Lithuania and the Russian part of Poland to Germany and Austria. It also had to recognise the independence of Ukraine, Georgia and Finland. Russia was plunged into civil war between the Bolsheviks and the 'White' armies (former Tsarist officers) backed by Great Britain, the United States, France and Japan. The Bolsheviks seized power in Georgia, Armenia and Azerbaijan, as well as Central Asia, in 1921. When Japan withdrew from Russia's Pacific coast at the end of 1922 the period of civil war ended.

The Bolsheviks had renamed Russia the Russian Soviet Federated Socialist Republic in 1918 with Moscow as the capital, but after the consolidation of Soviet power in Ukraine, Transcaucasia and Central Asia in December 1922, it became the Union of Soviet Socialist Republics (USSR). In 1933 the United States recognised the Soviet government, but unsuccessful attempts to form an alliance with Great Britain and France led to a non-aggression pact with Nazi Germany in August 1939. The Soviet Union annexed eastern Poland in September 1939, followed by Estonia, Latvia, Lithuania and territories in northern and eastern Romania (Bessarabia and Bukovina) in June 1940.

In 1941 Germany invaded the Soviet Union, capturing vast territories, to be finally expelled in 1944.

Soon after the liberation of the countries of Eastern Europe, Soviet-backed Communist regimes came to power, and in 1955 the so called 'Cold War' with the west began.

This doll represents a male costume worn near the Black Sea. He wears a black *curicurl* hat, white shirt with red buttons and red/black decoration at the cuffs and hem, red waist sash, brown jacket with black trim, blue trousers, black boots.

From 1988 a tremendous number of reforms in the Soviet Union culminated in many of the Soviet states demanding the right to become independent nations again. The Soviet Union did not impede the former satellites of East Germany, Poland, Czechoslovakia, Hungary, Bulgaria and Romania in their rush towards democratisation. In August 1991 Estonia and Latvia declared themselves fully independent; this was granted on 6 September 1991 along with independence for Lithuania. Several other republics — Ukraine, Byelorussia (Belarus), Azerbaijan, Uzbekistan, Kirghizia — also declared their independence, while Armenia, Georgia and Moldavia re-iterated earlier declarations of going their own way.
Capital Moscow.
Population 145.3 million, with 82.6 per cent Russian, 3.6 per cent Tartar, 2.7 per cent Ukrainian, 1.2 per cent Chuvash.

A 26.5-cm (10.5-inch) hard-plastic doll with a waxen look. The doll is dressed as a peasant in a tall red head-dress with a red/white spot babuska tied over it to one side, yellow blouse with red/white spot trim and gathered cuffs, red overblouse with yellow trim down the front and yellow braid and lace trim at the hem, blue/red plaid skirt with yellow/red braid trim and black ric-rac at the hem, red/white striped over-the-knee stockings, and black ankle boots.

Three traditional dolls of different times and materials. *Left* A plastic 'nodder'. The doll's head has a white moulded babushka; the gown is white moulded plastic with painted black braid decoration. *Middle* This straw doll labelled 'Made in USSR', is made of thin reed, with sisal hair and a plaited self band on the skirt. *Right* A 9-cm (3.5-inch) cloth doll from the 1930s–40s. The male doll has a crocheted hat, white shirt with red decoration, red sash, black trousers. It has 'Made in SOVIET UNION' on the base.

Religion Russian Orthodox, along with other Christian churches.
Language Russian is the predominant language.

St Lucia Caribbean

The second largest island in the Windward group of the West Indies, St Lucia is situated in the Caribbean between Martinique in the north and St Vincent in the south.

Like the other islands of the Windward group, St Lucia was first settled by the Arawak Indians, followed by the Caribs of South America. England and France both made attempts to colonise the island in the seventeenth century, alternating ownership until the islands was finally ceded to Britain in 1814. Slaves were imported from Africa until the trade was abolished in 1834.

Full internal autonomy was achieved in 1967, and full independence on 22 February 1979.
Capital Castries.
Population (1990) 200 000. 90.3 per cent are of African origin, 5.5 per cent mixed, 3.2 per cent East Indian, 0.8 per cent Caucasian.

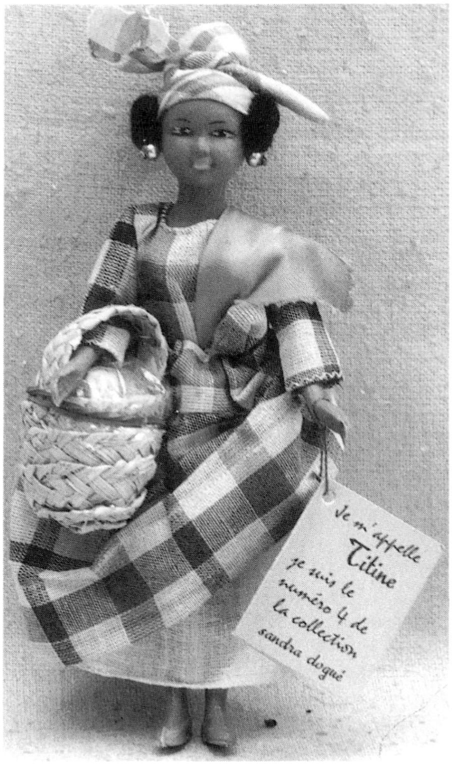

A plastic doll wearing a multi-check turban and matching dress hitched at one side to show the underskirt. A pink shawl is thrown over her shoulder. She carries a woven cane basket.

Religion 90 per cent Roman Catholic, 10 per cent Protestant.
Language English is the official language, although a local French-English creole is widely spoken.

St Vincent Caribbean

Situated 160 km (93 miles) west of Barbados in the Windward group of islands in the Caribbean, St Vincent and the associated Grenadines have an area of 388 square kilometres (150 square miles).

Like many of the Caribbean islands, St Vincent was first populated by the Arawak Indians who were displaced by the migrating Caribs.

The island was colonised by Europeans around the middle of the eighteenth century, and African slaves were imported as labour to work on the plantations. In 1795 the majority of the Caribs were deported by the British to the Bay of Honduras after they revolted against authority. Full internal self-government was introduced in 1969 and the country gained full independence on 27 October 1979.

Capital Kingston.
Population 105 000, with 25.7 per cent living in urban areas. 82 per cent of the population are of African origin, 13.9 per cent of mixed racial origins, and the remainder are Caucasian, Asian and Amerindian minorities.
Religion Christianity.
Language English is the official language, but a regional French patois is common.

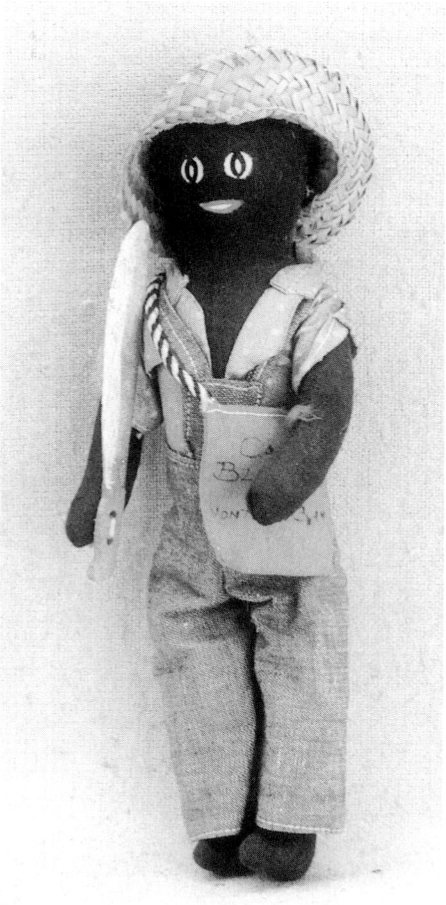

Sugar cane harvester. A 17.75-cm (7-inch) cloth doll wearing a straw hat, yellow shirt, denim overalls. He holds a machete in his right hand and has a bag over his shoulder.

Samoa (American Samoa and the Independent State of Western Samoa) South Pacific

American Samoa consists of five volcanic islands and two coral atolls in the South Pacific with a total area of 200 square kilometres (77 square miles).

Western Samoa, comprising two main islands and a number of smaller islands, has a total area of 2840 square kilometres (1097 square miles). Nineteen per cent of the land is arable, with 47 per cent forested.

Settled since around 800 BC by Polynesian peoples, the group of islands now known as American Samoa and the Independent State of Western Samoa was invaded by Fijians early in the thirteenth century.

In 1722 a Dutch explorer sighted the islands, but it was not until 1830 with the arrival of British missionaries that detailed records were kept. Britain, Germany and the United States all appointed representatives on the islands and began to vie with each other over commercial and legal privileges for their nationals. Then in 1872 the United States gained exclusive rights from the high chief to use the harbour of Pago Pago, on Tutuila, the main island in the eastern group.

The islands were divided in 1900 with Britain and Germany acquiring Western Samoa and America gaining the eastern section, American Samoa.

American Samoa The eastern islands became known as American Samoa in 1911. They were administered by the United States Navy until 1951, but are now under the US Department of the Interior. American Samoa is an unincorporated territory of the United States, making its people United States nationals but not citizens. In 1960 it was given selfgovernment, with certain powers reserved to the US Secretary of the Interior.

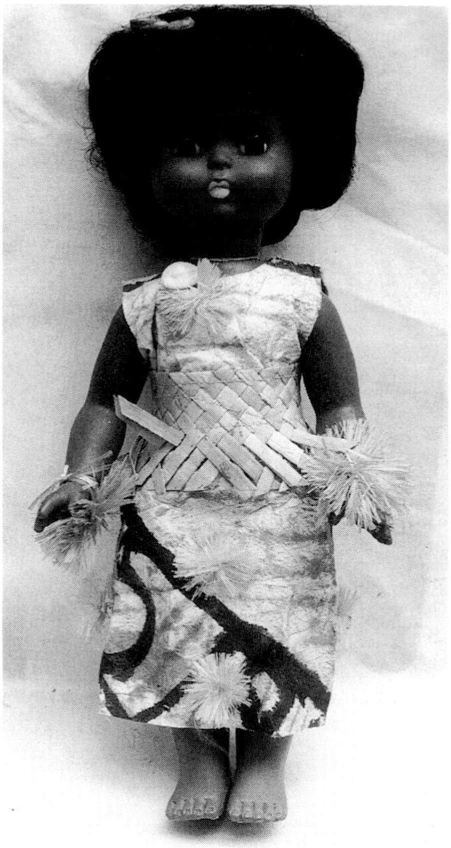

A 33-cm (13-inch) plastic doll. Her dress is made of tapa cloth, and has a wide woven palm leaf waistband and fine fibre pompons back and front. The doll wears similar pompons on her wrists, as well as a cowrie shell necklace.

Western Samoa Meanwhile, Germany renounced all claims to Western Samoa in 1914 and it was annexed to New Zealand on behalf of the League of Nations and the United Nations, and administered by New Zealand until 1962. Western Samoa became independent in January 1962 and authorised New Zealand to act as its foreign agent. It became a full member of the Commonwealth in 1970.

American Samoa
Capital Pago Pago.
Population 40 000 Samoans.
Religion Christian.
Language Samoan and English with most of the population bilingual.

Western Samoa
Capital Apia.
Population 185 000. Mainly Western Samoan and Maori, with 7 per cent Euro-

nesian (mixed European and Polynesian), and 0.4 per cent European.
Religion 99.7 per cent Christian.
Language English and Samoan are the official languages.

San Marino (Most Serene Republic of) Europe

The world's smallest republic, 20 kilometres (12 miles) west of the Adriatic. It has an area of 61 square kilometres (24 square miles) divided into nine castles or districts. Seventeen per cent of the land is arable.

The country claims to be the world's oldest republic, by tradition founded in the fourth century AD by a Christian stonemason who fled from Dalmatia to the Apennines. The community became one of Italy's many mini states, securing papal recognition in 1631.

The republic of San Marino declined the offer to join the unified Italy created in 1861, but it came under Fascist domination from 1923, and followed Italy in declaring war on Britain in 1940. San Marino abolished the Fascist system and declared its neutrality just before Italy surrendered in September 1943.
Capital San Marino.
Population 22 980, of which 90.1 per cent live in urban areas. 87.1 are Sanmarinese (citizens of San Marino) and 12.4 per cent are Italian.
Religion 95 per cent Roman Catholic.
Language Italian is the official language.

This plastic doll wears a black floral cap/scarf, white blouse with lace trim, purple skirt with lace trim, black lace-edged apron with painted floral decoration and the crest of San Marino.

Saudi Arabia (Kingdom of) Middle East

The Kingdom of Saudi Arabia occupies 89 per cent of the Arabian Peninsula, with borders to Jordan, Iraq and Kuwait in the north, Qatar, the United Arab Emirates and Oman to the east, and Yemen to the south, and shoreline to both the Red Sea and the Persian Gulf. It is divided into 14 provinces with a total area of 2 149 690 square kilometres (829 780 square miles). The 0.5 per cent of arable land is irrigated, and only 2 per cent of the land is forested.

The country was originally divided among a number of nomadic and semi-nomadic tribes with trading centres at Medina and Mecca (a pagan religious sanctuary). In the early centuries AD small Christian and Jewish communities were to be found but the majority of the people were animist.

Cloth dolls with painted features. *Man* This 28-cm (11-inch) doll wears a white head-dress with the traditional black coil, long white robe opened down the front over short white trousers. *Woman* The 24-cm (9.5-inch) doll wears a tall purple hat with silver braid edging. She has a sheer orange veil hiding her face. Over her head she wears a black shawl or cloak *(abaaya)* held with a clasp at the front. Underneath she has a purple blouse and lilac brocade skirt, with purple harem pants just seen beneath the skirt.

Then the prophet Muhammad, born in Mecca in 570 AD, founded Islam and most of what is modern Saudi Arabia became Muslim. After his death in 632 Islam moved out of Arabia to Damascus and Baghdad, splitting into two sects: Sunni and Shi'ite. Muslim unity in Arabia collapsed giving way to tribal rivalries and it wasn't until the invasion by the Seljuk Turks in 1174 that some order was restored. The Egyptian Mamelukes invaded the country in the sixteenth century but were soon overpowered by the Ottomans who established authority over most of the peninsula.

A compact in 1744 between a fervant Muslim preacher and an ancestor of the present rulers sought a return to Islamic purity. Riyadh was captured in 1765 and in 1803 the Saudis marched to the Hejaz, giving them authority over land from Hasa in the east to Hejaz in the west and Najran in the south. But the Ottoman sultan asked his Egyptian viceroy to reconquer the Hejaz; this they did, as well as reconquering the Najd, and in 1819 they destroyed the Saudi capital Dir'iyya. In 1838 the Egyptian viceroy returned to the Njad, defeating the Saudi ruler of the time and sending him captive to Cairo, from whence he escaped in 1843. The Saudi ruler reigned for a second 20 years, recovering most of the Njad and Hasa. By 1884 the Rashid family had conquered Riyadh and most of the Saudi clan had found refuge in Kuwait by 1890.

Today's kingdom dates from 1902 when a Saud took Riyadh one night with a small band, and by 1906 he had defeated the Rashid. During the next seven years he conquered the territory of Hasa, home of Shi'ite tribes. After World War I the reigning Saud, Abdul Aziz, expanded his domain taking in Hail and the Najd and with British support captured Mecca in 1924 and Medina in 1925. He took the title King of Hejaz in 1926 and announced the creation of the Kingdom of Saudi Arabia in September 1932.

Until oil was struck near Riyadh in 1937, most of Arabia had been free of foreign influence. Over the last 50 years, Saudi Arabia has often played an important role in world affairs: it assisted Egypt with money during the Suez crisis, supported the monarchists against Egypt, backed republicans in the civil war in North Yemen, and put pressure on the United States and other Western nations with an oil embargo after the war with Israel in 1973. The country now plays a

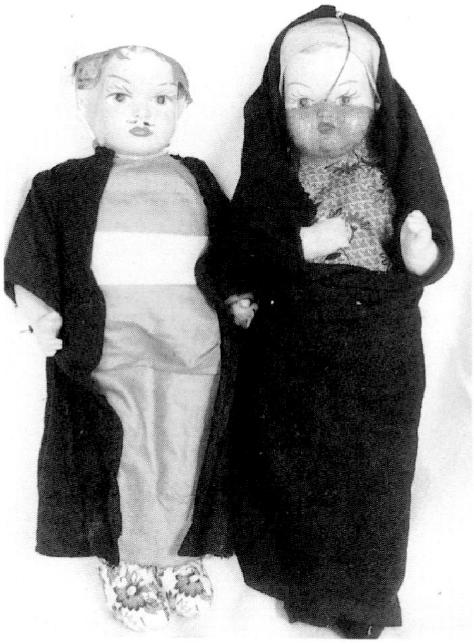

A pair of composition shoulderplate dolls (23 cm, 9 inches) with cloth bodies, bought in Saudi Arabia. The male doll wears a light blue pillbox hat with maroon crown, blue gown with lavender waist sash, dark blue outer garment, floral shoes. The female doll wears a blue headscarf, black shawl with a pin attached to her nose, red floral bodice, black skirt. (Private collection, Kempsey, New South Wales)

very active diplomatic and mediative part in the politics of the surrounding countries.

Capital Riyadh (royal capital); Jiddah (administrative capital).

Population 16.1 million, with 73 per cent living in urban areas. 90 per cent of the population are Arab, 10 per cent Afro-Asian.

Religion Almost 100 per cent Sunni Muslim, with a very small Christian minority.

Language Arabic is the official language, but English is taught in some secondary schools.

Scotland Europe

Scotland occupies the northern portion of the island known as Great Britain, and includes the islands of the Inner and Outer Hebrides, the Orkneys and the Shetlands. It has an area of 77 800 square kilometres (30 400 square miles).

The original inhabitants of Scotland were the Picts who frequently invaded the south (England), until the building of Hadrian's Wall by the Romans confined them to the north.

A doll with celluloid head and cloth body by Palitoy, England. He has a glengarry moulded as part of his head. The clothes are of oilcloth. The jacket is green with braid trim, the skirt a tartan check.

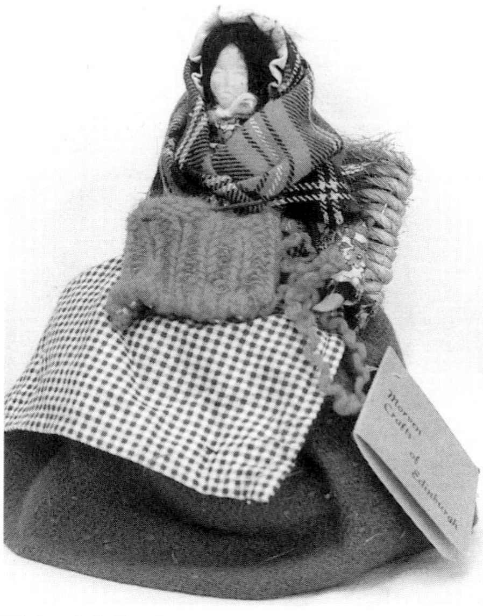

This doll by Morven Crafts of Edinburgh represents an eighteenth century Scottish highlander sitting in an Orkney chair — the wickerwork (represented in hemp) traditionally comes from Ross County. The doll's dark hair is covered by a white mob-cap tied at the neck, with over this a red tartan shawl. She wears a floral blouse, purple skirt, heavy grey underskirt, black stockings. She holds her red knitting on her check apron.

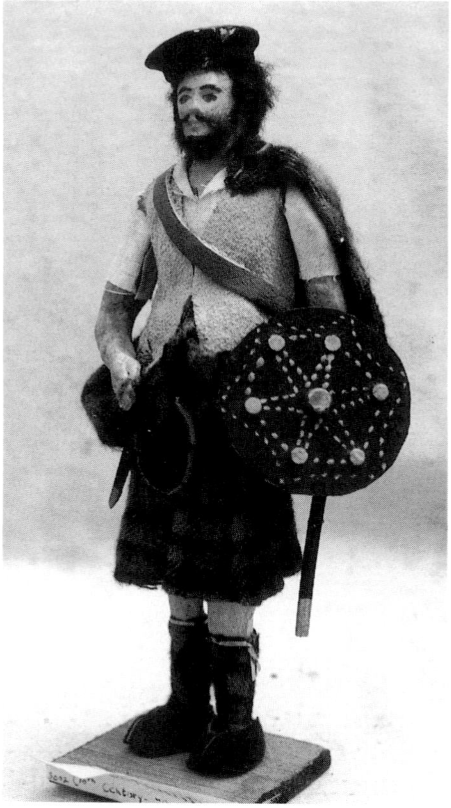

Rob Roy McGregor, a sixteenth century Scot. This handmade doll was bought in Oban, Scotland, in 1976. He wears a black 'bonnet', homespun shirt and leather jerkin, a short plaid over one shoulder and the kilt and sporran. In his left hand he holds a simulated leather *targe* (shield) and *claymore* (sword).

By the sixth century, Scots (Gaelic-speaking Irish), British, Angles and Picts formed the nucleus of the population of Scotland. Christianity was brought to the area in the sixth and seventh centuries. The Picts ruled for some time, but around the time of the Viking invasions the Scots became dominant, extending their domain into the realms of the Angles and British. From then on Scottish history remains obscure until about the twelfth century, and the introduction of feudalism.

From the late 1200s England invaded Scotland several times, but after the routing of the English at Bannockburn in 1314 Scotland again became an independent kingdom and remained so for two centuries. During the 1500s, Scotland was involved in wars both internal and external.

Then in 1567 James VI became King of Scotland and in 1603 ascended the throne of England. Religious persecution of the Scots, dating back to the 1500s, was

A German bisque-headed doll — A.M. 390 — dressed to represent a Scottish fishwife. She wears a tartan scarf, floral blouse, red/white skirt, black/white apron.

An English Chad Valley cloth play doll. She wears a tartan glengarry and a tartan dress.

An antique 'Schilling' type doll from the 1890s. The doll has glass eyes. He wears a black jacket over a white shirt with lace jabot at the neck, tartan kilt, and knit stockings.

finally ended with the revolution of 1688; in 1690 the Scottish Church was established and recognised as Presbyterian. In 1707 the Act of Union was passed and the history of Scotland became linked with that of England, except for the two unsuccessful Jacobite risings of 1715 and 1745.

Capital city Edinburgh (although Glasgow is larger).
Population 5.1 million.
Religion Church of Scotland and Presbyterian.
Language English, although Gaelic is still spoken in some areas.

Senegal (Republic of) Africa

Senegal is situated on the west coast of South Africa with borders to Mauretania in the north, Mali in the east, Guinea and Guinea Bissau in the south. It surrounds the small country of Gambia on three sides. An area of 196 190 square kilometres (75 729 square miles) is divided into 10 regions. Twenty-seven per cent of the land is arable with 31 per cent forested.

A brown cloth doll in her festival dress of mauve and silver turban and long all-enveloping overdress. Underneath she wears a green gown. Around her neck is a gold necklace and she wears gold bangles at the wrists. (Courtesy Jenny Miller, New South Wales)

Senegal's earliest inhabitants were ancestors of the Wolof and Serer black pastoral ethnic groups. North African traders called it the 'Land of the Blacks'. The country was named after Zenegar Berbers but Muslim Arabs had become a major influence in the Senegal valley by eleventh century AD, with the king of an important gold-rich kingdom being converted to Islam. Senegal was incorporated into the vast Mali empire which extended westwards to the Atlantic by the fourteenth century. But the Mali empire had disintegrated by the end of the sixteenth century and Senegal was dominated by smaller kingdoms that occupied the region between the Senegal and Gambia valleys.

Portuguese merchants took gold and slaves from Senegal at the end of the fifteenth century. But the French had replaced the Portuguese, Dutch and English traders by the mid-seventeenth century, setting up a trading post in 1637 in St Louis and taking over the fortified island of Goree in 1677. Five thousand slaves were exported annually through

Goree at the height of the slave trade. The French established a sequence of river forts along the Senegal Valley, but as they expanded inland met with resistance from a group of Islamic reformists trying to establish an Islamic state. By the end of the nineteenth century French forces had overcome all resistance.

At the beginning of this century France organised its various West African colonies into the federation of French West Africa with its administrative centre in Dakar (the capital of Senegal). Senegal was the only French colony that enjoyed the same status as a French metropolitan department and its citizens were allowed to vote and elect a deputy to the French parliament.

By the late 1950s, although many African politicians wanted to conserve the unity of the federation, France's policy was to allow the colonies to become independent. In August 1960 Senegal became the independent Republic of Senegal after breaking away from the Mali Federation formed in June 1960.

Capital Dakar.

Population 7.5 million, with 35 per cent living in urban areas. Wolof 36 per cent, Fulani 18 per cent and Serer 17 per cent.

Religion 91 per cent Sunni Muslim, 6 per cent Christian, 3 per cent traditional animist beliefs.

Language French is the official language, with other ethnic languages also spoken.

This doll has blue flowers in her hair, and wears a white blouse decorated with embroidery and lace, blue bolero with gold braid and button trim. Her skirt of woven multi-striped material is finely pleated at the back. She wears a blue apron beautifully hand embroidered and finished with braid edging.

The doll wears a flower in her hair, a white embroidered blouse with red trim, red vest and yellow trim, red striped skirt, black apron embroidered with flowers, black stockings, gold shoes.

Serbia Europe

Situated in southeastern Europe, Serbia (part of Yugoslavia from 1929 to the 1990s) shares borders with Croatia, Hungary, Romania, Bulgaria, Macedonia, Albania and Bosnia-Hercegovina. It has an area of 55 968 square kilometres (21 604 square miles).

Serbia was settled by the Thracians as early as 2000 BC, coming first under Greek control, then under Roman rule from 168 BC to 9 AD. With the decline of Rome in the fourth century, the area came under the nominal control of the Eastern empire at Constantinople, but was laid waste in the fifth century by invading Huns, and the Avars in the sixth century. Slavs arrived in the region in the sixth and seventh centuries to become vassals of the Byzantine empire after 626 AD. During the seventh century two Slavic tribes, the Croats in the north and the Serbs in the south, came to prominence.

At the turn of the tenth century the Eastern Orthodox Christian Serbs were absorbed into the Bulgarian empire, but later enjoyed a period of autonomy under Byzantine suzerainty. A Serbian empire was created in 1165, but fell prey to the Ottoman Turks in 1389.

After the Turks failed to take Vienna in 1683, Ottoman power in the Balkans began to decline, with the Turks ceding Hungary, Transylvania, Croatia and large parts of northern Serbia to the Austrian Hapsburgs. The Serbian territories were regained by the Turks in 1739, but after an uprising by the Serbs (1804–13), the Russians in 1829 obliged the Turks to respect Serbian autonomy. The Serbian state was refounded as an hereditary princedom in 1830 and after the Treaty of Berlin in 1870 the country received recognition of its independence from Turkey. Serbia, then a Balkan kingdom, had its borders increased by the treaty of Bucharest in 1913.

After World War I the Serbian monarchy united Serbia and Montenegro with the former Austro-Hungarian territories of Slovenia, Dalmatia, Croatia, Bosnia, Hercegovina and Vojvodina into the Kingdom of Serbs, Croats and Slovenes in December 1918. In 1929 the country's name was changed to Yugoslavia (Land of the South Slavs).

From 1941, although overrun by Germany and its allies, Yugoslavia was plunged into civil war involving Croatian nationalists who wanted an independent state of Croatia. The Germans happily exploited the hatred between the Croats and the Serbs. A provisional government was formed in 1943 which later established the Federative People's Republic of Yugoslavia and abolished the monarchy in November 1945. A constitution modelled on the Soviet constitution of 1936 was adopted in January 1946.

Kosovo and Vojvodina were given the status of semi-autonomous provinces within Serbia (but are currently demanding independence). By the late 1980s, Serbia, which favoured a centralised state, inevitably came into conflict with Slovenia and Croatia, which favoured greater decentralisation.

The changes sweeping the Soviet Union and Eastern Europe inevitably touched Yugoslavia. Three major religions, eight major ethnic groups, two alphabets, four languages, and ancient animosities all combined to create a volatile situation by the end of the 1980s. On 25 June 1991 Croatia and Slovenia declared their independence, but this was suspended until October 1991. The fighting between Serbia and the other former states of Yugoslavia unfortunately continues.

Capital Belgrade.
Population 9.3 million.
Religion Predominantly Christian — Eastern Orthodox.
Language Serbian, with English and German widely understood. The Cyrillic alphabet is used.

Sikkim Asia

This small Indian state with an area of 7299 square kilometres (2820 square miles) in the Himalaya is bounded in the west by Nepal, in the south by Bengal (now part of India), and in the north and east by Bhutan. Sikkim was under British protection before World War II, but when India gained independence in 1947 it became an Indian state, and has one seat in each of the parliaments. Sikkim has the smallest population of any Indian state.

Capital Gangtok.
Population 315 682.
Religion Buddhism.

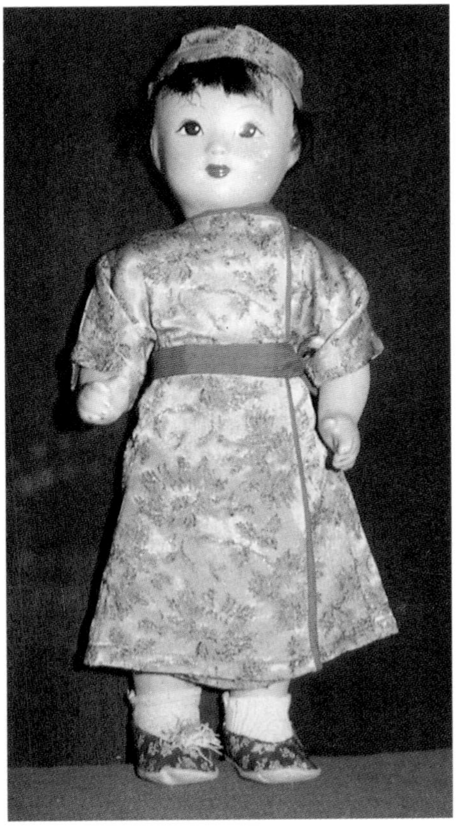

A composition doll with cloth body wearing a shaped blue skull cap, longish blue robe edged with red, and red waist sash. Incidentally the robe should cross over the other way.

Singapore (Republic of) Asia

Located off the southernmost point of the Malay Peninsula, the island country of Singapore is only 124 kilometres (77 miles) north of the Equator. Besides the main island of Singapore the country encompasses 57 smaller islands, with a total area of 620 square kilometres (239 square miles). Four per cent of the land is arable and 5 per cent forested.

First mentioned in the Malay Annals as the busy fourteenth century trading centre Temasak (Sea Town), it became known as Singa pura (Sanskrit for City of the Lion) at about the time that rival expanding empires of Java attacked. The island was divided between them and by the end of the fourteenth century Singapura was destroyed.

Satay man, a cloth doll (13 cm, 5.25 inches) sitting. This doll depicts a Singaporean stall holder who cooks satays while you wait. He wears a yellow turban, cream shirt with high collar, cream trousers, short green wrap-around skirt over the top and trousers, green sandals. In front is the small stove on which he cooks satay sticks.

For the next 400 years the island was almost deserted until the opening up of trade routes to the east. The strategic value of the island as a base and a challenge against Dutch monopoly was recognised by Sir Stamford Raffles, an employee of the East India Company, which established a trading settlement on Singapore in 1819.

The Anglo-Dutch Treaty of 1824 clarified the island's position and Singapore, Malacca and Penang were incorporated into the Straits Settlements in 1826; in 1867 the island came under direct control of the British Colonial Office.

After the Japanese invasion in World War II Britain re-established control of the island in 1945, with a desire to administer the whole Malay peninsula as a single unit. The colony of the Straits Settlements

Cloth dolls (21 cm, 8.25 inches) with painted features. The man wears a gold/blue scarf/turban caught at the side, long blue jacket with a wide blue/gold brocade wrap-around cummerbund, blue trousers and two-strap sandals. He has a white/green/red sash over his shoulder. The woman wears her hair piled on top of her head, with a metal floral decoration at the front. She wears a thigh-length jacket of dark floral fabric with a waist pocket, wrap-around skirt of the same material, scarf around her neck. She carries a red handbag on her left arm.

was dissolved and Singapore became a separate crown colony. In 1955 a new constitution gave Singapore partial selfgovernment and by 1957 full internal government had been achieved. In 1959 the State of Singapore was established with full selfgovernment.

In 1963 the Federation of Malaysia was formed, with Singapore a constituted state, but due to internal problems between mainland Malaysia and Singapore, the Malaysian parliament in August 1965 approved Singapore becoming an independent state within the Commonwealth. Singapore became a republic in December 1965 retrospectively dated to 9 August 1965.

Capital Singapore City.

Population (1990) 2.7 million, all of whom live in urban areas. 76.4 per cent Chinese, 14.9 per cent Malay, 6.4 per cent Indian and 2.3 per cent other nationalities.

Religion Buddhism, Taoism, Islam, Christianity and Hinduism. Most of the Chinese population adhere to Buddhism, the Malays to Islam.

Language English is the official language with Malay the national language. Mandarin (Chinese) and Tamil are also spoken.

Slovakia (Republic of) Europe

The eastern half of what was Czechoslovakia from 1918 until the early 1990s, Slovakia has borders to Poland, Ukraine, Hungary and the Czech Republic. Dense forests cover 40 per cent of Slovakia.

The Slav ancestors of the Czechs and Slovaks arrived in the area between the fifth and the seventh centuries AD, and were converted to Christianity during the ninth century. Slovakia was incorporated into the Kingdom of Hungary at the end of the ninth century, a condition that lasted until the end of World War I in 1918.

With the collapse of the Hapsburg Empire, the independent country of Czechoslovakia was formed, consisting of the former Austrian provinces of Bohemia and Moravia as well as Slovakia. The Slovaks resented being dominated by the Czechs, and an independent Slovak state was declared in March 1939; this state was to be occupied by the Germans within a few months. The Slovaks began a national uprising in August 1944, resisting the German occupiers until late October 1944.

Roshava region, eastern Slovakia. The woman wears a red scarf, blouse with a wide lace-frilled collar and finely pleated sleeves, black vest with braid trim. Her skirt is white, and her apron is white with braid trim. The man wears a black *curicurl* hat with flat crown and blue tassel, white shirt with lace collar, black tie, jacket and breeches trimmed with blue cord, knee-length black boots.

Orava region near the Polish border. A 1930s composition doll with glass eyes. She wears a dark head-dress, white blouse trimmed with red ribbons, red/white shawl with multi-coloured fringe of red/yellow/blue/black trim, white/pink floral apron with blue braid hem trim.

A 28.5-cm (11.25-inch) composition doll. She wears a red turban head-dress. Her blouse has a finely pleated lace collar and fancy pleated sleeves with braid and broderie lace trim. Her waistcoat is dark green with gold medallion and braid trim. A black pleated skirt has two braid streamers edged in gold hanging down at the back. Her pleated brocade apron is lace trimmed with a green braid waistband and bow.

Ruzomberok-Libtov region. Plastic dolls (17.75 cm, 7 inches). The man wears a black fur hat with white top and blue tassel, white shirt with yellow braid trim, white jacket trimmed with yellow braid and blue stitching, white trousers also trimmed with blue, knee-length black boots. The woman wears a white headscarf with yellow braid trim and bow at the back, white blouse with sleeves gathered at the elbow and yellow lace trim, blue skirt with yellow braid and white lace trim and braid shoulder straps. She has a large yellow bow as part of her waist sash. Her shoes are black.

In March 1945 a proclamation decreed the equality of Czechs and Slovaks, but the Communists emerged as the strongest force in May 1946, and the country came under Soviet dominance. In January 1969 a federal system was introduced with separate autonomous Slovak and Czech governments. Communist power over the whole of Czechoslovakia ended in 1989.

In July 1992 Slovakia voted to withdraw from Czechoslovakia and became the independent country of Slovakia.

Capital Bratislava.
Religion Predominantly Roman Catholic.
Language Slovak is the official language, with Hungarian and Czech also spoken.

Spain (Spanish State) Europe

Situated in southwestern Europe, encompassing most of the Iberian Peninsula, Spain has an area of 504 782 square kilometres (194 846 square miles). Spanish territory also extends to the Canary Islands in the Atlantic, Balearic Islands in the Mediterranean, and the cities of Ceuta and Melilla on the northern Moroccan coast. Thirty-one per cent of the land is considered arable and about the same area is forested.

Celts crossed the Pyrenees about 1000 BC, and Phoenician trading settlements were established in Spain before the end of the eighth century BC. The coast was colonised by the Greeks from the seventh century BC, who were conquered in turn by the Carthaginians in the third century BC. Pacified by the Romans in 27 BC, Spain remained a Roman province until overrun by Germanic tribes in the fourth century AD.

The conversion of their king to Christianity in 587 helped integrate the Visigoths, and they adopted the Romano-Spanish language in the seventh century. Visigoth power ended when the Moors conquered the peninsula in 711 and introduced Islam. Beginning in 962, the Christian reconquest culminated in victory in 1212 with the Moors confined to Granada; Granada was finally taken in 1492.

Southern Italy came under Spanish rule from 1501 to 1504 and the Low Countries were inherited in 1504. In the 1500s Spain conquered the Aztecs in Mexico and destroyed the Inca empire in

Mallorquin The male doll wears a black flat hat over a blue headscarf and has a matching blue neckerchief and cummerbund; white shirt with deep pointed collar, short black jacket with gold buttons, brown/black striped full breeches, white stockings, black shoes, and castanets in both hands. The female doll has a white lace head shawl with lace edging. She wears a black bodice and gold and cream brocade skirt, white stockings, black shoes, and has castanets in her hands.

Malaguena The woman has her hair done in a roll down her back and tied with a red ribbon. She wears pearl earrings and a red flower. Her red and white striped dress has a top frill at the front, frills at the back, and an under frill on the sleeves. The skirt has an under frill of pink with gold trim. She wears a black apron, gold bracelets and has castanets with streamers in her hands. The male doll wears a flat black hat, striped neckerchief, white open-neck shirt, black waistcoat, red cummerbund, dark blue trousers with white cuffs, black shoes laced to the knee with red/yellow yarn. He strums a guitar.

Segoviana The male doll wears a wide-brimmed black hat with cord band, white shirt, blue brocade waistcoat with black lapels and gold chain, under a black velvet jacket with braid edging, a red cummerbund over black knee breeches, white stockings with black lacing, black shoes. He wears a flowing black cape with wide collar and has a cane in his left hand. The female doll wears a tall blue lace hat with black brocade front, red pompon trim and a lace mantle; black blouse/jacket with brocade trim at the front and cuffs. Her red velvet skirt is trimmed with gold and black braid and fancy braid at the hem. She has white painted stockings, black shoes, and holds a short staff.

Salmantina The doll wears a white mantilla shawl, gold necklaces with medallions, black brocade shawl with yellow fringing. Her black blouse has gold decoration on the sleeves and lace cuffs. She wears a black skirt very richly embroidered on the lower portion with red/gold hem. Her apron is also richly embroidered, with green side-trim and blue/white pleated hem portion above dark blue fringing.

A lovely old painted bisque K * R 126 doll made in Germany and dressed in a Spanish outfit of black felt hat, white shirt with black bow, and red and yellow felt suit. (Courtesy Dawn Moonie, Brisbane)

Peru, expanding its overseas empire in both the Americas and Asia (the Philippines), and by 1580 Portugal had also been brought under Spanish rule.

The northern portion of the Low Countries (The Netherlands) won independence in 1581. Spain attempted to invade England with an armada of 130 ships in 1588, only to be decisively beaten by the British. Portugal regained its independence in 1640, and Spain lost its Italian possessions in 1714 to Austria, and Gibraltar to Britain. Spain's American colonies (in revolt from 1810) had by 1830 won independence, except for Cuba and Puerto Rico. The first national parliament (Cortes) was convened in 1810. In 1895 rebellion in Cuba led to the United States gaining possession of Cuba, Puerto Rico and the Philippines.

Remaining neutral during World War I and World War II, Spain was nevertheless caught up in its own Civil War between 1936 and 1939. Although parliament was revived in 1942, the dictatorship which arose in 1936 continued until 1975, when the monarchy was restored and general elections were held for the first time since 1936.

A beautiful felt doll (Lenci?) with black hair, wearing a wide-skirted dress of deep yellow and orange felt, and red shoes. (Private collection)

Spain began to transfer its Moroccan possessions to an independent Morocco in 1956, culminating in the return of Ifni in 1969, but the enclaves of Ceuta and Melilla on the Moroccan coast were retained. Spain granted Equatorial Guinea its independence in 1968, and in 1970 when Spain withdrew from Western Sahara it was the end of Spain's colonial history.

Capital Madrid.

Population 39.4 million, with 75.8 per cent living in urban areas. Spanish 73 per cent, Catalan 16 per cent, Galician 8 per cent, Basque 2 per cent, with an estimated several hundred thousand Gypsies.

Religion Roman Catholic 97 per cent, with an estimated 300 000 Muslims and 13 000 Jews.

Language Castilian Spanish is the official language; Basque, Catalan, and Galician are spoken in various areas of Spain.

South Africa (Republic of) Africa

Occupying the southern tip of the African continent, South Africa is divided into four provinces and has an area of 1 233 404 square kilometres (476 094 square miles) which also includes the African homelands of Ciskei, Transkei (in the southeast) and Venda (in the north) whose 'independent' status is only recognised by South Africa. South Africa totally surrounds the independent country

Transkei A 15-cm (6-inch) black hard-plastic doll. She wears a tall yellow turban with bead braid trim, long orange blanket cape with white and blue bead braid edging and bead trim on the back. Her orange skirt has a white front panel with blue bead trim. The skirt is trimmed with black braid bands and beads down the front and around the hem. The doll wears red/white bead anklets, and a white bag hangs by a bead strap from her waist.

'Voortrekkers' *Left* A 15-cm (6-inch) plastic doll wearing a white *voortrekker* bonnet gathered at the back and with a bow at the side, and a check dress with white shawl collar fastened at the front. *Right* A 17-cm (6.75-inch) plastic doll wearing a wide-brimmed pink hat and a pink dress with white lace shawl. She carries a carpet bag.

Zulu A 14.5-cm (5.75-inch) black hard-plastic doll with red turban head-dress with bead trim, silver earrings and anklets, bead necklace, silver and bead bangles. She wears an orange top, black leather skirt, and bead belt.

These two lovely felt dolls, so beautifully finished and dressed with fancy bead weaving, were made at the Red Cross Rehabilitation Centre in Durban. The doll on the left has a fancy bead hairdo and bead and feather necklace. Her skirt is black with embroidery and bead trimming. The doll on the right has a similar skirt, but a very fancy head-dress and shawl all of coloured beads.

Two very intricately made and designed dolls by the **Ndebele** tribe of South Africa. The doll on the left is fully decorated with beadwork and is very colourful. The doll on the right has a red/white bead 'head', gold banded necklet, beaded front lap in white/red/black and wears a cloak of brown and tan with beaded ornamentation. (Courtesy Jenny Miller, New South Wales)

Durban An 11.5-cm (4.5-inch) hard-plastic doll. These colourful dolls depict the colourful ricksha men that were a common sight around the streets of Durban early this century. The doll wears an elaborate head-dress of embroidered red felt and red and white feathers. Two white pieces of plastic piping represent the horns often found on these head-dresses. He wears a white felt costume richly embroidered with beads.

of Lesotho and partially that of Swaziland. It has borders with Namibia, Botswana, Zimbabwe and Mozambique. Ten per cent of the land is arable with 3 per cent forested.

The San (Bushmen) and Khoikhoi (Hottentots) lived as hunters and gatherers around 8000 BC in the area that is now modern South Africa. By the time of European contact the Koikhoi had developed a pastoral culture and by the fifteenth century sophisticated gold and copper mining industries had been developed by the Bantu-speaking people, as well as an active East African trade network.

A Portuguese navigator is the first documented European to have sailed round the southern tip of the African continent in 1488 and by 1652 the Dutch East India Company had established a colony at the Cape of Good Hope. The early settlers were first known as Boers and later Afrikaaners; interbreeding between them and the San and Khoikhoi led to a new ethnic group, the Cape Coloureds. From the Cape the settlers ventured inland encountering the Bantu-speaking Xhosa people, but cattle raiding by the Xhosa during the eighteenth century led to intermittent wars between the two factions for almost a century.

The British captured the Cape in 1795, relinquishing control in 1802 to recapture it four years later. Resisting British domination, in particular the emancipation of slaves in the Cape Colony, the Afrikaaner farmers migrated northwards from 1830 to 1834, in what is known as the Great Trek.

Transvaal was proclaimed a British colony in 1838, Natal in 1843 and the Orange Free State in 1854. Transvaal and the Orange Free State gained independence from British colonial rule in 1850, to become British protectorates for a short period when seeking protection from the Zulus in 1879.

After the discovery of diamonds in 1868 and gold in 1886, black migrant labour from the homelands was extensively used along with imported labour from India; this became the basic pattern of labour use in these two industries, which continues even today.

The Boer Republic resisted British attempts to absorb it into the South African unity. The Boers first defeated the British in the 1881 Boer War and between

This 14.5-cm (5.75-inch) black hard-plastic doll has a tall black turban with bead trim, silver earrings and bangles, bead necklace. Her gold-coloured shawl is draped over her left shoulder. She wears a golden-yellow skirt with two brown bands, and a white apron with brown band trim.

Ndebele A 15-cm (6-inch) hard-plastic doll wearing a tall orange head-dress stuffed and trimmed with beads; wide red/white/black band at the base, and orange/yellow at top. She has a red/white/black front bib under a beautiful cape of red/white/black/blue small beads. Her orange skirt also has a bead trim.

1899 and 1902 they made attacks on both Natal and Cape Colony, but British counter-offensives turned the tides of war. Transvaal and the Orange Free State, as a result of a treaty of 1902, were incorporated into the British Empire, but four years later were granted selfgovernment. In May 1910 the Union of South Africa was established as a British dominion, but blacks were excluded from the vote.

After supporting Britain during World War I, South African troops forced German Southwest Africa (Namibia) to capitulate in 1915 and in 1919 the former German colony became a mandate administered by South Africa.

During the 1920s and 30s many acts of parliament gave more protection and rights to the white population and less and less to the black. South Africa voted in 1948 to reduce ties with Britain, at the same time increasing the power of the Afrikaaner and preserving white supremacy. The policy of apartheid was introduced in 1948, and several racial acts were introduced over the following years, including the establishment of black homelands. South Africa left the Commonwealth in May 1961. Between 1958 and 1966 the government had established 10 homelands comprising 13 per cent of all land for African ethnic groups. Transkei in 1963 was the first to gain selfgoverning status. Later four homelands were granted a so-called independence: Transkei in 1976, Bophuthatswana in 1977, Venda in 1979 and Ciskei in 1981; but this is not recognised outside of South Africa.

Trade unions were legalised in 1979, and in 1982 the new prime minister began to liberalise apartheid: many aspects of so-called petty apartheid were either eliminated or simply ignored. South Africa, in a determined bid to end the country's isolation, has from 1989 entered into a period of rapid and ongoing reform including a non-racist constitution. In May 1994, after the first general election when all adults could vote, South Africa's first black president, Nelson Mandela, was elected.

Capital Pretoria.

Population 34.5 million, plus 8.1 million living in the homelands. Black 68 per cent, white 18 per cent, coloured 11 per cent, Asian 3 per cent.

Religion Black Christian Churches 31 per cent, Dutch Reform 23 per cent, Roman Catholic 15 per cent, Hindu 3 per cent, Muslim 2 per cent, with an estimated 120 000 Jewish.

Language Afrikaans and English are the official languages; Xhosa, Zulu, Swazi and Ndebele are the most common African languages, with at least four Indian dialects.

South Korea See Korea.

Southwest Africa See Namibia.

Soviet Union See also Armenia, Azerbaijan, Belarus, Estonia, Georgia, Kazakhstan, Latvia, Lithuania, Moldova, Tajikistan, Turkmenia, Ukraine, Uzbekistan.

Sri Lanka (Democratic Socialist Republic of) (formerly Ceylon) Asia

Situated south of the Indian subcontinent, the island country of Sri Lanka has an area of 65 610 square kilometres (25 325 square miles) divided into 9 provinces. Sixteen per cent of the land is arable, while 37 per cent is still covered in tropical vegetation and open woodlands.

Traces of stone age settlements dating back to around 10 000 BC have been found throughout Sri Lanka. From the 1st century BC to the thirteenth century AD a complex irrigation-based civilisation flourished, after which the centre of power shifted to the highlands.

Two cultural groups, the northern Hindu Tamils and the southern Buddhist Sinhalese (whose ancestors migrated from India about 500 BC), live together on the island, not always in harmony.

A succession of European powers influenced the coastal regions: first Portugal from 1600 until 1658, The

A rich **Kandy** couple, 25.5-cm (10-inch) cloth dolls. The man wears a gold brocade four-cornered hat with jewel on top, gold brocade shirt and jacket. Under the jacket he wears a green/gold/white padded waistband over his red/gold wrapped trousers, with white trousers underneath. He wears white socks and silver shoes. His jewellery includes a gold bead necklace with large medallion, beaded ring. The female doll has hair decoration, and wears earrings, a gold bead necklace with bead medallion, gold bangles. She wears a red cropped jacket with side peplum, and sari, both embroidered in gold. She has a silver bag and sandals.

Netherlands until 1795; then from 1815 after the conquest of the Kandyan kingdom the entire island came under British rule.

Ceylon's (Sri Lanka's former name) constitutional development took place with very little trouble. The National Congress was formed in 1919 and the Tamil Congress in 1921, and they remained two moderate elite organisations. Britain introduced a new constitution in 1947 in anticipation of the country's independence, which was achieved in February 1948.

In 1954 it was proposed that Sinhala be made the country's sole official language, much to the chagrin of the Tamils. In 1972 a new constitution was proclaimed leaving the parliamentary system intact but declaring the country a republic and changing its name from Ceylon to Sri Lanka. A new presidential system was enshrined in a new constitution in 1978.

From 1983 continual conflict has flared between the Sinhalese majority of the south and the northern Tamil minority.

Tea picker, a 25.5-cm (10-inch) cloth doll. She wears a check headscarf, over which is hung the basket to hold the freshly picked tea leaves. She wears a short cerise blouse and purple and yellow sari. In front is a simulated tea bush.

A 23-cm (9-inch) cloth doll. She wears earrings and a necklace, a short dark grey top, and a wrap-around mauve and purple skirt with peplum. She carries a basket on her head for fruit or vegetables.

Capital Colombo.
Population (1990) 17.2 million, of which 21.1 per cent live in urban areas. 74 per cent Sinhales, 18 per cent Tamil, 7 per cent Moor, 1 per cent Burgher, Malay and Veddha.
Religion 69 per cent Buddhist, 15 per cent Hindu, 8 per cent Christian, 8 per cent Muslim.
Language Sinhala is the official language; but both Tamil and Sinhala are national languages.

Swaziland (Kingdom of) Africa

With an area of 17 363 square kilometres (6702 square miles), the landlocked country of Swaziland is surrounded by South Africa on three sides and Mozambique on the fourth. Eight per cent of the land is arable, 6 per cent forested.

In the sixteenth century Bantu-speaking people migrated south along the Mozambique coast of eastern Africa. Then a group of Swazi, who had originally settled in the south, were moved

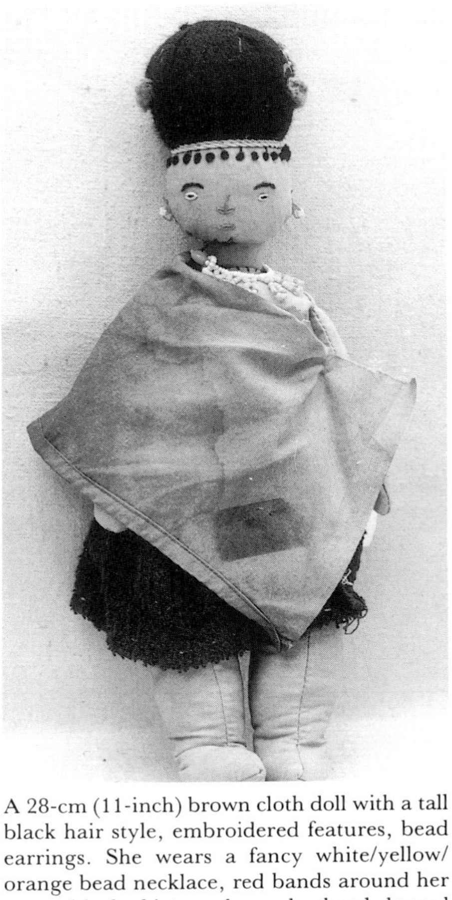

A 28-cm (11-inch) brown cloth doll with a tall black hair style, embroidered features, bead earrings. She wears a fancy white/yellow/orange bead necklace, red bands around her torso, black skirt, and purple shawl draped over her right shoulder.

This brown cloth doll has a high hairdo with yellow band at the forehead, embroidered features and large earrings. She wears a large bead necklace, black skirt, and multicoloured floral shawl trimmed in yellow draped around her shoulders. (Courtesy J. Miller, New South Wales)

Hard-plastic dolls. *Left* The female doll wears a white fur head-dress, bead necklace and wrap around grass skirt; she has a baby on her back held by her wide yellow/white bodice. The male doll wears a fur head-dress with ornament at the front, bead necklace, fur front panel, fur anklets, and holds a fur shield and spear.

north under pressure from the Zulus. The Swazi sought British support in the mid-nineteenth century to limit expansion by the Zulus and settlement by the Transvaal Boers who had obtained concessions over much of Swaziland by the 1880s.

A provisional government of British, South African and Swazi representatives was decided on in 1888, with Britain assuming sovereignty in 1894. Transvaal administered the country from 1903, until Swaziland, along with Basutoland and Bechuanaland, were all placed under one High Commission. Limited selfgovernment was granted to Swaziland in 1963, with full independence achieved in September 1968.

Capital Mbabane.

Population (1990) 800 000, with 26.3 per cent living in urban areas. 97 per cent are African, 3 per cent European.

Religion 60 per cent Christian, 40 per cent traditional customs and beliefs.

Language English and Swazi (Siswati) are the official languages, with 90 per cent of the people speaking Swazi.

Sweden (Kingdom of) Europe

Occupying the western half of the Scandinavian Peninsula, Sweden has an area of 449 964 square kilometres (172 786 square miles) divided into 24 counties *(Lan)*. Fifteen per cent of the country lies north of the Arctic Circle.

Sweden takes its name from the

Decorative wooden dolls. The detail on these dolls is painted onto their turned bodies. The clown at left is painted olive green with mustard yellow and white spots and has red/yellow yarn hair and black hat. The middle doll has a pink painted body with well-painted pink flowers and green leaves on a black painted apron, and wears a large pink bow at the back of her head. The right-hand doll has a painted red dress, blue/white/black painted apron, and a lace panel held on with brass studs. Her arms are movable.

Four dolls by the famous Swedish dollmaker Charlotte Weibull, Malmo. *Left* A female doll with 14-cm (5.5-inch) cloth body, wire arms, wooden lower body on base. She wears a red scarf, beige blouse, red waistband, green underskirt, woven skirt of yellow/pink with decorative banding. She carries a woven cane basket. *Centre left* This 20-cm (8-inch) female doll wears a red pleated halo head-dress, white blouse with lace-edged collar, fawn waistcoat edged in green with black insert and jewelled decoration, red skirt, multi-striped apron, white stockings, and wooden sabots. *Centre right* The 17.75-cm (7-inch) male doll wears a wide-brimmed black hat with blue cord band, white shirt, blue waistcoat, black brocade tie, white jacket with bead buttons at the sides and blue/white trim at the hem, white socks, and wooden sabots. He carries a wooden fiddle and bow. *Right* A 16.5-cm (6.5-inch) cloth head and torso, wooden stake below. She wears a red hat, red neck scarf, green dress, and plaid apron.

Germanic Svear people whose early kingdom in the seventh century AD extended from where Stockholm now stands to much of central Sweden. Swedish warriors and traders penetrated deep into Russia and as far as Constantinople during the great Viking expansion of 800–1100. Christianity, introduced by German and English missionaries, was fully established by the middle of the twelfth century.

Swedish rule of Finland was confirmed by a treaty in 1323, and in 1397 Sweden and Norway were absorbed into the kingdom of Denmark. During the reign of Gustav I Vasa (1523–60) Sweden became independent although southern Sweden and Norway remained under Danish rule.

With the acquisition of Estonia in the sixteenth century, followed by that of Poland through marriage, Swedish power in the Baltic was well established. In the seventeenth century Sweden vanquished the threatening armies of Poland and Russia, annexed Polish Livonia and deprived Russia of access to the Baltic. When Sweden defeated the Hapsburg-led

Two traditional wooden dolls. The lefthand doll is a troll covered in brown fur with pink hair and a string of wooden beads around its neck. The righthand doll is a wooden 'Viking' complete with horned helmet, brass shield, bushy beard, and spear. Circa 1970s.

forces in 1631, it ensured the eventual defeat of Hapsburg ambition in northern Europe, and by 1645 the Danes had been driven out of southern Sweden. An absolute monarchy was created in 1679.

Spectacular Swedish victories against the Danes, Russians and Poles turned into disaster after an invasion of Russia; advancing enemies, including Prussia and England-Hanover, threatened Sweden's very survival. Sweden was forced in 1718 to sign peace treaties ceding most of its southern and eastern possessions, with Russia obtaining Estonia, Livonia, Ingria and Finnish Karelia. Russia became the dominant power on the Gulf of Finland.

A new parliamentary constitution of 1723 gave more authority to the Riksdag (parliament) than to the crown.

Sweden's alliance with Britain during the Napoleonic Wars led to Russia conquering Finland in 1809. At the Congress of Vienna (1814–15) Norway was transferred from the Danish crown to Sweden, although Finland remained part of Russia. Sweden lost its remaining possession in Germany.

The old four-chambered Riksdag was replaced by a two-house parliament based on equal rights in the 1860s. But endemic rural poverty in the late nineteenth century caused large-scale emigration to North America. Severe strains in the union of Sweden and Norway culminated in Norway becoming fully independent in 1905.

Sweden remained neutral during both World Wars I and II.

Capital Stockholm.

Population (1990) 8.5 million, of which 91 per cent are Swedish, 3 per cent Finnish, approximately 15–17 000 Lapps, 2000 Gypsies, 16 000 Jews. In 1987 there were large numbers of people from other countries, including Yugozlavia 39 000, Poland 15 000, Turkey 23 000, Iran 20 000, Germany 12 000, Chile 12 000.

Religion Protestant 89 per cent, with 2 per cent Roman Catholic.

Language Swedish is the official language, although Finnish is also spoken and English is taught in most schools.

Switzerland (Swiss Confederation) Europe

A landlocked country in central Europe, Switzerland has an area of 41 293 square kilometres (15 939 square miles) divided into 23 cantons. Ten per cent of the land is arable with 26 per cent forested.

Known to have been under Roman rule from 58 BC, the area of what is modern Switzerland became part of the Swabian lands around 600 AD after being penetrated by Germanic tribes in the fifth century AD.

Passing to Burgundian rule in the ninth century, the Swiss cantons that emerged after the Dark Ages enjoyed a certain amount of autonomy. They then became a province of the Holy Roman Empire from 1233, to come under the over-lordship of the Hapsburgs in 1273. The Austrian encroachments on Swiss liberties were not welcomed, causing three of the autonomous cantons to join with other cantons against the Austrians; after a long struggle Switzerland gained virtual independence within the Hapsburg Empire by late in the fifteenth century.

The Reformation caused religious wars within Switzerland from 1520 to 1540, with some cantons embracing Calvanism, while others remained loyal to Rome.

Benefiting from France's victory in the Thirty Years War (1618–48), the Swiss Confederation achieved full independence in 1648. But Switzerland was invaded by French revolutionary armies in 1798 and converted into a centralised Helvetic Republic. Power was restored to the cantons in 1803 after mediation by Napoleon.

In 1815, at the Congress of Vienna, the

A carved wooden doll dressed in **Appenzell** costume. She wears a black head-dress with white lace brim trimmed with flowers. She has large lace sleeves trimmed with black bows, black waistcoat with white trim and braid shoulder pieces, black skirt, and blue apron with lower self frill. (Courtesy J. Coleman)

Cellulon dolls (25.5 cm, 10 inches), circa 1970. The male doll wears a flat black hat trimmed with flowers and red ribbon, white shirt, red waistcoat with gold braid trim and silver buttons. He has yellow knee breeches, brown leather braces with ornamented cross strap, lemon waist scarf with orange trim, white socks, black shoes. The female doll wears a straw hat with red cord band, white blouse, black waistcoat with wide square braid collars edged in black, and brocade showing underneath the black front lacing. Her red waist sash is worn over a red skirt and striped apron, with her canton's emblem at the hem; white socks and black shoes.

Left The 25.5-cm (10-inch) epoxy plastic and cloth doll wears a small black skull cap with gold braid edging, white blouse with lace collar. Her red jacket is shaped at the back and has a black shawl collar, black lacing over inner black plastron, and white lace cuffs. She has a pleated red skirt, black apron with embroidered trim, white stockings, black shoes. *Right* A 19-cm (7.5-inch) doll from **Berne** dressed in a straw hat with red flower trim, white blouse; red vest with black collar and trim, laced in black over a yellow insert. She wears a blue skirt with red hem trim, red/white apron, white stockings, black shoes.

Far left **Lowenthal** The 14.5-cm (5.75-inch) plastic doll wears a black and silver head-dress, black dress, white lace-edged shawl, white apron with floral braid trim, gold cross at her neck, black shoes. *Left* **Appenzell** The 19.5-cm (7.75-inch) plastic doll wears an upstanding lace head-dress with yellow centre and red ribbons. She has a white blouse with braid collar held by a gilt buttons, and silver chain. Her black waistcoat has black lacing and gilt button trim; red pleated skirt, blue brocade apron, white socks, black shoes. *Middle* A 10-cm (4-inch) all-wooden jointed doll wearing a white hooded jacket with red lining inside the hood, red lacing down the front, and the Swiss emblem on the pocket; brown trousers; red socks and brown shoes. It has a metal tag on the jacket. *Right* **Uri** The 19.5-cm (7.75-inch) plastic doll wears a black net upstanding hat with lace edging, white blouse, black waistcoat with black lacing over maroon insert, blue shawl, black skirt, brocade apron, white socks and black shoes. *Far right* The 14.5-cm (5.75-inch) plastic doll wears a black bonnet with black lace brim; white blouse gathered at the elbow with lace cuffs and a square white collar with lace edge. She has a black waistcoat with brocade front trim and silver buttons, black skirt, blue apron, black shoes.

Geneva A celluloid doll wearing a straw hat with lace under the brim, tied under the chin with yellow ribbon; mauve brocade dress with brocade front bands; dark olive apron.

Swiss Confederation was re-affirmed, was joined by Geneva (a separate republic) and Valais, and declared perpetually neutral. A new constitution in 1848 (modelled on that of the United States) gave central government substantial powers but also guaranteed cantonal rights in important areas. Neuchatel (previously a principality under Prussia) joined the Confederation in 1857.

The horrors of the Franco-Austrian war of 1859 impelled Henri Dumant of Geneva to found the International Red Cross in 1864; and Swiss neutrality, observed during both World Wars, enabled Switzerland to play a major humanitarian role during those years.

Capital Bern.

Population (1990) 6.7 million, with Swiss nationals consisting of 47 per cent ethnic German, 20 per cent French, 4 per cent Italian, 1 per cent Romanasch and 1 per cent other nationalities.

Religion 49 per cent Roman Catholic, 48 per cent different Protestant denominations, 0.3 per cent Jewish.

Language Of the four national languages, 65 per cent speak German, 18.4 per cent French, 9.8 per cent Italian, 0.8 per cent Romansch. Also 1.6 per cent speak Spanish and 0.6 per cent Turkish.

Syria (Syrian Arab Republic) Middle East

Situated on the far east coast of the Mediterranean, with borders to Turkey, Iraq, Jordan, Lebanon and Israel, the Syrian Arab Republic has an area of 185 180 square kilometres (71 480 square miles) divided into 14 governates. Twenty-eight per cent of the land is arable with 3 per cent forested.

Although the heritage of the area includes Assyrian, Babylonian, Persian and Greek empires, its history as an independent state dates back to the seventh century AD. Captured from the Byzantine empire in 634 AD by followers of the prophet Mohammed, Damascus became the centre of a Muslim community. Later, as the capital, Damascus was the hub of an empire which extended to Spain and India. At that time the Christian majority was largely unaffected by its Muslim rulers. When the Umayyad dynasty was overthrown in 750 AD, the capital was moved to Baghdad, and Syria became very vulnerable.

Christian states established in Syria and Palestine by European crusaders in the eleventh century were short lived as Saladin won military supremacy at the end of the twelfth century.

Under Ottoman empire control, Syria was not governed as one province, but included Aleppo and Damascus in competition. With the end of World War I and the collapse of the Ottoman empire in 1918, Syria was placed under French

The male doll is dressed in a white head-dress with red crown, black gown with white sleeves and gold braid trim at the front, gold belt. He wears an enveloping black cape with gold embroidery. The female doll wears a black headscarf with gold decoration; black face veil; black and gold brocade dress with gold braid decoration at the front, cuffs and hem, gold cord at the waist. (Courtesy Jenny Miller, New South Wales)

mandate authority in 1920. The French divided it into several zones: Alecandretta for the Turks, Aleppo and Damascus for the Sunni Muslims and Jabal Druze for the Druze.

Syria attained full independence in 1946. Much of Syria's modern history has been shaped by its opposition to the state of Israel, and its increasing involvement with Lebanon.

Capital Damascus.
Population (1990) 12.6 million, with 49 per cent in urban areas. 90.3 per cent are Arab; 9.7 per cent Kurdish, Armenians, Turkish, Circassian and Assyrian.
Religion 74 per cent Sunni Muslim; 16 per cent Alawite, Druze and other Muslim sects; 10 per cent Christian.
Language Arabic is the official language and is spoken by 89 per cent of the population.

Tahiti See French Polynesia.

Taiwan (Republic of China) (formerly Formosa) Asia

The island republic of Taiwan is situated 130 kilometres (81 miles) off the southeast coast of mainland China. Divided into 16 counties *(hsien)*, the republic comprises Taiwan Island, the P'eng-hu Lein-tao Islands to the east, Lau Hou and Lu Tao,

Dolls bought in the 1970s, made of cloth over wire armature, with pressed fabric faces. The 19-cm (7.5-inch) female doll has grey hair done in a bun at the back. She wears a black headband with front ornament, blue brocade jacket with black frogging, black trousers, small brown brocade shoes. She carries a woven basket. The male doll has grey hair and beard. He wears a black hat with velvet brim and red pompon on the apex, black waist-length jacket frogged down the front, long dark green skirt with splits to the knees, white trousers, black shoes.

Quemoy, Matzu and some smaller islands to the north. It has an area of 36 179 square kilometres (13 965 square miles), with 55 per cent forested.

Originally inhabited by Malayo-Polynesian aborigines, the island was exploited by Europeans because of its strategic value during the fifteenth century, and was brought under mainland Chinese control in the seventeenth century. After the Sino-Japanese war of 1894–5 Taiwan was ceded to Japan, but with the defeat of Japan in World War II, the island reverted to China.

The Taiwanese revolted against Chinese rule in 1947. With the Chinese Communists occupying the mainland, the Nationalist forces fled *en masse* to Taiwan towards the end of 1949, establishing the Republic of China. The United States assisted the island with its economic development, and from January 1951 recognised the Nationalist Chinese government in Taiwan as the only legal

Wood and cloth dolls with painted faces (14 cm, 5.5 inches). *Left* The female doll wears a decorated blue head-dress with fringe ornament on each side. She has a brown/blue brocade top with cream cuffs, blue striped skirt. Apricot fabric is wound round the wooden base underneath. *Centre left* The male doll wears a tall black head-dress with side wings, long tan robe with cream cuffs. Black base underneath. *Centre right* The female doll wears a black head-dress with cream cuffs, orange trim and black breast decoration is curved up at each side. The red base is decorated with yellow. *Right* The male doll wears a black hat, segmented on top, with a turned-up brim; blue gown; black sleeveless jacket frogged in red with a blue design on the front; and black waist sash.

Five cloth and plastic dolls dressed in traditional gowns. Dolls of this type are freely available in many shops, particularly in 'Chinatown' in the larger cities.

representative of China. But by 1971 the People's Republic of China (Communist China) was gaining international recognition, and in 1979 the United States also recognised the regime. During 1987–88 the Taiwanese government began encouraging the opening of informal relations with the People's Republic of China.

Six decades of civil war against the mainland Communists was formally abandoned when a 43-year state of siege was lifted in May 1991.

Hill tribe doll (32 cm, 12.5 inches) has black yarn hair trimmed with flowers and beads. She wears strings of beads around the neck, red blouse with black and white trim, green buttons and yellow fringe. Her red wrap-around skirt is edged in black with yellow and green trim. She has a yarn waistband tied at each side, black leggings with white trim and green tassels.

Capital Taipei.
Population (1990) 20.2 million, with 72 per cent living in urban areas. 84 per cent of the population is Taiwanese, 2 million mainland Chinese, with an estimated 332 000 (Chinese) aborigines.
Religion 2.05 million Taoists, 3.56 million Buddhists, over half a million Christians.
Language Mandarin is the official language, but South Fukien and Taiwanese dialects are commonly spoken, as well as various aboriginal dialects.

Tajikistan (Republic of) Central Asia

Tajikistan was once part of Turkestan. The original inhabitants were probably Aryan, but were overrun by the Huns, and also suffered invasions from China, Tibet and Mongolia.

Around 1812 Russian incursions began against the Muslim khanates of Central Asia, although the final conquest of that region took most of the century. Tajikistan was one of five Islamic nations — including Turkmenistan, Uzbekistan, Kazakhstan and Kirgizstan — annexed by the Russian empire during the nineteenth century. It was quickly seized by the Communists after the revolution in Russia, and in 1922 became part of the Russian Federated Soviet Socialist Republics, and later, in 1924, the Tajikistan SSR. Tajikistan became independent in 1991.
Capital Dushanbe.
Population 4.8 million, with Tajik 58.8 per cent, Uzbek 22.9 per cent, Russian 10.4 per cent, Tartar 2.1 per cent.

Doll wearing a pillbox hat with a scarf extending from it. Her peach dress features painted black decoration. She is also wearing a dark grey sleeveless jacket and red trousers.

Thailand (Kingdom of) (formerly Siam) Asia

Situated in the west of the Southeast Asian Indo-Chinese Peninsula, and also stretching from the north to halfway down the Malay Peninsula, Thailand has an area of 514 000 square kilometres (198 404 square miles). The country is divided into 73 provinces or *changwat* and has borders to Burma and Laos in the north, Cambodia in the east and Malaysia in the south. Thirty-four per cent of the land is arable, with 30 per cent forested.

People from the northern parts of Burma and the Yunnan province of China migrated to the heart of modern Thailand between the seventh and eleventh centuries. A kingdom was established in north central Thailand in 1238 AD, signalling 200 years of expansion, and as Thai culture and identity developed the

Cloth dolls (24 cm, 9.5 inches) by Bangkok Dolls, representing the Ayudya period. The female doll has earrings and a bead necklace, green top, sheer gold fabric worn over her shoulder, and a gold brocade belt with large ornament at front. She wears a green and gold design skirt wrapped around — left over right — with six narrow pleats at the front edge; gold scuffs. She holds a paper circlet in her right hand. The male doll wears a gold jacket with gold brocade collar and front edge, wide gold and silver brocade waist sash, blue/gold draped trousers with red/gold undertrousers, black pointed shoes.

Cloth dolls (23 cm, 9 inches) by Bangkok dolls. *Left* The doll wears an elaborate black turban with woven braid trim, silver band necklace, silver chain earrings, silver medallion at the neck. Her black jacket has a pink furry trim, red/white cuffs, maroon tassels at the sides. She wears a black waist sash with wide embroidered ends, tied at the back; black back drape and multicoloured embroidered trousers. *Right* **Yap** tribe The doll wears a rolled black turban, gold neck rings, black crossover jacket with white trim, black trousers. He has a yellow bag with black strap and bands slung over his shoulder, and carries a musical instrument.

Cloth dolls by Bangkok dolls. *Left* 'Fruit vendor'. The 25.5-cm (10-inch) doll wears a traditional woven straw hat, green jacket, striped wrap-around skirt (red background), and carries a yoke with two cane baskets of vegetables. *Right* 'Klong fruit and vegetable vendor'. A kneeling doll in a wooden boat, dressed in the traditional straw hat, red jacket, brown-background striped wrap-around skirt, and holding an oar in her left hand.

E-Kaw weaver, a 14-cm (5.5-inch) sitting cloth doll. She wears a high head-dress with silk tassels, silver neck jewellery, black jacket with silver/green/gold bands on the sleeves, short skirt with silver braid bands, green sash with medallion trim, green trousers. As she weaves the surplus is held in the woven straw baskets.

Cloth dolls. *Left* The doll has a colourful head-dress of yellow and red pompons and silver medallions, blue gown and trousers trimmed with red and silver bells at the neck. *Right* The doll is similarly dressed, but in white and red.

Khmer empire of Angkor receded. In the late thirteenth and fourteenth centuries Thai influence expanded southwards.

A new state, Ayuthia, emerged during the mid-fourteenth century and prospered, conquering Angkor and taking Burmese land to the west, Thai principalities in the north and Malay territories in the south.

Contact with Europe began in the sixteenth century, and after Portugal's conquest of Malacca in 1511, Portuguese missionaries, adventurers and traders began arriving in Siam (Thailand's old name). Ayuthia soon became entangled in the rivalries and intrigue between Dutch and Portuguese traders, and a French mission was accepted as a counterbalance in the late 1600s.

After a Burmese invasion in 1767, Ayuthia was razed and a new Thai state was founded. When the present-day dynasty was founded in 1781, the capital was relocated to Bangkok.

During the eighteenth and early nineteenth centuries attempts were made to re-impose authority over southern Laos, western Cambodia and northern Malaysia. In 1892, by establishing a modern monarchy, giving Laotian and Cambodian territory to France, and Malay territory to Britain, Siam was the only Southeast Asian country to avoid colonial control.

A bloodless coup in 1932 led to a European-style constitutional monarchy. Siam adopted the name Thailand in 1939. During World War II, the governing regime collaborated with the Japanese when they invaded Thailand in 1941.

In 1958 an authoritarian regime was imposed, which abolished the constitution and elections. This state of things persisted until the 1970s when a democratic government was formed.

Capital Bangkok.

Population 55.7 million, with 19.8 per cent living in urban areas. 75 per cent are Thai, 14 per cent Chinese, 11 per cent other.

Religion 95.5 per cent adhere to Theravada Buddhism, the national religion. Muslims, Hindus, Sikhs and Christians make up the remaining 4.5 per cent. Confucianism is also practised.

Language Thai (also known as Siamese) is the official language.

Tibet Asia

Tibet, an autonomous region of the People's Republic of China with an area of 1 221 600 square kilometres (471 500 square miles), shares its southern borders with India, Burma, Bhutan and Nepal, and elsewhere adjoins China.

The early history of Tibet is largely legend. Buddhism was introduced in the seventh century, and after suffering a decline was revived in the fourteenth century when the strict monastic order was founded with the Dalai Lama as head.

In 1253 the eastern part of Tibet was conquered by Kublai Khan. The first Europeans to visit the country were Portuguese Jesuits in the sixteenth and seventeenth centuries. Other travellers followed but were not welcomed by the independent Tibetans, who feared annexation by the government of India. A British expedition reached Lhasa in 1904, after which a treaty was concluded between Britain and Tibet.

In 1910 China attempted to impose effective rule. Then in October 1950 the Chinese army entered Tibet and in 1951 Tibet was re-annexed, becoming a so-called autonomous region of China.

Capital Lhasa.
Population 2.2 million.
Language Tibetan (re-instated as a official language in 1988).
Religion Predominantly Buddhist.

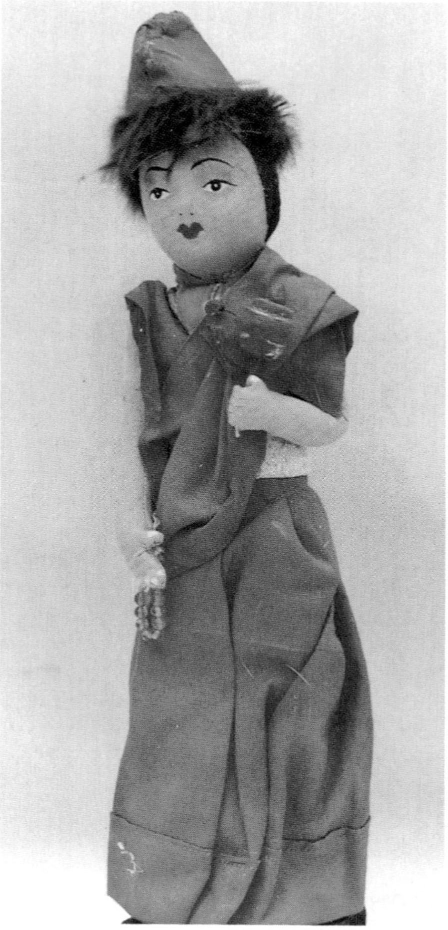

'Lama', a 25.5-cm (10-inch) cloth doll. He wears a red cardboard pointed hat with fur brim, blue brocade scarf, green brocade waist sash, long red skirt pleated at the front to the left side, red drape over his shoulder. He holds a prayer wheel in his left hand, prayer beads in his right.

Cloth dolls (25.5 cm, 10 inches). *Left* The doll has gold earrings, a high-necked mauve striped blouse, long blue brocade wrap-around gown, necklace of beads and a medallion. She wears a multi-striped apron over a pink sash, and has long boots painted on her cloth legs with the upper and sole painted of carved wood. She holds a staff in her hands. *Right* The male doll wears an earring, blue neckscarf, knee-length jacket of blue/khaki/green/white/black stripes. The cloth legs and wooden feet are painted to represent boots and leggings. He has a dagger held by a purple waist sash.

Cloth dolls. The female doll wears a bead necklace, blue blouse, colourful tabard, wine skirt, red shoes. The male doll has a wine brocade hat, wine brocade jacket and trousers, painted shoes. (Courtesy Nepal Pavilion, Expo 88)

Tonga (Kingdom of Tonga) Pacific Ocean

Consisting of an archipelago of some 172 islands, 650 kilometres (404 miles) east of

A carved wooden doll on a wooden base, 17.75 cm (7 inches) overall. The doll has a stump body and is carved from one piece of wood except for the arms, which are also wood. The hair is carved and the facial features are inked in. The doll wears a long multicoloured jacket over a wrap-around skirt of the same material, wide woven waistband held with a black cord. The doll was carved on the island in 1970.

Fiji in the South Pacific, Tonga has a total area of 748 square kilometres (289 square miles). Although surface water is negligible, 25 per cent of the land area is arable, with 12 per cent forested.

Tonga has been inhabited by Polynesian peoples for about 3000 years, and the line of ruling dynasties dates back to 950 AD. The Dutch were probably the first Europeans to make contact with the islands in the seventeenth century, followed by the British when Captain Cook named them the Friendly Islands in the eighteenth century. After a period of civil wars that ended in the late 1800s, a unified and independent nation emerged. Christianity was introduced by Wesleyan missionaries in 1822, and within a few years most of the population had become Christian.

Although Germany, Britain and the United States had recognised the country's independence, a treaty was signed between Britain and Tonga in 1900 to ward off German advances, at the same time enabling Tongan foreign policy to be conducted by a British consul.

In 1958 Tonga and Britain signed a new treaty of friendship; in 1970 Tonga became completely independent of Britain and joined the Commonwealth.

Capital Nuku'alofa.
Population 100 465, with 31.8 per cent living in urban areas. 98 per cent are Polynesian Tongan, with about 300 Europeans.
Religion Christianity.
Language Tongan and English.

Trinidad and Tobago (Republic of) Caribbean

The southernmost of the Windward Islands group in the Caribbean, Trinidad is situated approximately 11 kilometres (7 miles) north of the Venezuelan coast. With an area of 4828 square kilometres (1863 square miles), Trinidad is 32 kilometres (20 miles) south of its neighbour Tobago (300 square kilometres (116 square miles). Fourteen per cent of the republic's land is arable, with 44 per cent covered in tropical rainforest.

The earliest inhabitants of Trinidad and Tobago were the Arawak and Carib Indians. The islands were discovered by Colombus in 1498 and claimed for Spain. Although Trinidad was colonised it remained underdeveloped until it was seized by the British in 1797.

African slaves worked the sugar and cocoa plantations at first, but with the abolition of slavery in 1834 there was a shortage of labour. This was overcome with the importation of Indian, Chinese and Madeiran workers, many of whom settled in the country permanently.

Although Tobago was settled by Europeans in the mid 1600s, it was not until 1814 that it was confirmed a British possession. Tobago remained a separate colony from Trinidad until 1888 when the two were linked.

Ministerial government was introduced in 1959, followed by full internal self-government in 1961. Trinidad joined the Federation of the West Indies in 1958, but left after Jamaica seceded. The islands gained independence in August 1962.

Capital Port-of-Spain.
Population (1990) 1.3 million, of which 94 per cent live in Trinidad. 43 per cent are black, 40 per cent East Indian, 14 per cent mixed race, 1 per cent white, 1 per cent Chinese, 1 per cent other.
Religion 36.2 per cent Roman Catholic, 23 per cent Hindi, 13.1 per cent Protestant, 6 per cent Muslim.
Language English is the official language, although Hindi, Spanish and French are also spoken.

A 26.5-cm (10.5-inch) cloth doll wearing a white hat with feather and tulle under the brim and tulle band. She wears earrings and a necklace, yellow/white blouse, tulle shawl, red skirt with check flounce and 'Trinidad' printed on it. She carries a white handbag.

Tunisia (Republic of) Africa

Covering an area of 163 610 square kilometres (63 153 square miles) and divided into 18 governates, Tunisia is situated in North Africa with shoreline to the Mediterranean, and borders with Algeria in the west and Libya in the east. Twenty per cent of the land is arable with 4 per cent forested.

Tunisia was inhabited by Zenata Berbers (nomadic horsemen), when Phoenician sailors founded Utica and other trading posts in 1101 BC and Carthage in 814 BC. Carthage's power along the Mediterranean coast lasted until 264 BC and it was finally destroyed by the Romans in 146 BC. The nomadic shepherds (Numidians) who had remained in the mountain regions were included with Carthage in the Roman province of Africa Nova.

A 19-cm (7.5-inch) hard-plastic doll with blue sleeping eyes and black (Arabic) painting around the eyes and on the face. The hands and feet are painted with red stain. The doll wears a grey/blue and silver shawl and dress. She has a silver chain and medallion from which hangs a silver hand pendant engraved with a star. She wears a woollen waist sash. (Courtesy Sherry Morgan, Clearwater, Florida, USA. Photograph: J. Maxson)

Overrun by the Vandals in 439 AD, the area was conquered by the Byzantine empire in 534, and Byzantine rule lasted for 100 years in spite of frequent rebellion by the Berbers. Later an Arab conquest brought Islam to North Africa. Tunisia was devastated by conquering tribes from Egypt in the eleventh century. Then in 1230 the Hafsid dynasty was founded, an amir proclaimed and the country was renamed Tunisia after the new capital Tunis.

In 1574 Tunisia became an Ottoman province, with the Italian, French and English fighting for control of it in subsequent centuries. The country became a French protectorate in 1883, and was occupied by the Axis in World War II until driven out by British forces in 1943. Tunisia finally gained its independence on 20 March 1956.

Capital Tunis.

Population (1990) 8.1 million, with 52.8 per cent living in urban areas. 98 per cent are Arab, 1 per cent European, and less than 1 per cent Jewish.

Religion Islam is the state religion, with 98 per cent Sunni Muslim, and 1 per cent are Christian.

Language Arabic is the official language, with French and Berber widely used.

Turkey (Republic of) Middle East

Situated on the cusp of the continents of Asia and Europe, in the area many refer to as Asia Minor or the Middle East, Turkey has an area of 779 452 square kilometres (300 868 square miles). With coastline to the Black Sea and the Mediterranean, Turkey has borders to Syria and Iraq in the south, Iran in the east, and Georgia, Armenia and Azerbaijan in the north. Thirty per cent of the land is arable with 26 per cent forested.

Turkey's history dates to the time when 16 Turkish tribes became a powerful force in Asia and Europe between 2000 BC and 1500 AD. Asia Minor was won from the Persians in the fourth century BC as Alexander the Great expanded his empire as far east as India. An eastern capital was established at Constantinople early in the fourth century AD when the country was incorporated into the Roman empire.

One of the Turkish tribes embraced Islam in the seventh century and Islam had spread to the area of modern Turkey by the eleventh century, when the region was part of both the Byzantine empire and the Greek Christian world. A victory over the Byzantines in 1071 enabled one of the 16 tribes to form a sultanate in 1098, which repulsed Christian crusaders in the twelfth century, but disintegrated in the thirteenth century before the Mongol hordes.

The Ottoman Turks became dominant in Anatolia in the thirteenth and

A 19-cm (7.5-inch) plastic doll dressed in a red head-dress covered with yellow brocade, light blue shirt, blue jacket with floating sleeve panels (all embroidered), gold neckband, wide silver brocade waistband, navy blue knee breeches, black boots with gold painted ornamentation. He holds a shield in his left hand and a sword in his right. (Courtesy Vera Woodhead, Queensland)

Cloth dolls (11.5 cm, 4.5 inches sitting). The female doll is dressed in a tall head-dress covered with braid and gold medallions on the bottom rim. She has a full-sleeved yellow blouse and baggy pants, red shoes, multi-coloured stole over her shoulders and down the front. The male doll is dressed in a white turban around a multicoloured braid centrepiece. He wears a full white shirt and trousers, red shoes, wide orange waistband, and multicoloured stole.

Fortune teller, a cloth doll (14 cm, 5.5 inches sitting). She wears a white headscarf with red dots, dark brown jacket with gold braid trim over cream blouse, and tan trousers. She has cards set out on the floral cushion she is sitting on. (Courtesy Vera Woodhead, Queensland)

Caliph, a cloth doll (12.75 cm, 5 inches sitting) with a long flowing beard. He wears a dark pink turban decorated at the top and front, dark pink shirt, a wide yellow waistband, white waistcoat, striped trousers, and red pointed-toe shoes. He is sitting on a white cushion, and has a long sword in his right hand and a tray of goods on his lap. (Courtesy of Vera Woodhead, Queensland)

Plastic and wire dolls (19 cm, 7.5 inches). *Left* The female doll wears a blue head-dress tied at the back, long multi-striped jacket of white/orange/brown, apricot harem pants, silver belt, gold-painted pointed shoes, and holds a plate with three candles in each hand. *Centre* The male doll wears a tall red fez, long white jacket over a striped shirt with neckband, wide green sash, long white skirt over white trousers. *Right* The doll wears a red plastic fez, face veil, long blue jacket edged in gold, gold belt, purple harem trousers, gold pointed shoes. She holds a lace-edged parasol in her right hand.

fourteenth centuries, and after they had conquered Thrace, Macedonia, Bulgaria and Serbia their leader was recognised as sultan in 1396. Although defeated by the Mongols in 1402, Ottoman power was restored about 20 years later, and within 30 years had overthrown what was left of the Byzantine Empire, storming Constantinople in 1453. This city, now called Istanbul, became the Ottoman capital.

Greece, Montenegro, Serbia, Bosnia-Hercegovina, Walachia (Romania) and Bukovina soon came under Ottoman control, followed by Christian Trebizond, and Crimea. In the years between 1481 and 1512 Moldavia and Bessarabia were captured, and during the following eight years Kurdistan, Mesopotamia, Palestine, Syria, Hejaz and Egypt were added to the empire. Suleiman, who ruled from 1520 to 1566, conquered the Black Sea littoral, Baghdad, the Greek islands of Rhodes, Samos and Chios, Belgrade, Hungary and tried to besiege Vienna in 1529.

The Ottoman navy became the scourge of Christian ships in the Mediterranean. Although the millions of Christians who came under Ottoman rule were granted religious tolerance, failure to pay Ottoman taxes was not tolerated.

Left A wire armature doll with painted plastic head and hands. The doll wears a white turban with red top, long navy blue robe, purple/yellow/gold underrobe with red waist sash, baggy dark brown pants. He holds a musical instrument. *Centre* This female doll has a wooden bead head, cloth over wire armature body and limbs (20 cm, 8 inches). She wears a high orange and yellow head-dress covered with a figured scarf that half covers her face. She has a long dark orange and yellow striped coat split at the sides to the waist and trimmed with gold and lace at the cuffs, gold belt with large buckle, blue harem pants, and blue shoes. She carries a ewer on her right shoulder. *Right* A 17.75-cm (7-inch) doll with clay head, wire armature body. She wears a tall hat with scarf tied at the back, long brocade coat of yellow/gold/purple trimmed with silver. She has a gold belt, blue floral apron trimmed with lacy, navy blue/white floral harem pants, and carries a ewer on her right arm.

But although Crete was captured in 1669 and the Ukraine in 1678, the empire's territorial power began to decline with the fall of Buda (1686) and of Belgrade in 1688. Most of Hungary, Transylvania and Croatia were ceded to Austria in 1699, followed by Podalia to Poland, and Dalmatia and the Morea to Venice.

After a war with Russia (1768–74) the Crimea and Azov were lost and the Ottoman Empire recognised Russia's right to protect Christian Moldavia and Walachia, followed by Bessarabia and western Georgia (1787–1812), Serbia gained autonomy in 1817, while France established a protectorate over Algiers, and Egypt became selfgoverning. Further wars ensued between 1853 and 1878 and the empire was forced to recognise the independence of Romania, Serbia and Montenegro, the autonomy of Bulgaria, Austrian protectorates over Bosnia-Hercegovina, a British protectorate in Cyprus, and Russia's acquisition of the Caucasus. In the 1880s Thessaly was ceded to Greece, a French protectorate was established over Tunisia (1881), Britain occupied Egypt (1882) and Bulgaria became independent.

A war with Italy (1911–12) lost the empire Libya and the Dodecanese Islands, and also the Balkan States (1912–13), followed by most of the remaining Ottoman territories in Europe; these went mainly to Greece and Serbia, except for Albania which became an independent state. After World War I, in 1920, Turkey accepted the loss of its Arab territories in the Middle East which were mandated to Britain and France, and an independent Armenian republic was created.

In October 1923 a Turkish republic was declared with Ankara as capital, with a new constitution in 1924. In succeeding years many state institutions and laws were westernised, Arabic script gave way to the Latin alphabet and Western dress became obligatory.

Turkey remained neutral during World War II except for the last months, but took no active part. A new constitution in November 1982 reaffirmed Turkey's democratic, secular and parliamentary identity.

Capital Ankara.

Population (1990) 56.7 million, with 53 per cent living in urban areas. 83 per cent are Turkish, 12 per cent Kurdish, 3 per cent other.

Religion 98 per cent Muslim.

Language Turkish is the official language, spoken by 90 per cent of the population, with Kurdish and Arabic also spoken.

Turkmenistan (Republic of) Central Asia

The original inhabitants of Turkmenistan, which was once part of Turkestan, were probably Aryans who were overrun by the Huns, and also suffered invasions from China, Tibet and Mongolia.

Around 1812 Russia moved against the Muslim khanates of Central Asia, and over the nineteenth century five Islamic nations were annexed by the Russian Empire, including Turkmenistan. The Russian Revolution did not significantly change Turkmenistan's status, and by 1922 the country had become part of the Russian Federated Soviet Socialist

Female doll wears a red head-dress, caftan and trousers. Male doll wears a white fur hat, striped coat, fawn tousers and red boots.

Republic; it became the Turkmenistan SSR in 1924.

Turkmenistan became an independent republic in 1991 after the break-up of the USSR.

Capital Ashkhabad.

Population 3.4 million, consisting of Turkmen 68.4 per cent, Russian 12.6 per cent, Uzbek 8.5 per cent, Kazakh 2.9 per cent.

Uganda (Republic of) Africa

The landlocked country of Uganda is situated on the Equator in East Africa, surrounded by Zaire to the west, Sudan to the north, Kenya to the east, and Rwanda and Tanzania to the south. It has an area of 236 040 square kilometres (91 111 square miles) divided into 10 provinces. Twenty-three per cent of the land is arable with 30 per cent forested.

Hand axes found in Uganda have been dated to 50 000 BC, but it was not until the first millennium BC that agriculture was developed in the region. By the fourteenth century, a centralised kingdom had been founded with its capital at Bega.

European explorers entered the country of Buganda (1856–84) followed by missionaries. At the same time Islam was introduced by traders from Sudan. The territory of present-day Uganda (incorporating Buganda and 28 other ethnic groups) came under British influence in

A brown cloth doll with a wide headscarf around her hair, long earrings, multi-banded gold necklace. She has a dusky pink jacket with large medallion trim, floral skirt, and sheer scarf around her waist.

1886. Administered by a trading company until 1893, it was then formally incorporated as a British protectorate. In 1900 Buganda was given a degree of autonomy.

When the Ugandans were given a majority in the protectorate's executive and administrative councils in 1955, it signalled independence was on the way. At independence in 1962 Britain imposed a federal constitution, giving considerable autonomy to the four kingdoms (including Buganda) and 10 administrative districts. A new republican constitution in 1966 abolished all kingdoms.

Capital Kampala.

Population (1990) 18 million, with 14 per cent living in urban areas. 99 per cent are African (Ganda, Teso, Nkole, Nyoro and Soga peoples), 1 per cent European, Asian and Arab.

Religion 33 per cent Roman Catholic, 33 per cent Protestant, 18 per cent animist, 16 per cent Muslim.

Language English is the official language, but 70 per cent are Bantu-speaking. English and Swahili are both commonly used, but Luganda (Ganda) is most widely acknowledged.

Ukraine (Republic of) Europe

Situated in eastern Europe, with coastline to the Black Sea, Ukraine has borders with the Russian Federated Republic, Moldova, Romania, Hungary, Slovakia, Poland and Belarus. It has an area of 604 000 square kilometres (233 144 square miles).

When Norse warriors and merchants spread through the region to the Black Sea at the end of the ninth century, a unified Russian state emerged as Kievan Rus, centred on Kiev. In the twelfth century Kievan Rus power declined as a result of

A 28-cm (11-inch) wax-like plastic doll bought in 1973. He wears a charcoal-grey *curicurl* hat, white shirt painted to simulate embroidery on the stand-up collar and down the front; yellow jacket edged in mustard yellow at the cuffs, front and hem; red sash, navy blue breeches, black boots.

Both dolls are plastic and cloth. *Left* The male doll wears a *curicurl* hat; long white shirt embroidered at the front, sleeves and hem; braid belt, brown bolero with yellow braid trim, white trousers, beige leggings, brown shoes. He carries a woven bag over the right shoulder. *Right* The male doll wears a tall black curicurl hat; white jacket embroidered at the front, sleeves and hem; green sash, white trousers, blue leggings, and brown shoes. He carries a liquor jug in one hand and a mug in the other.

Left A 16.5-cm (6.5-inch) plastic doll with cloth body. The male doll wears a grey curl hat, white shirt with red trim, red/white striped sash, full purple trousers and black boots. *Right* A 17.75-cm (7-inch) doll with plastic torso, cloth upper arms and legs. She wears a green/white floral babushka, red jacket with yellow front trim and green print sleeves, blue plaid wrap-around skirt over a white decorated underskirt, green apron with brown trim, and high red boots.

internal power struggles and external pressures. Overrun by the Tartars (1237–40), it became part of the vast Mongol-Tartar empire.

Ukraine, the original Cossack state of the thirteenth and seventeenth centuries, joined with the Muscovites in 1654 to become part of the Russian empire. It became independent again in March 1918, but only for four years, as it was one of the first regions to become a Soviet Socialist Republic.

It was a member of the United Nations in its own right from 1945. In August 1991 Ukraine, along with many other former Soviet autonomous regions, declared its independence.

Capital Kiev.
Population 51.2 million. 73 per cent are Ukrainian, 21.1 per cent Russian, 1.3 per cent Jewish.
Religion Catholicism is common in Ukraine; 3 million were legally allowed to register as congregation in 1989.
Language Ukrainian.

Ulster See Northern Ireland.

United Kingdom See England, Scotland, Wales and Northern Ireland.

United States of America
North America

Situated in the continent of North America, the United States shares borders with Canada in the north and Mexico in the south, and has coastlines to the Pacific and Atlantic Oceans as well as the Gulf of Mexico. It has an area of 9 372 614 square kilometres (3 617 829 square miles), which includes the state of Alaska to the northwest of Canada, and Hawaii in the central Pacific.

The Amerindian tribes are believed to have crossed the Bering Straits from Asia to the Americas, establishing cultures in North America ranging from the nomadic dwellers of the plains (prairies) to the elaborate civilisations in Mexico.

The voyages of Christopher Colombus in the fifteenth century opened up North America to European contact. Although the Spanish settled in the south of North America and the French and English established fur trading settlements in Canada, the area between the two was largely shunned.

In 1587 Sir Walter Raleigh made an

These carved wooden dolls belong to the rich heritage of the Appalachian area of the USA. They have hand-carved features and hair, and are jointed at the neck, shoulders, hips and knees. Their simple homespun clothing puts them in the 1940–50 era. The woman (23.5 cm, 9.25 inches) is dressed in a black sunbonnet, blue/white floral dress, black apron. The man (24 cm, 9.5 inches) is dressed in a wide-brimmed black hat, blue shirt and denim overalls.

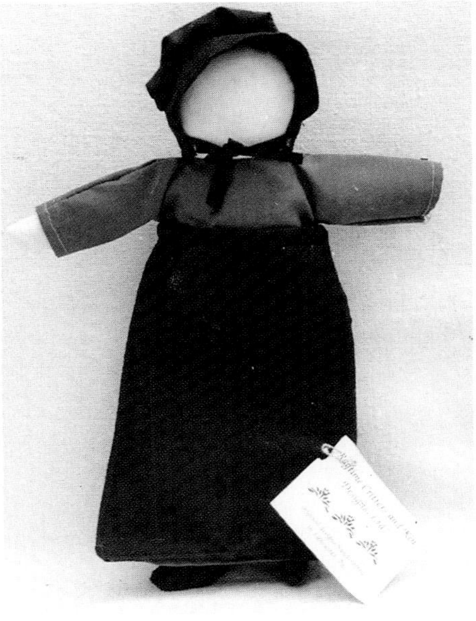

Pennsylvania, Amish A 25.5-cm (10-inch) cloth doll bought in 1991 in the Amish area. She wears a black bonnet, green dress, black apron and shoes. Her tag reads 'Ragtime Critters & Kin Designs Ltd'. Part of the proceeds of the sale of these dolls goes towards buying farms for Amish people.

Southern cotton-picker, a 30.5-cm (12-inch) brown cloth doll with black curly hair, painted features (circa 1940s). She wears a black/white floral dress with a red bandana tied around her neck, white apron with blue ric-rac trim and waistband. She has a long white bag to take the cotton balls slung around her waist.

Hawaii A brown plastic doll dressed in a green bodice, green 'grass' skirt, with yellow lei.

attempt to establish a colony on an island off the coast of Virginia. Although it was unsuccessful it fired the imagination of the British who, for the next 50 years, established colonies along the coast stretching from Maine to Georgia; these small colonies had little or no connection with London, being mainly private business ventures.

The British eventually moved to establish authority in each of the then 13 colonies. The Seven Years War (1757–63) had definite results, for when the French were defeated they ceded their remaining possessions in Canada and all the land west of the Mississippi to Britain. In 1763 France ceded Louisiana to Spain, which in turn ceded Florida to Britain.

The Townshend Duties and the Tea Act in 1769 provoked American settlers to rally for independence, leading to frequent clashes culminating in the Boston Tea Party of 1773. When the British parliament over-reacted in 1774, trying to suppress any rebellion, it had the opposite effect, uniting the 13 colonies against Britain. Open fighting broke out between British troops and settlers.

On 4 July 1776 representatives of the 13 colonies signed a Declaration of Independence from Britain. Britain initially had the upper hand in the war that followed, but their defeat at Yorktown in 1781 marked the effective end of the war, and in 1783 Britain recognised American independence.

The 13 colonies quickly divided again although they remained loosely linked under the Articles of Confederation (1777). The American Constitution of 1788 was the world's first written constitution and is the basis of the present United States of America.

In 1800 Philadelphia was replaced as capital by the newly created city of Washington DC (District of Columbia). One of the administration's first acts was to reject Britain's 1763 treaty with the Indians, and the great drive west to lands between the Appalachians and the Mississippi began. In 1803 Louisiana was purchased from the French and in 1818 the Oregon Territory was ceded to the United States by Britain. Texas joined the Union in 1845 after a short period as an independent state, and in 1850 New Mexico, Arizona, California, Utah and Colorado were acquired from Mexico.

When gold was discovered in California in 1848–49, the westward expansion received further impetus. A mixture of treaty, deception and war dispossessed many of the Indian nations from their native lands, causing trouble between Indians and settlers.

Industrial revolution in the north strengthened the institution of slavery used extensively on the southern cotton plantations. By the middle of the nineteenth century many wanted the abolition of slavery, and until the 1865 assassination of Abraham Lincoln, who endorsed the abolition of slavery, the southern states in 1861 seceded from the Union, forming the Confederate States of America (South Carolina, Mississippi, Florida, Alabama, Georgia, Louisiana, Texas, Virginia, Arkansas, Tennessee,

'Mammy dolls' whose base is actually a black rubber bottle teat, with simple embroidered features (which required considerable skill). These small dolls originated in the southern states of the USA and were still being made into the 1940s. Relatively scarce, they are prized for their charm by collectors of regional dolls. Both dolls are dressed in red/white, the one on the left in check, the other in stripes; both have white aprons and shawls, and red bandanas on their heads. (Author's collection)

A group of hard-plastic dolls. The female doll on the left is by Carlson and represents 'Betsy Ross', who designed the American flag. She is dressed in a white mob-cap, floral dress and white apron, and holds the flag she designed in her right hand. The Indian doll was also made by Carlson, who dressed many dolls in American Indian costume. The male doll on the right represents a 1776 American in all his finery. The doll on the right is dressed to represent Hawaii.

Hopi Indian weaver, a 4.5-cm (1.75-inch) sitting cloth doll. This simple doll, dressed in a blouse and skirt, sits at a simple wood and cane loom on which is a woven square outside her wooden teepee. Circa 1920–30. (Author's collection)

Three 'Skookum' dolls. *Left* This 15-cm (6-inch) doll with celluloid mask face has black hair, a headband, wooden beads, Indian rug, check skirt, pipe legs. *Centre* This 24-cm (9.5-inch) doll has black hair, a painted headband, coloured top, Indian bead necklace, Indian blanket, grey skirt, wooden legs and painted grey mocassins. *Right* A 12-cm (4.75-inch) papoose on a board. The doll still has an attached stamped label from the 1920s. He has a composition mask face, black hair, leather headband and bands around his yellow blanket. The board is decorated with painting.

An original **Chippewa** Indian child's doll. The doll is 30.5 cm (12 inches) tall and is made with a cloth body, leather face and moccasins. The doll's gown is of fine leather. Black cloth at the back of the head represents hair. The doll has bead eyes and mouth, and the gown and moccasins have very simple painted decorations. (Author's collection)

Seminole Indian, Florida A 'stump doll' with head, torso and body in one piece, separate movable wooden arms (circa 1920–30s). The head is carved and painted with black hair. The doll wears a multi-string bead necklace, red blouse with mauve sleeves, multicoloured cape of mauve/pink/green bands with red hem. The skirt is also multicoloured, in gathered bands — mauve at the waist with top banding of red/black; then narrow gathered bands of white/red/mauve, top banding of blue; blue/pink/mauve (blue top band); and black hem. (Author's collection)

North Carolina were all part of the Confederation). The resulting American Civil War lasted four years, until the southern states surrendered in 1865. In 1866 slavery was formally abolished throughout the United States by the Thirteenth Amendment.

The Spanish-American War of 1898 catapulted the United States out of its isolationism, and after the war the United States became a major power in the Caribbean and the Pacific with the acquisition of Puerto Rico, Guam, the Philippines and control of Cuba. In the following years the Hawaiian Islands were annexed in 1898, the Panama Canal opened in 1914 and the Danish Virgin Islands were acquired in 1916.

The United States remained neutral for the first three years of World War I, but were an important factor in the last year helping to force Germany to accept an armistice. The United States again stayed neutral when World War II broke out in Europe but entered the war on 7 December 1941 when Pearl Harbour in the Hawaiian Islands was bombed by the Japanese. At the end of the war in the Pacific, the United States took part in the final signing of the surrender by Japan in August 1945.

Although the American blacks had been freed from slavery by the Civil War they had no civil rights and were subjected to racial discrimination and segregation. The Civil Rights Act of 1964 finally gave black people the same constitutional rights as other Americans.

Shocked into the space race by the initial Soviet successes, the United States set out to send a manned mission to the moon. Their aims were fully realised when US astronaut Neil Armstrong set foot on the moon on 20 July 1969.

The American Indian populations are concentrated in Oklahoma, Arizona, New Mexico, California and North Carolina with more than 50 per cent living in reservations. The Navajo reserves alone cover 6 879 900 hectares (17 000 233 acres) and support 150 000 people.

Capital Washington DC.

Population (1990) 251.4 million, of which 85 per cent are white, 12 per cent black,

Kachinas. Both are made of light carved wood. *Left* Carved in wood and then painted, the Kachina has a bright orange head, yellow torso, blue skirt with white panel, and string of beads around its neck. *Right* 'Chief' by L. Mitchell (on the base), a 15-cm (6-inch) wooden Kachina bought in Tombstone, Arizona, in 1991. The Kachina has feathers on the head, around the neck and in the hand. The head is richly ornamented in white/black over red and blue. The front apron is painted leather, and the boots are blue leather.

'Indian Craft Koasati', also known as **Coushatta** Indians, Elton, Louisiana. An Indian girl grinding corn. The doll is 10.75 cm (4.25 inches) tall and made of cloth. She has black hair, red gown, blue bead necklace, brown boots. The grinding pestle, well and stand are all cleverly made from woven straw.

3 per cent other races including 1.3 million indigenous American Indians.
Religion Protestant 55 per cent, Roman Catholic 30 per cent, Jewish 3 per cent, Eastern Orthodox 2 per cent, Muslim 2 per cent.
Language English is the official language. Spanish and 30 other languages are also spoken.

Indian dolls by Carlson. The five hard-plastic dolls are dressed in various costumes depicting different Indian tribes. The costumes are all made of soft leather and embroidered with beads.

Three **Shoshone** Indian craft dolls made from leather and cloth, and correctly dressed to represent: *left* an Indian brave; *centre* an Indian maiden; and *right* an Indian medicine man. All are beautifully decorated with Indian beadwork. (Private collection, Tasmania)

Uruguay (Eastern Republic of Uruguay) South America

Situated on the east coast of South America, Uruguay is divided into 19 departments with a total area of 176 220 square kilometres (68 021 square miles). It has borders to Brazil in the north and Argentina in the west. Eight per cent of the land is arable with only 4 per cent forested.

The Spanish took very little interest in the area as they could find no gold or silver, and only a few Indians to exploit. Then in 1680 the Portuguese founded the Colonia do Sacremento to further their smuggling operations in Argentina, and the Spanish founded Montevideo in 1726 as a belated response.

With settlement came the development of cattle ranching, and a struggle for

Cloth dolls (21.5 cm, 8.5 inches). The female doll wears a lace mantilla, red bodice with blue edging and floral sleeves with red cuffs, black floral skirt. She holds a wooden guitar. The male doll wears a black hat with wide brim, white shirt, red waistcoast with yellow trim, blue felt and leather belt, brown check trousers with white leather chaps passed between the legs from the front and crossed over at the back, white boots.

independence from Spain which lasted for nearly 30 years. The Autonomous Government of the Eastern Province was established in 1811, only to be suppressed by the Portuguese, and the area was then annexed to Brazil. In 1828 Uruguay gained its independence through the mediation of Great Britain, which saw Uruguay as a buffer zone between the rivals Brazil and Argentina. But for over 40 years civil war divided the country as two factions, the 'Blanchos' and the 'Colorados' tried to gain territory from each other through courting support from Argentina and Brazil. A formal territorial agreement was concluded in 1896.

Europeans had migrated to the country in the 1830s and 40s and they represented 40 per cent of the total population by 1880. With the growing demand for meat and wool, the land-owning elite entered politics. José Batlle y Ordóñez, a Colorados leader, achieved power in 1903, and succeeded in establishing economic growth with increased government control, and also managed to restrict the power of the presidential office in favour of a council of national administration.

Periods of dictatorship and coups followed, but in 1947 Luis Batlle Berres became president and Uruguay entered

Cloth dolls. *Left* The female doll wears a blue floral dress, white knotted neck scarf, white apron, skirt with lace trim, red shoes. *Centre* The male doll wears a white headband, white shirt, short black jacket with embroidery trim, white and black striped serape, red belt with silver ornamentation, brown trousers with white chaps. A pair of wooden bolas hang from his belt. *Right* The male doll wears a wide-brimmed black hat, cream neckerchief knotted at the neck, orange/white striped shirt, brown serape, dark brown trousers, beige boots. He holds a string with bolas. (Courtesy Jenny Miller, New South Wales)

another period of prosperity, enjoying the highest per capita income in Latin America at that time. A military takeover of 1973 lasted until 1984, when democracy was reinstated with an elected president. In 1988 the first free elections for 18 years were held.
Capital Montevideo (nearly half the population live in the capital).
Population (1990) 3 million, with 86.2 per cent living in urban areas. 88 per cent are white (of Iberian and Italian origin), 8 per cent mestizo, 4 per cent black.
Religion Christian 68 per cent, Jewish 2 per cent, 30 per cent are unaffiliated.
Language Spanish is the official language, spoken by 97 per cent of the population.

USSR See Russia.

Uzbekistan Central Asia

Uzbekistan, a landlocked country in southern Eurasia, abuts Turkmenistan, Afghanistan, Tadjikistan, Kirgizstan and Kazakhstan. It has an area of 447 000 square kilometres (172 542 square miles).

Uzbekistan was one of five Central Asian Islamic nations annexed by Russia during the nineteenth century which became part of the Russian Federated

Plastic dolls (28.5 cm, 11.25 inches). The female doll has four black braids and wears a black cap with beaded blue/white band, long striped jacket with yoke and blue edging, yellow bolero with gold decoration, red trousers with blue/white cuffs, and red shoes. The male doll wears a black cap with white decoration around the rim, white shirt, navy and white jacket, red sash, blue trousers tucked into red boots.

Soviet Socialist Republic in 1922. Uzbekistan became the Uzbek SSR.

When Uzbekistan became independent in 1991, it adopted a flag carrying the Islamic crescent.
Capital Taskent.
Population 19 million, with 68.7 per cent of the population Uzbeks, 10.8 per cent Russian, 4.2 per cent Tartar, 3.9 per cent Tajik and 1.9 per cent Karakalpah.

Vanuatu (Republic of) South Pacific

Formerly the Anglo-French Condominium of the New Hebrides, Vanuatu is located in the South Pacific 2250 kilometres (1406 miles) northeast of Sydney, and west of Fiji. The archipelago of Vanuatu consists of 13 large islands and 70 islets with a total area of 14 760 square kilometres (5697 square miles). Only 1 per cent of the land is arable.

Inhabited from 5000 BC by Melanesian peoples, the islands were first visited by Europeans, the Portuguese, in 1606. They were systematically explored by Captain Cook in 1774 when he named them the New Hebrides.

Brown plastic doll dressed in traditional tapa cloth, decorated with black and white painted designs.

In the nineteenth century both Britain and France developed trading posts on the islands and in 1887 they set up a joint naval commission to govern them. British and French citizens were given political dominance over the indigenous peoples in 1906, when the Anglo-French Condominium was formalised. The islands remained comparatively isolated until World War II, when two major bases were established there for the Allied drive in the Pacific.

A bitter struggle for independence began in 1971, including an armed rebellion in May 1980; the islands finally achieved independence on 30 July 1980, and became the Republic of Vanuatu.
Capital Port Vila.
Population 142 600, with 14.5 per cent living in urban areas. 94 per cent are indigenous Ni-Vanuatu of Melanesian origin, 4 per cent French; 2 per cent Australians/New Zealanders, Vietnamese, Chinese and other Pacific islanders.
Religion 80 per cent Christian. Traditional animist beliefs account for the bulk of the remainder, although the Cargo Cult is pre-eminent on the island of Tanna.
Language Bislama, (pidgin) English and French are all official languages, and Melanesian dialects are also spoken.

Vatican (Vatican City State) Europe

Seat of the Holy See, the Vatican City State lies wholly within the city of Rome, Italy. It is the world's smallest state with an area of only 0.44 square kilometres (0.17 square miles). It is the seat of government of the Roman Catholic Church and a repository of human heritage and artistic development.

Nero had many Christians killed on the site in early Christian times, and according to tradition the Apostle Peter was buried here. The emperor Constantine built a church on the site between 324 and 349 AD. In 852 walls were added to protect the church from the Saracens. After the abandonment of Avignon, France, as the papal residence, the Vatican became the seat of papacy in 1377. New walls enclosing a considerably larger territory were built from 1540 to 1640.

The papacy's temporal authority (dating from the eighth century) had extended into much of central Italy by the sixteenth century. The papal states were incorporated into the emerging Italian states from 1859.

Successive popes refused to leave the Vatican until February 1929, when a Treaty was signed with Italy recognising the Holy See's sovereignty in the Vatican State. From 1973 the Vatican has established diplomatic relations with over 100 countries.

Capital Vatican City.
Population 1000.
Religion Roman Catholicism.
Language Italian and Latin.

'Guardia del Papa', a doll by Eros, Italy. He wears a ceremonial silver helmet with red plume, silver breastplate, red/yellow/blue costume, black boots, and carries a ceremonial pike at his right side.

Papal guards. *Left* 'Guardia del Papa', a cloth and plastic doll by Eros, Italy. The doll wears a blue beret, white frill at the neck, blue/red/yellow striped jacket, black belt, blue/red/yellow knee breeches, blue/yellow gaiters. He holds a ceremonial pike in his right hand. *Centre* A celluloid doll of the 1930s. He wears a navy beret, red/yellow/blue jacket with lace collar, full red/yellow/blue trousers tucked into yellow/black boots. *Right* An 8.25-cm (3.25-inch) plastic doll 'Roma' on the base, very simply dressed to represent a papal guard.

Venezuela (Republic of) South America

Fronting the Caribbean Sea, Venezuela is located in northern South America and has an area of 912 050 square kilometres (352 050 square miles). Three per cent of the land is arable, with 39 per cent forested.

The country was named Venezuela (or little Venice) by an explorer who was following in Colombus's footsteps in 1499 and saw the huts of the indigenous Indians built on stilts on the swampy shore of Lake Maracaibo.

First settled by the Spanish about 1500, development was at first slow as there was no gold and considerable resistance from the indigenous Indians. In 1528 Spain allowed the German banking house of Welser to settle and develop the country, but resumed control in 1556, founding the future capital Caracas in 1567. Responsibility for the area passed from Santo Domingo to the Viceroyalty of New Granada (1739–1819).

Spanish neglect in the sixteenth and seventeenth centuries led to illicit trading with the French, English and Dutch, which Spain tried to eradicate by granting a monopoly to the Guipuzcoana Company of Basque merchants in 1728. This created resentment among American-born Spaniards who declared independence in July 1811 (one of the first Latin American countries to do so), but it took 10 years of civil war before independence was secured in 1821.

The hero of the campaign, Simon Bolivar, went on to assist in the liberation of Colombia, Ecuador, Peru and Bolivia. In 1830 a new constitution guaranteed true independence for Venezuela. After oil was discovered in 1920, Venezuela went through a period of prosperity followed by political turmoil.

Capital Caracas.
Population (1990) 19.6 million, with 85.7 per cent living in urban areas. 67 per cent are mestizo, 21 per cent white, 10 per cent

Dolls with felt heads and felt-covered wire bodies, bought in the early 1970s. The 14.5-cm (5.75-inch) female doll carries a woven basket on her head. She has a white blouse with wide lace collars, red waistband, full yellow-patterned navy skirt with lace edging, red scuff shoes. The male doll wears a black hat, white jacket with red and blue band down the front and white trousers (his *liqui-liqui* — Venezuelan man's suit); black scuffs known as *alpargatas*. He holds a pair of *maracas*.

black, and 2 per cent Indian and Amerindian.
Religion Christianity: 96 per cent Roman Catholic, 2 per cent Protestant.
Language Spanish is the official language, and 30 separate languages are spoken by the Amerindians.

Vietnam (The Socialist Republic of) Asia

With an area of 329 560 square kilometres (127 210 square miles), Vietnam is situated on the eastern coast of the Indo-Chinese Peninsula in Southeast Asia. Twenty-two per cent of the land is arable, with 40 per cent forested.

The Vietnamese people are thought to have originated from an ethnic group in southern China who moved south. In 214 BC a military garrison was established by the Han Chinese in northern Vietnam, and the area of present-day Vietnam was annexed to a Chinese province a century later. The region attained nominal independence in 939 after 1000 years of Chinese domination.

The Vietnamese gradually expanded southward from the Red River delta, populating most of the Mekong delta by the eighteenth century. The country was divided into three basic regions: Cochin China in the south, Annam in the centre, and Tonkin in the north. From the seventeenth century a sizeable Catholic community had been established in the area, particularly by the French. Recurrent persecution gave France an excuse to capture Saigon in 1859, and within eight years the French had completely conquered southern Vietnam, which became the French colony of Cochin China. France secured Hanoi in 1883 and took over Annam and Tonkin in 1884 as protectorates, uniting them into a single country in 1887.

A pair of 38-cm (15-inch) war-time dolls. *Left* The doll wears her hair piled to the front and top of the head. She wears a long satin brocade gown split to the waist, gold necklace, long lemon trousers, brown sandals. *Right* The doll wears a dark blue brocade gown, cream headband, and cream trousers.

Resistance to French domination continued until Japan occupied Vietnam in 1940. When Japan surrendered in August 1945, the short-lived Democratic Republic of Vietnam was declared on 2 September 1945, with Hanoi as capital. Vietnam was temporarily divided into two zones under the Potsdam agreement: the north was occupied by the Chinese who recognised Hanoi, while British troops in the south re-armed the French troops interned by the Japanese and took control of Saigon. In March 1946 a compromise agreement was signed between the French and the Vietnamese government, recognising the Democratic Republic as a 'free state' within the French Union.

France established the 'State of Vietnam' with Saigon as capital in 1948. This new state was recognised by western nations, whereas the Communist nations officially recognised the Democratic Republic, which partly or wholly controlled rural Tonkin and Annam, and large areas of Cochin China.

After a siege lasting 55 days, 10 000 French troops surrendered in northwest Tonkin on 7 May 1954, and peace negotiations opened in Geneva. Vietnam was divided into two, to be re-united after elections in July 1956; this was rejected and the country remained divided into the US-supported South and the Communist North.

In August 1964, after claiming that its vessels had been attacked by Vietnamese patrol boats in the Gulf of Tonkin, the USA launched air attacks on the North, and by the end of the year thousands of US forces were stationed in Vietnam. High casualties and disenchantment led to peace talks in 1969. Further negotiations occurred in 1973, but the war only ended with the fall of Saigon and the defacto re-unification of the country in April 1975.

Vietnam was officially re-unified on 2 July 1976 under the name of the Socialist Republic of Vietnam.
Capital Hanoi.
Population (1990) 70.2 million, with 19 per cent living in urban areas. 87.3 per cent are Vietnamese, 2 per cent Chinese, 1.5 per cent Thai and 1.4 per cent Khmer.
Religion Buddhism is the principal religion — 55.3 per cent; Roman Catholic 7 per cent and Muslim 1 per cent.
Language Vietnamese is the official language, written with a Roman script with added tonal markings. Chinese, Khmer, French, English, Russian and a variety of local dialects are also spoken.

Virgin Islands (British Virgin Islands and United States Virgin Islands) Caribbean

Although the Virgin Islands belong to the same archipelago, they come under two different administrations. The islands to

This brown plastic doll carries a woven cane basket on top of her check headscarf. Her green floral dress is tucked up at one side to show her white underskirt. She has a yellow shawl collar to her dress.

the west, mainly St Croix, St Thomas and St John (and some 50 islets), with a total area of 352 square kilometres (136 square miles), are an unincorporated territory of the United States. The group of islands to the northeast is the British Virgin Islands with an area of 150 square kilometres (58 square miles), a dependent territory of the United Kingdom. The main island is Tortola.

The islands were first inhabited by the Arawak Indians, then by the Caribs who migrated northward from mainland South America. Columbus discovered the islands in 1493, but there was no European settlement until the seventeenth century, although the islands had been used as bases by English and Dutch privateers before then.

British Virgin Islands When Tortola, the main land of the group now known as the British Virgin Islands, was settled in 1672 the group was formally annexed by Britain, and African slaves were imported to work on the plantations. In 1773 the islands were granted their own government and house of assembly. Slavery was abolished in 1834 and with this the economy took a downturn. The House of Assembly was elected from 1867, and from 1872 to 1956 the islands were administered as part of the Federal Colony of the Leeward Islands. Greater internal selfgovernment was introduced in 1977.
Capital Road Town.
Population (1989) 12 124.
Religion Christianity.
Language English is the official language.

United States Virgin Islands The Danes used the island of St Thomas as a trading post in 1665, with the Danish West India Company enlarging its possession in 1718 by colonising St John and buying St Croix from France in 1773. In 1746 the Danish crown assumed responsibility for the islands. African slaves were used as labour on the large plantations until slavery was abolished in the Danish West Indies in 1848.

In 1867 Denmark entered into negotiation with the USA for sale of the islands, but a 1902 treaty was rejected by Denmark; the sale eventually took place in 1916. The islands were transferred to US military administration in 1917 and US citizenship was granted in 1927. Civil administration replaced naval control in 1931 and in 1968 the islands were given the right to elect their own governor.
Capital Charlotte Amalie.
Population (1989) 109 105.
Religion Christianity.
Language English is the official language, although Spanish and a creole are both widely spoken.

Wales Europe

With an area of 19 097 square kilometres (7460 square miles), Wales occupies the southwest of Britain, with England to the east. Wales, along with England and Scotland, make up Great Britain, and these three along with Northern Ireland are the United Kingdom.

The Roman conquest of 43 AD had little cultural effect upon the semi-barbarous tribes of the Welsh hills. During the next few centuries Christianity was introduced and the Welsh came into contact with the Saxon English; and by the end of the fourth century Scots had formed settlements in Wales. By 600, except for the far west, most of Britain had fallen to Germanic invaders.

The period following the Norman conquest saw the steady progress of the Normans into Wales, and although they failed to subjugate the entire area, by 1093 they exercised control over many Welsh communities. The Welsh princes held out for a time in the hills, but a military defeat in 1282 enabled the English king to give his heir Edward, born at Caernavon in 1284, the title Prince of Wales.

Henry VIII's reign saw the full annexation of Wales, under acts of parliament of 1536 and 1543. From then on, Welsh history was tied to that of England and later of Scotland.
Main city Cardiff.
Population 2.8 million.
Language English is the official language, but 19 per cent of the population can speak or read Welsh.

Hard-plastic dolls (16.5 cm, 6.5 inches) 'Empire made'. The female doll wears a tall black truncated cone hat with white lace under the brim, black/red check shawl, black skirt, white lace-trimmed apron, black shoes, white socks. The male doll wears a flat wide-brimmed black hat, white jabot, white shirt with lace cuffs, red crossover sleeveless jacket with the red Welsh dragon emblem, red/black kilt-like skirt, white socks, and black shoes.

Left 'Welsh Chorister', a 12.75-cm (5-inch) wooden peg doll, bought beside Carnarvon castle in 1976. She wears a black hat with lace under the brim, white blouse, red shawl, blue skirt, white apron. She holds a song book in her hands. *Right* 'Winkle Seller', a 17.75-cm (7-inch) plastic doll bought in Wales in 1976. She wears a white cap with white lace brim under a basket on her head (for carrying winkles); a red/white blouse, red/white/black shawl, red/white panniered overskirt (opened down the front), black and white striped skirt and long trousers, white apron with pockets. She carries a narrow basket on each arm.

Western Samoa See Samoa.

Yugoslavia See Bosnia-Hercegovina, Croatia, Macedonia, Montenegro, Serbia.

Zimbabwe (Republic of) (1911–64 Southern Rhodesia; 1964–79 Rhodesia; 1979–80 Zimbabwe Rhodesia) Africa

The landlocked republic of Zimbabwe is surrounded by Zambia to the north, Mozambique to the east, South Africa to the south and Botswana south and east. Divided into 8 provinces, the republic has an area of 390 580 square kilometres (150 764 square miles), with 7 per cent of the land arable and 62 per cent forested.

Remains of stone age cultures have been found in Zimbabwe dating back 500 000 years. In the first millennium AD Bantu-speaking peoples arrived in the region, driving the San (Bushmen) into the desert. The first Europeans are thought to have reached the region in the sixteenth century, followed by an abortive search for gold by a Portuguese military expedition. Around 1830 a second migration of Bantu-speakers, fleeing the Zulus, arrived in Zimbabwe. Carving out a kingdom in the Zulu pastoral tradition, the Ndebele subdued the indigenous Shona tribes. British and Afrikaaner hunters, traders and prospectors moved north from South Africa, along with missionaries, during the nineteenth century.

After a Ndebele ruler had been duped by the British South African Company into signing away African land rights in 1890, the country became known as Southern Rhodesia and was administered by the company. But a referendum held in 1922 resulted in it becoming a self-governing colony in 1923 rather than joining the Union of South Africa. During the 1930s several discriminatory legislative measures reinforced white rule in the country.

The Central African Federation was formed in 1953 from Northern Rhodesia (Zambia), Southern Rhodesia (Zimbabwe) and Nyasaland (Malawi), but it broke up in 1963 as Zambia and Malawi made rapid progress towards independence. Southern Rhodesia's formal application for independence was rejected in 1962 by the British government, but in November 1965 it unilaterally declared independence. Then from 1972 to 1979 the country was racked by guerilla warfare, until an agreement was finally hammered out on a transition to independence based on majority rule.

'Drummer'. The doll has a fur head-dress, black/blue/white shirt, red trousers. He sits with a drum between his knees. (Courtesy J. Miller, New South Wales)

A 20-cm (8-inch) doll completely made of woven straw, with features embroidered in fine straw. The doll carries a bundle of sticks on her head. She wears a pink blouse, yellow shawl holding a baby on her back along with a wooden spear. She has a woven black skirt trimmed with beads.

In April 1980 Zimbabwe became an independent republic within the Commonwealth. Since then it has played an important role in international efforts to stabilise the region and end apartheid in South Africa.

Capital Harare.

Population 10.1 million, with 27 per cent living in urban areas. 98 per cent are African (71 per cent Shona, 16 per cent Ndebele), 1 per cent white, 1 per cent Asian or of mixed race. At the end of 1980 there were 135 000 refugees from Mozambique in Zimbabwe.

Religion 50 per cent pursue Christian/local beliefs, 25 per cent Christianity, 24 per cent indigenous beliefs, and there is a small Muslim minority.

Language English is the official language, but Shona and Ndebele are widely spoken.

Index

aboriginal, Australian, 14, 15
aboriginal, Japanese, 80
Abyssinia, 11
AFGHANISTAN, 11
Africa, 12, 28, 36, 46, 48, 59, 91, 100, 102, 107, 136, 147, 150
Ainu (Japan), 80
ALBANIA, 11
ALGERIA, 12
Alsace Lorraine (France), 52-3
Alt Wien (Vienna), 16
Amager (Denmark), 43-4
American Indians, 152-4
American Samoa, 11, 127-8
Andra Pradesh (India), 43, 67-8
ANDORRA, 12
Arab Republic of Egypt, 48
Aran (Ireland), 73
Araucanian Indian (Chile), 31
ARGENTINA, 13-14
ARMENIA, 13
Ashanti (Ghana), 58
Asia, 11, 18, 21, 26-7, 30-1, 64, 69, 82, 84, 88, 109, 114, 125, 133, 138, 144, 146-7, 157
Asia Minor, 7, 13, 55
Assam Khasi (India), 25
Atlantic Ocean, 30
AUSTRALIA, 13-15
AUSTRIA, 15-16
Automaton, 79
AZERBAIJAN, 16-17

BAHRAIN, 16-17
Baitz dolls (Austria), 15
banana leaf doll, 87
Bangkok dolls (Thailand), 27, 144-5
BANGLADESH, 17-18, 23
Banjara (India), 68, 124
BARBADOS, 18
Basutoland, 18
Bavaria, 56, 58
bead & shell dolls, 28
BELARUS, 18-19
BELGIUM, 19-20
benefit dolls, 8, 32, 35, 101
Bengal, 21
Bengkulu (Indonesia), 70
Benquet (Philippines), 15
Berlin (Germany), 56
Bethlehem, 111
Bigoudenne (France), 54
Bihar (India), 67
bisque doll (French), 41, 53, 96, 122
bisque doll (German), 49, 54, 58, 83, 108-9, 131, 136
Black Forest (Germany), 56-7
BOLIVIA, 21
Bondo (India), 68
Borneo, 84
BOSNIA-HERCEGOVINA, 21-2
BRAZIL, 22
Brides, 23-25, 35, 49, 72, 83, 109
Britain/British, 30
British Virgin Islands, 157-8
Brittany (Bretagne), 52-3
Bruxelles (Belgium), 20
BULGARIA, 25-6
BURMA, 26-7
Byelarus/Byelorussia, 18

Calabria (Italy), 76
CAMBODIA, 27-8
CAMEROON, 28
CANADA, 28-9
CANARY IS., 30
Cannes (France), 53
Capri (Italy), 77
Caribbean Ocean, 62-3, 78, 95, 120, 127-8, 147, 157
CELEBES, 30
celluloid dolls, 12, 20, 42, 52-3, 56-7, 76, 102, 104-6, 118, 130, 142, 153
cellulon dolls, 100, 141
Central America, 62, 64, 95, 111
Central Asia, 149, 155
CHANNEL IS., 30-1
CHILE, 31
china-headed doll, 54
CHINA, 31-5, 101
clay dolls, 21, 35, 42, 51-2, 63, 72, 74, 78, 84, 90, 113-14, 116-17, 120
clay/latex doll, 14
cloth dolls, 17-18, 23, 27, 31, 38-43, 45-9, 52, 57, 59-61, 63, 65, 71-3, 78, 83-4, 88, 91-2, 96, 100, 103, 105, 108, 110, 114-15, 117, 119, 121, 123, 125, 127-9, 131, 133, 139-40, 143-8, 151, 154-5
COLOMBIA, 35-6
composition dolls, 11, 31-6, 40, 54, 65, 105, 130-1, 133
Connemara (Ireland), 73
COOK IS., 36
Copenhagen (Denmark), 43
CORNWALL, 36
cornleaf dolls, 63
Côte d'Azur (France), 53
CÔTE D'IVOIRE, 36-7
Cracow (Poland), 24
CRETE, 37
CROATIA, 37-8
CUBA, 38-9
CYPRUS, 39-40
Czechoslovakia, 41
CZECH REPUBLIC, 40-1

dance, 41-3, 52, 87, 108, 122
Daruma dolls (Japan), 81
Delhi (India), 25
DENMARK, 43, 45
DJIBOUTI, 44
DOMINICA, 44-5
Donegal (Ireland), 73
Door of Hope dolls, 32, 35
Dublin (Ireland), 72
Durban (S. Africa), 137

ENGLAND, 36, 47-8, 59
epoxy dolls, 37, 142
Eros dolls (Italy), 101
Eskimo (Canada), 28-9
ESTONIA, 48
ETHIOPIA, 48-9
ethnic dolls, 7-8
Europe, 11-12, 15, 18-19, 25, 30-1, 37, 39, 43, 47-8, 50-1, 55, 59, 65, 72, 75, 88-9, 92-4, 97-9, 103, 108, 116, 118, 122, 125, 129-30, 132, 140-1, 150, 158

Federal Republic of Germany, 55, 58
felt dolls, 15, 34, 102, 136-7, 156
FIJI, 49
FINLAND, 50-1
fisherfolk dolls, 43, 52, 73, 119, 131
Flanders (Belgium), 20
Florence/Firenze (Italy), 76
folk dolls, 7-8
FRANCE, 51-5
FRENCH POLYNESIA, 55

gaucho, 13
geisha, 80
Genoa (Italy), 75
GEORGIA, 55
German Democratic Republic, 58
GERMANY, 45, 55-8, 120
GHANA, 58-9
'God of Plenty' (Bolivia), 21
Gold Coast (Africa), 59
Great Britain, 47, 59
GREECE, 37, 39, 59-61, 120
GREENLAND, 61-2
GRENADA, 62
GUATEMALA, 62-3
Guernsey (Channel Is.), 30
Gujarat (India), 67
gypsy, 68, 124

HAITI, 63
Hakarta doll (Japan), 80-1
Hashemite Kingdom of Jordan, 83
Hawaii (USA), 64, 152
Hedebo (Denmark), 43
Hellenic Republic (Greece), 59
Himachal Pradesh (India), 34
Hina doll (Japan), 79
historical dolls, 8
Hokkaido (Japan), 80
Holland, 103-5
HONDURAS, 64-5
HONG KONG, 50, 64-5
HUNGARY, 23, 65-6
Hunza (Pakistan), 111

ICELAND, 66
Ichimatsu Ninyo doll, 81
Igorots (Philippines), 115
INDIA, 25, 42-3, 50, 67, 101, 120, 122
INDONESIA, 69-70, 82, 84, 120-1
Inuit (Eskimo), 28-9
International dolls, 7, 8
IRAN, 70
IRAQ, 71-2
IRELAND, 47, 72-3
ISRAEL, 73-5, 120
ITALY, 75-8, 101
Ivory Coast, 36, 78

Jakarta (None), 69
JAMAICA, 78
Jammu & Kashmir, 25, 84
JAPAN, 28, 78-81, 122
JAVA, 69, 82-3
Jawa, 82
Jay Dolls (Ireland), 72
Jericho (Jordan), 83-4
Jersey (Channel Is.), 31
JORDAN, 83
Jute dolls, 18, 76

KALIMANTAN, 84
KASHMIR, 84-5
Kathiawara (India), 69
KAZAKHSTAN, 85
KENYA, 85-7
Kerala (India), 25
Kibbutz, 74
Kime Kama Ninyo (Japan), 81
Kokeshi doll, 82
KOREA (South), 22, 42, 87-8, 101

lacemaker doll (Belgium), 19
LAOS, 88
LAPLAND, 88-9
Las Palmas, 30
LATVIA, 89
leather dolls, 28, 46, 61, 100, 153-4
LEBANON, 90-1
Lenci dolls, 34, 136
leprechaun, 72, 75
LESOTHO, 91
LIBERIA, 91-2
LIECHTENSTEIN, 92
LITHUANIA, 41, 92-3
LUXEMBOURG, 92-3

MACEDONIA, 93, 94
Madame Alexander doll, 21
Madeira (Portugal), 102, 119
Madhya Pradesh (India), 67
MALAYSIA, 94
MALTA, 94-5
Marken (Netherlands), 104
MARTINIQUE, 95-6
Masai tribe, 87
Matrouska dolls, 125
Mero (Philippines), 115
MEXICO, 95-7
Middle East, 7, 70-1, 73, 83, 90, 129, 148
Milano/Milan (Italy), 75-6
Mizoram (India), 67
MOLDOVA, 97
MONACO, 97-8
MONGOLIA, 98
MONTENEGRO, 98-9
Mor Danmark (Denmark), 44
MOROCCO, 24, 100
MORAVIA, 99-100
Mountie/Mounted Police, 29
Munich (Germany), 56-7
Museum/s, 9, 24-5, 42
MUSICIANS, 75, 101-2, 114, 123, 126, 135, 140
Myanmar (Burma), 26-7

Naga, 68
NAMIBIA, 102
Napoli (Italy), 75
National dolls, 7-8
Ndebele tribe, 137-8
NEPAL, 102-3, 122
NETHERLANDS, 103-5
NEW CALEDONIA, 105-6
New Guinea, 106
New Hebrides, 106
NEW ZEALAND, 106-7
NIGERIA, 107
Ninyo dolls, 80-1
Nippon, 78
NORTHERN IRELAND, 49, 72, 108
North America, 18, 28, 38
North Atlantic, 66
NORWAY, 23, 108-9
Nubian, 49

Opera dolls, 34
Orissa State (India), 42

Pacific Ocean, 36, 49, 55, 69, 82, 84, 105-6, 112, 116, 146
PAKISTAN, 67, 109
PALESTINE, 111
PANAMA, 111-12
papier mâché doll, 33
PAPUA NEW GUINEA, 112-13
Paris (France), 52
Pedigree dolls (Aust), 49, 112
PERU, 113-14
Persia, 70, 113
PHILIPPINES, 23, 114-16
PITCAIRN IS., 116
POLAND, 23, 116-18
Policemen, 29, 47, 52, 97
PORTUGAL, 102, 118-19
Prince Edward Is. (Can), 29
Provence (France), 52-3
PUERTO RICO, 120
Punjab, 25
puppet doll, 69

Rajasthan (India), 42, 67-8
Ravca doll (France), 52
Reliable dolls (Canada), 29
RELIGION, 8, 21, 49, 51, 57, 59, 70-4, 120-2, 146, 151, 156
resin dolls, 23, 73, 108, 123
Rhine (Germany), 57
Rhodes (Greece), 60
Rhodesia, 159
Rogarth dolls, 47
ROMANIA, 122-4
ROMANY (Gypsies), 124-5
Rosnaes (Denmark), 43
rubber dolls, 50-1, 152
RUSSIA, 41, 125-7
Russian Federated Republic, 125

ST. LUCIA, 127-8
ST. VINCENT, 128
SAMOA, 128-9
Samuri (Japan), 79
Sailor dolls, 47, 52
Samburu tribe (Kenya), 85
SAN MARINO, 129
Santhal (India), 68
Santons (France), 51
Sardinia (Italy), 76-7
SAUDI ARABIA, 129-30
Schmider Trachten dolls, 56
SCOTLAND, 42, 130-1
SENEGAL, 131-2
SERBIA, 132-3
Shankars Doll Museum, 24-5, 42, 124
Siam, 144
Sicily (Italy), 76-8
Sienna (Italy), 75
SIKKIM, 133
SINGAPORE, 133-4
Sinta (Indonesia), 70
Slavonica, 38
Sligo (Ireland), 73
SLOVAKIA, 41, 134-5
snake charmer, 69
Sofia (Bulgaria), 26
Sorrento (Italy), 75
SOUTH AFRICA, 136
South America, 21, 31, 35, 45, 113, 115, 156
Southern Rhodesia, 159
South Korea, 42, 138
South Pacific Is., 42, 112, 128, 155
Southwest Africa, 138
souvenir dolls, 7-8, 47, 50, 82
Soviet Union, 138
SPAIN, 42, 135-6
SRI LANKA, 41, 121, 138-9
straw dolls, 45, 70, 96, 120-1, 127
Sulawesi, 30
Swaggie (Swagman) doll, 14
SWAZILAND, 138-40
SWEDEN, 140-1
SWITZERLAND, 120, 141-2
SYRIA, 46, 142-3

Tagalog (Philippines), 115
Tahiti, 55, 143
TAIWAN, 143-4
TAJIKISTAN, 144
Tamilnadu (India), 67
THAILAND, 42, 122, 144
TIBET, 120, 146
TONGA, 146-7
Transkei (S. Africa), 136
TRINIDAD & TOBAGO, 147
Tripura (India), 67
Troll dolls, 50, 109, 141
tourist trade dolls, 50
TUNISIA, 147-8
TURKEY, 23, 39, 148-9
TURKMENISTAN, 149-50
Tyrol, 76

UGANDA, 150
UKRAINE, 150-1
Ulster, 59, 108, 151
Union of Myanmar, 26-7
United Arab Republic, 46
United Kingdom, 151
UNITED STATES, 121, 151-3
URUGUAY, 154-5
U.S.A., 121, 151-3
U.S.S.R., 13, 155
US Virgin Is., 157-8
Uttar Pradesh (India), 25
UZBEKISTAN, 155

VANUATU, 155
VATICAN, 156
VENEZUELA, 156-7
Venice (Italy), 76
Vienna (Austria), 16
VIETNAM, 157
VIRGIN IS., 157-8

WALES, 59, 158
Warsaw (Poland), 116-17
wax dolls, 7
wax-like dolls, 13, 71, 127, 150
Weibell dolls, 140
West Cork (Ireland), 72
Western Samoa, 128, 158
West Indies, 18, 44
White Russia, 18
wooden dolls, 14, 26, 30, 32, 35, 45, 51, 58, 64, 75, 82, 86-7, 102, 106-7, 112, 116-18, 121, 125, 140-1, 143, 151, 153-4

yarn dolls, 108-9
Yamato Ninyo (Japan), 80
Yugoslavia, 158

ZIMBABWE, 159
Zulu, 137